Developing I

Developing Research Writing is designed to encourage, inspire and improve the advisory practice of providing writing feedback. This book provides insights and advice that supervisors can use to advance their support of their research students' writing, and at the same time, survive increasing supervisory demands.

Book parts are framed by empirical supervisor and doctoral student experiences and chapters within each part provide multiple approaches. The carefully chosen contributors are specialists on research writing and doctoral pedagogy, who guide the reader through the key stages of providing feedback. Split into nine key parts, the book covers:

- starting a new supervision with writing in focus;
- making use of other resources along the way;
- encouraging style through control of language;
- writing feedback on English as an Additional Language (EAL) writing;
- Master's and Honours smaller projects' writing feedback;
- thesis by publication or performance-based writing;
- maintaining and gathering momentum;
- keeping the examiner happy;
- writing feedback as nudging through identity transition.

The parts cohere into a go-to handbook for developing the supervision process. Drawing on research, literature and experience, *Developing Research Writing* offers well-theorized, yet practical and grounded advice conducive to good practices.

Susan Carter is Senior Lecturer in the Centre for Learning and Research in Higher Education (CLeaR), University of Auckland, New Zealand.

Deborah Laurs is Senior Learning Advisor in Student Learning *Te Taiako*, Victoria University of Wellington, New Zealand.

Developing Research Writing

A Handbook for Supervisors and Advisors

Edited by
Susan Carter and
Deborah Laurs

Routledge
Taylor & Francis Group
LONDON AND NEW YORK

First published 2018
by Routledge
2 Park Square, Milton Park, Abingdon, Oxon OX14 4RN

and by Routledge
711 Third Avenue, New York, NY 10017

Routledge is an imprint of the Taylor & Francis Group, an informa business

British Library Cataloguing in Publication Data
A catalogue record for this book is available from the British Library.

Library of Congress Cataloging-in-Publication Data
A catalog record for this book has been requested

ISBN: 978-1-138-68814-8 (hbk)
ISBN: 978-1-138-68815-5 (pbk)
ISBN: 978-1-315-54198-3 (ebk)

Typeset in Palatino
by Florence Production Ltd, Stoodleigh, Devon, UK

Contents

Illustrations

FIGURES

TABLES

Who we are

Contributors' biographical details

EDITORS

Susan Carter is Senior Lecturer in the Centre for Learning and Research in Higher Education (CLeaR), University of Auckland, New Zealand. She coordinated the Student Learning Centre Doctoral Programme from 2004 to 2012, and now facilitates the supervision seminar series within CLeaR. Understanding gained from years of working with doctoral students, including individual consultations, translates into support for supervisors. She also provides workshops for academics on research writing. Susan regularly contributes to the *DoctoralWriting SIG* online forum (https://doctoralwriting.wordpress.com/), and her most recent publications include *Structuring your Research Thesis* (with Ian Brailsford and Fran Kelly; Palgrave MacMillan, 2012) and *Developing Generic Support for Doctoral Students: Practice and Pedagogy* (with Deborah Laurs; Routledge, 2014).

Deborah Laurs has been Senior Learning Advisor in Student Learning *Te Taiako*, Victoria University of Wellington, New Zealand, since 2001. Her doctorate examined the representation of adolescents in 20th-century NZ young adult fiction and she has taught widely in English literature, media, communication studies and creative writing programmes. She provides one-on-one consultations for doctoral students at all stages of the thesis journey, and also oversees campus-wide research skills seminars and workshops, leads thesis-writing intensives, has supervised master's and doctoral students, and contributes to supervisor training. Together with Susan Carter, she co-edited *Developing Generic Support for Doctoral Students: Practice and Pedagogy* (Routledge, 2014).

Both editors also contributed chapters.

CHAPTER AUTHORS

Claire Aitchison is a Senior Lecturer in the Teaching Innovation Unit, University of South Australia, Australia. She has worked in various capacities in higher education supporting doctoral students and their supervisors for more than 25 years. In addition, as a consultant, her research and work with academics and supervisors are focused on improving practices for the development of research writing and publications.

Sarah Barradell is a PhD candidate in the Faculty of Education and Social Work at the University of Sydney, as well as a Lecturer in Physiotherapy, School of Allied Health, College of Science, Health and Engineering, La Trobe University, Australia.

Liz Beddoe is an Associate Professor in Education and Social Work, University of Auckland, New Zealand. Her teaching and research interests include critical perspectives on social work education and professional supervision. Her recent books include *Challenges in Professional Supervision* (with Allyson Davys; Jessica Kingsley Publishers, 2016), *Social Work Practice for Promoting Health and Wellbeing: Critical Issues* (with Jane Maidment; Routledge, 2014), and *Social Policy for Social Work and Human Services in Aotearoa New Zealand: Diverse Perspectives* (with Jane Maidment; Canterbury University Press, 2016).

John Bitchener is Professor of Applied Linguistics at the Auckland University of Technology, New Zealand, where he is supervising 12 doctoral candidates. He has published widely in leading journals and is author of five books including *Written Corrective Feedback in Second Language Acquisition and Writing* (with Dana R. Ferris; Routledge, 2012) and *Written Corrective Feedback for L2 Development* (with Neomy Storch; Multilingual Matters, 2016).

Barbara Bolt is Professor in Contemporary Arts and Culture, and Associate Dean (Research) and Co-Director of the Creative Arts Therapies Research Unit, in the Victorian College of the Arts and the Melbourne Conservatorium of Music, the University of Melbourne, Australia. As a practising artist and art theorist, she has written extensively on artistic research and its ethical implications. She is author of *Art beyond Representation: The Performative Power of the Image* (I.B. Tauris, 2004) and *Heidegger Reframed: Interpreting Key Thinkers for the Arts* (I.B. Tauris, 2011), in addition to four co-edited volumes. Her website is www.barbbolt.com/

Eva M. Brodin is an Associate Professor in Educational Sciences, Lund University, Sweden, where she is also a Senior Lecturer in the Department of Psychology and works as an Educational Developer in the field of doctoral supervision at the Division for Higher Education Development. She is also a Research Fellow at the Centre for Higher and Adult Education, Stellenbosch University, South Africa. Her research is directed towards doctoral students' development of critical and creative thinking and academic identity, and organizational support for doctoral students.

Rachael Cayley is an Associate Professor in the Teaching Stream, School of Graduate Studies, University of Toronto, Canada. She teaches academic writing and speaking to graduate students. She also writes about academic writing for graduate students in her blog, *Explorations of Style* (www.explorationsofstyle.com). Her current research concerns dissertation boot camps and their role in facilitating the development of an academic writing identity.

Lisa Chant (Māori tribal affiliation Ngati Whatua) is a Senior Education Consultant and Senior Lecturer at the Tai Poutini Polytechnic, New Zealand, and a Senior Fellow of the Higher Education Academy (UK). She obtained her PhD in Community Health from the University of Auckland. Her areas of teaching expertise include medical humanities, politics and public policy, university teaching and learning, indigenous and Māori studies, and media.

Sarah C. Cornelius is a Senior Lecturer in Education at the University of Aberdeen, United Kingdom. She has a wide range of interests in post-compulsory education and digital learning. An experienced supervisor at PhD and master's levels, Sarah coordinated the supervision of master's students for 5 years, exploring and developing approaches to the delivery of support for students and supervisors.

Martin East is an Associate Professor and Associate Dean (Research) in Education and Social Work, University of Auckland, New Zealand. His work on an Ako Aotearoa National Project Fund team (https://akoaotearoa.ac.nz/best-practice-supervisor-feedback) has shaped and influenced his thinking about effective feedback on postgraduate students' writing.

B. Liezel Frick is an Associate Professor in the Centre for Higher and Adult Education, Department of Curriculum Studies, Stellenbosch University, South Africa. Her research focuses on doctoral creativity, early career researcher development, and supervisory practices in doctoral education.

George D. Gopen (JD and PhD, Harvard) is Professor Emeritus of the Practice of Rhetoric at Duke University, United States, where he founded the University Writing Program and taught for 30 years. He is recognized as one of the world's premier writing consultants, having developed his wholly new Reader Expectation Approach to the English Language for students and for clients in all professions. For more information, see his website, www.GeorgeGopen.com

Barbara M. Grant is an Associate Professor in Critical Studies in Education, University of Auckland, New Zealand. She teaches and researches in the field of higher education and has run many workshops on supervision for institutions in Aotearoa/New Zealand over the past 20 years. Her research and writing interests lie in the pedagogies of graduate research supervision, as well as academic identities and work, research methodologies for education and the social sciences, and academic writing.

Cally Guerin is an Academic Developer in the Faculty of Arts, University of Adelaide, Australia. She has worked and published in doctoral education since 2008, currently delivering a research skills programme for doctoral students. With Claire Aitchison and Susan Carter, she is a founding editor of the *DoctoralWriting SIG* blog (https://doctoralwriting.wordpress.com/). Recent publications include *Writing Groups for Doctoral Education and Beyond: Innovations in Practice and Theory* (co-edited with Claire Aitchison; Routledge, 2014) and *Research Literacies and Writing Pedagogies for Masters and Doctoral Writers* (co-edited with Cecile Badenhorst; Brill, 2016).

Andrea Haines is a Senior Tutor in the Centre for Tertiary Teaching and Learning (CeTTL), University of Waikato, New Zealand. She focuses on providing support for doctoral students through the Doctoral Writing Conversations programme and individual consultations. She has a particular interest in the writing needs of thesis students and how these can be met through peer support and targeted language programmes.

E. Marcia Johnson comes from a background in eLearning and Applied Linguistics, and is Director of the Centre for Tertiary Teaching and Learning (CeTTL) at the University of Waikato, New Zealand. Marcia and her team have introduced a number of cross-disciplinary, cohort-based initiatives to improve the student experience of learning, particularly doctoral writing and academic integrity. In particular, their weekly Doctoral Writing Conversation programme has facilitated the development of a range of strategies to help PhD students become successful thesis writers.

Margaret Kiley holds an adjunct position in the Research School of Humanities and the Arts, Australian National University, with a conjoint position at the University of Newcastle, Australia. Her research and teaching focus on the education of future researchers. In addition to working in further/higher education in Australia, Indonesia, Malaysia and the UK, she has presented workshops on research education and training in New Zealand, Canada and the United States, while publishing extensively on doctoral practice.

Vijay Kumar is a Senior Lecturer in the Higher Education Development Centre, University of Otago, New Zealand. His research interests include feedback practices, postgraduate supervision, doctoral examination and academic writing. Vijay has published extensively, including *A Handbook for Postgraduate Supervision* (with B. H. Huat; Universiti Putra Malaysia Press, 2011).

Anne Lee has worked as an independent consultant specializing in doctoral supervision with universities in Europe (including the UK and Scandinavia),

Africa and the Middle East. She leads programmes at the University of Stavanger, Norway (where she was appointed an Associate Professor in 2015), the University of Bristol, UK (where she is an Honorary Research Fellow) and Roehampton University in London (where she is a Senior Research Fellow). Her website is located at www.drannelee.wordpress.com. Her publication record includes *Successful Research Supervision: Advising Students Doing Research* (Routledge, 2012).

Juliet Lum is Head of Higher Degree Research Learning Skills at Macquarie University, Australia. She is overseeing the programme of training courses and workshops for PhD candidates across campus, and delivering the Research Communications unit for the university's Master of Research programme. Previously, she worked as a dialogue designer for Syrinx Speech Systems, and as a project manager for language technology company, Appen.

Jane Maidment is an Associate Professor in Human Services and Social Work, University of Canterbury, New Zealand. She is a registered social worker and has teaching and research interests in the fields of education, practice skill development, older persons, and using craft as a vehicle for social connectedness. She has published extensively in national and international journals, and co-authored, with Liz Beddoe, *Mapping Knowledge for Social Work Practice: Critical Intersections* (Cengage, 2009) and *Social Policy for Social Work and Human Services in Aotearoa New Zealand: Diverse Perspectives* (Canterbury University Press, 2016).

Inger Mewburn is an Associate Professor and Director of Research Training in the Division of Research, Australian National University, Australia. She specializes in the study of research education and research student support. She is a Senior Fellow of the Higher Education Academy (UK), and a regular guest speaker on research issues both at universities and in the mainstream media. Her main research interests are PhD graduate employability, doctoral education, design teaching and digital academic practices. She publishes scholarly works on research students and their experiences, and edits and contributes to *The Thesis Whisperer* blog: https://thesiswhisperer.com/

Rowena Murray is Professor of Education and Director of Research at the University of the West of Scotland, United Kingdom, and Principal Fellow of the Higher Education Academy (UK). She graduated with MA (Hons) from the University of Glasgow and a PhD from Pennsylvania State University, where she studied Rhetoric and Composition. Her teaching and research focus on academic writing. Her works include *How to Write a Thesis* (3rd edition, Open University Press, 2011), *Writing for Academic Journals* (3rd edition, Open University Press, 2013), *The Handbook of Academic Writing* (with Sarah Moore; Open University Press, 2006) and *Writing in Social Spaces* (Routledge, 2014). Her research has been funded by the British Academy, the Carnegie Trust and the Nuffield Foundation.

Sandra Nicol is a Lecturer (Scholarship) in the School of Education, University of Aberdeen, United Kingdom, and a Senior Fellow of the Higher Education Academy (UK). Her background is in primary education and she became a Chartered Teacher (master's level) in 2005 before working in the higher education sector. She was Director of the University of Aberdeen's Chartered Teacher Programme between 2008 and 2013. She currently teaches both undergraduate and postgraduate students and has had a research focus on how to support students and supervisors undertaking master's work-based projects and dissertations.

Alet P. Olivier is a Lecturer at the Postgraduate School, University of the Free State, South Africa. She is currently pursuing her PhD on authorial voice at the University of Pretoria. Her teaching and research interests include plagiarism, research writing and facilitation at all postgraduate levels, and in particular a pedagogical approach to the instruction of voice in advanced academic writing.

Anthony Paré is a Professor and Head of the Department of Language and Literacy Education at the University of British Columbia, Canada. Before this, he worked at McGill University for over 30 years, where he chaired the Department of Integrated Studies in Education, directed the Centre for the Study and Teaching of Writing, and edited the *McGill Journal of Education*. He examines academic and workplace writing, situated learning, school-to-work transitions, the development of professional literacies, and doctoral education. He is presently researching the supervisory dyad and its role in the rhetorical apprenticeship of doctoral students.

Tai Peseta is a Senior Lecturer in Education Innovation at the University of Sydney, Australia. For many years, she was part of a university-wide programme for the professional development of supervisors. Currently she is supervising five research students, and working on two funded projects in research and doctoral education: one of these revitalizes the idea of stewardship for the Australian PhD; and the other explores access and equity as a problem for knowledge in doctoral curricula.

Sharon Sharmini is a Lecturer in the Department of English, Faculty of Modern Languages and Communication, Universiti Putra, Malaysia. She gained her PhD from the University of Otago, New Zealand. Her research interests include doctoral assessment, graduate writing and sociolinguistics.

Paul J. Silvia is the Lucy Spinks Keker Excellence Professor at the University of North Carolina at Greensboro, United States. He is the author of two books about writing (*How to Write A Lot* [2007] and *Write It Up* [2015], both from APA Books), several research articles about the psychology of creativity and the arts, and at least one arcane blog.

Sue Starfield is Professor in the School of Education and Director of the Learning Centre, University of New South Wales, Australia. She has co-authored *Thesis and Dissertation Writing in a Second Language: A Handbook for Supervisors* (with Brian Paltridge; Routledge, 2007) and co-edited *Doctoral Writing in the Creative and Performing Arts* (with Brian Paltridge and Louise Ravelli; Libri, 2014).

Elke Stracke is an Associate Professor in the Faculty of Education, Science, Technology and Mathematics, University of Canberra, Australia. She is an applied/educational linguist and teaches TESOL/Foreign Language Teaching courses. Her current research interests focus on two areas: motivation, blended and independent language learning and their relationship with learner autonomy; and feedback, assessment and peer learning in postgraduate supervision practice.

Helen Sword is Professor and Director of the Centre for Learning and Research in Higher Education (CLeaR), University of Auckland, New Zealand. Trained as a literary scholar, she publishes on the writing practices of faculty and PhD students from across the disciplines. Her recent books include *Stylish Academic Writing* (Harvard University Press, 2012), *The Writer's Diet* (University of Chicago Press, 2016), and *Air & Light & Time & Space: How Successful Academics Write* (Harvard University Press, 2017). She has also developed two interactive online writing tools, the Writer's Diet Test and the Writing BASE. For more, see www.helensword.com and www.writersdiet.com.

Pat Thomson (PhD, PSM, FAcSS) is Professor of Education at the University of Nottingham, United Kingdom, and Convenor of the university's Centre for Research in Arts Creativity and Literacies. A former head teacher, she brought to higher education an interest in the pedagogies of academic writing and reading. Her own writing addiction has produced 20 edited books and monographs – four on academic writing and three on research methods – as well as her blog *patter* (https://patthomson.net). She runs workshops around the world on academic writing, alongside her day job of researching and teaching about the arts and school and community change.

Gina Wisker is Professor of Higher Education and Contemporary Literature, and Head of the Centre for Learning and Teaching, University of Brighton, United Kingdom. Specializing in postgraduate study and supervision, she has published *The Postgraduate Research Handbook* (2nd edition, Palgrave Macmillan, 2008), *The Good Supervisor* (2nd edition, Palgrave Macmillan, 2012) and *Getting Published* (Palgrave, 2015). Gina also teaches, supervises, researches and publishes in 20th-century women's writing, particularly postcolonial writing, Gothic and popular fictions, with prolific publications.

'Ema Wolfgramm-Foliaki is a Lecturer in the Centre for Learning and Research in Higher Education (CLeaR), University of Auckland, New Zealand. She contributes a Pasifika pedagogy to staff development. Her thesis highlights specific forms of literacy practices underpinned by Tongan cultural values and beliefs. Her current research centres on widening participation for first-in-the-family students' success. Funded by the Worldwide Universities Network (WUN) and supported by partner universities, the project aims for improved Pasifika success in higher education and in the wider society.

Linlin Xu is a Lecturer in the School of Foreign Languages, Chongqing University of Posts and Telecommunications, China, and is currently pursuing her PhD at the University of Auckland, New Zealand. Her research interests include written feedback, doctoral writing and intercultural doctoral supervision.

Acknowledgements

We thank Ako Aotearoa (the New Zealand National Centre for Tertiary Teaching Excellence) Northern Hub for funding and the steer towards a focus on practice. Their funds enabled professional analysis of the data that thread through this book, and employment of John Wei, an invaluable research assistant, whom we thank for his diligence and engagement.

Susan thanks her CLeaR colleagues, and Deborah, her colleagues at Student Learning; both workplace centres gave committed support as we worked together again.

The University of Auckland's Faculty of Education and Social Work awarded Susan 6 months' research and study leave in which to pull the book together and meet with some of the contributors worldwide. Ro and Mo, thanks, too, for experiences within Loch Winnock.

Neale, thanks for coming along on Susan's leave as the perfect travelling companion; Axel, thanks for keeping Deborah's home fires burning while she too worked on this project.

We also acknowledge the many supervisors and students whose voices are included in this book and others who enrich our daily work. Thanks, too, for all the interesting conversations about writing that occurred along the way.

Our contributors were prompt and patient, and we warmly acknowledge their insights and expertise that enhance this comprehensive book. Routledge have again given us excellent midwifery to ensure that this book safely finds your hands.

Introduction

Opening the books on research writing feedback

Susan Carter and Deborah Laurs

> If, rather than just telling me what you think, you ask me:
>
> - What do you think of this piece of writing?
> - What is the purpose/what were you trying to achieve?
> - What is the writing doing here?
> - What are its strengths?
> - What do you think isn't working/needs improving?
> - What do you need to do next to develop this further?
> - What do you think of the tone you're taking here?
>
> ... then I would probably come up with most of the feedback you were going to give me myself.
>
> (Doctoral student participant)

The above words of advice from a confident student who took part in a recent research project at a New Zealand research-intensive university make supervising the doctoral writing process seem so easy. Yet supervisor participants in the same study, which triggered this book, assured us that, from their perspective, the reality is not that easy. Supervisors said of their students:

'They can't write.'

'They won't write.'

'They do write, but badly.'

> *'Students whose first language is not English are just awful. But local students are often even worse.'*
>
> *'They don't follow advice.'*
>
> *'They become unduly emotional about advice, even when it is given kindly and with lots of positive feedback.'*

Our 12 and 13 years of respective experience (as supervisors, as learning advisors, and as academic developers) working with doctoral students and supervisors led us to research doctoral writing feedback. We knew there were challenges. Our experience confirms Badenhorst and Guerin's (2016: 3–15) argument that research writing's complexity is often invisible to students and to academics; that academic writing remains deeply conservative despite graduate profile calls for creativity; and that the historic privileging of 'detached' scholarship causes psychological hardship for many. Of the 1247 accredited doctoral supervisors whom we invited to tell us about their supervision experience through an anonymized digital questionnaire, 226 of them did—the quotations above reflect six fairly typical responses. The sample size allowed a check for discipline difference around specific aspects of doctoral writing support. Surprisingly, despite epistemological differences, social negotiations around doctoral writing feedback present similar challenges across disciplines (Carter, Kensington-Miller and Courtney, 2017). Commonalities of experience prompted our desire to pull together experts in academic writing and doctoral pedagogy to create a book that might encourage, inspire, and improve practice. Many chapter authors are less theoretical and more grounded here than in their work elsewhere, writing for an audience of practitioners across the disciplines rather than educationalists. This book is framed by our empirical study: representative survey participants' voices (both supervisors and doctoral students [n=80]) open each part, anchoring chapter-authors' expertise, reflections and advice with accounts from the field.

Readers are likely to identify with participant supervisors' experiences. Several respondents commented that supervisory input is under-rewarded, under-appreciated by the academic system, and exacerbated by the layers of administration associated with rigorously-enforced completion constraints. Bureaucratic checks and time-limits serve to protect doctoral students (a valuable and relatively vulnerable stratum of the university), but supervisors felt that such protection came at their expense. Our findings' most significant theme is that supervision was perceived to *'take too much time'* (221 respondents), with different aspects of writing feedback identified as particularly *'time-consuming'* (20). Supervisors frequently also mentioned students' failure to take advice, so that *'it did sometimes feel like Groundhog Day'*. One supervisor participant summed up:

> *I have no problem with a student's DECIDING not to follow advice and providing a reason—that's great. Most often, though, students ignore advice—and other academics*

> *note this too—because they do not understand it, find it too hard or are in non-productive mode.*

That frustration was counter-balanced by other supervisors' awareness of students' emotional trials with writing. At the same time, there was acknowledgement that supervisors cannot side-step their responsibility to give honest feedback: *'Sometimes you need to say something isn't working at exactly the point when the student least wants to hear it.'*

We also surveyed doctoral students [n=80] about their experiences of receiving feedback on their writing. Students were asked to identity both helpful and unhelpful feedback that they received. Generally their tone was less exasperated than that of supervisors—but emotions often lay below the surface of well-considered responses: *'Feedback . . . is particularly helpful when it doesn't cause me to become disheartened and feel as if I have been pouring hours of work into something which will be re-worked to an unrecognizable state'.* Comments often confirmed sensitivity about feedback on their writing. Given their high investment in the process, students often take comments on their writing personally (Laurs, 2010), regarding critique as an attack, which then undermines their confidence (Can and Walker, 2011).

Commonly, students wanted feedback on their ideas, their content and their structure, and felt short-changed when they received only grammar and typo corrections instead. Although a handful of students really appreciated attention to grammar, most pointed out that they could revise surface-level problems themselves, or get help elsewhere (student learning services, peers or friends). They most valued advice that afforded them access to the supervisor's expertise with the academic genre and discipline itself.

Students confirmed that they looked for clear, concrete advice that enabled them to progress. They found it helpful *'when the critique and questions asked were specific and showed me where I needed to address gaps in structure and content'.* They criticized the emptiness of vague, overly-general statements such as *'keep going'*, and the absence of explicit guidance on how to improve: *'I was a little confused if the feedback was only "?"'.* Another student spelt out the limitation of *'general comments in the margin like: "you need to unpack this more" or "you don't need to tell me everything about this" with no further elaboration'.* Sometimes students fixate so much on producing the perfect draft that they become blocked, avoiding meeting with or submitting work to their supervisor at all. This theme in our data confirms other studies revealing students' frustration with vague feedback saying that the written work is inadequate, without explaining how to improve it (Yeh, 2010). For clarity about what was needed, students also appreciated the provision of exemplars and models.

Doctoral students quite often require help in interpreting supervisors' comments. Usually students only submit written work to their supervisor because they think it is reasonably good. That catch-all supervisory comment *'unclear'* is spectacularly unclear itself. In reality, the reasons why writing might not be clear are many, including faulty grammar and syntax, inaccuracy of terms or lack of specificity, structure or disciplinary know-how. Sometimes abstract nouns proliferate where concrete terms would be stronger (Sword, 2007, 2012). Jumbled prose often signals problems at deeper conceptual levels concerning theory, epistemology or logic. Without guidance, students are unlikely to recognize how to improve their writing, and may address the wrong one of the inadequacies just listed. Fixing grammar won't help if logic remains faulty.

Students disliked extremes in the quantity of feedback, too much or not enough. One student described feeling overwhelmed *'when I am given feedback on everything at once. One thousand comments in the margins'*. Conversely, another noted that *'On one chapter I had a five-word comment and less than a minute of verbal feedback'*. Unsurprisingly, students appreciated promptness and clear communication about turnaround times: *'it is helpful for the supervisor to be honest about likely turnaround times and periods when they are relatively free to review work'*. And, of course, *'very negative'* or *'harsh'* feedback is unhelpful—there were lots of comments on how *'devastating'* this was, sometimes signalling reluctance to submit further writing.

Our data, then, reveal prickliness on both sides of the writing feedback relationship, a discomfort endorsed by literature. Hardy and Clughen's review reveals a chorus of confusion and anguish regarding thesis writing on the part of both students and academics (Hardy and Clughen 2012: 25–54). Anthony Paré's (2011) research into 30 supervisors at work identified that very good supervisors often 'lack the linguistic and rhetorical vocabulary' (2011: 66), resulting in 'fuzzy' feedback that their students can't understand: 'despite their good intentions and thoughtful efforts, the supervisors . . . struggled to help students write' (2011: 71). Our own experience confirms Paré's (2011) findings as fairly typical: academic experts often have little interest in, or experience of, fine-tuning the mechanics of rhetoric, and are unable to move students from feelings of personal inadequacy to effective written expression (Aitchison et al., 2012). Some don't see writing development as their sphere of duty. This book argues that it should be.

Increasing internationalization complicates writing feedback, with international students reporting that they feel alienated (Ali and Kohun, 2007), second-class (Morley, 2003) and under-supported (Strauss, 2012). Approaches to thinking are culturally based (Robinson-Pant, 2010): the doctoral thesis genre requires students to critically present their views in accordance with an Anglo-centric dialogic convention that has little tolerance for the discursiveness often present in other cultures. We did not ask supervisors in our survey about experience with students who have English as an Additional Language (EAL), but 66 mentioned this as a significant factor in writing support.

There is relatively little guidance available to supervisors on giving clear directive feedback on writing. Useful handbooks advise doctoral students on research learning (Dunleavy, 2003; Phillips and Pugh, 2005; Wisker, 2008) and on writing (Aitchison and Paré, 2012; Murray, 2011; White, 2011), including how to structure a thesis (Carter, Kelly and Brailsford, 2012). Paltridge and Starfield (2007) offer suggestions for those supervising EAL students, which mainly relate to mechanics of language, as does John Bitchener (2013). Students increasingly make use of social media concerning doctoral writing, potential resources that supervisors are often not aware of (Guerin, Aitchison and Carter, 2016). Relatively few books, however, offer practical, scaffolded strategies on giving feedback.

Supporting doctoral writing is not solely a matter of fostering English language proficiency: supervisors face challenges, such as maintaining writing momentum, encouraging students to find their voice and helping them to become savvy about discipline-specific epistemologies. Ongoing supervisory support, together with a clear acknowledgement of the iterative, dialogic nature of the process—drafting and re-drafting in response to targeted feedback—are significant for timely completion of thesis-writing.

Ultimately, doctorates are judged primarily on the merits of the thesis. Targeted feedback is crucial throughout the 3–4-year process during which students hone their thinking and writing skills. Building on a foundation of supervisor and doctoral student experiences, this book provides insights and advice on a range of factors that supervisors could consider, and act upon, to provide effective feedback on research students' writing, and survive increasing supervisory demands. We have brought together specialists on research writing and its associated pedagogy. They present chapters arranged in book parts addressing different aspects of writing support. Together, the parts create a single handbook for research writing development. Supervisor and student comments from our survey participants head up the short prefaces to the nine different aspects of writing feedback covered here.

The book begins with a foundation for ongoing good writing and feedback. Part I advises on commencing the supervisory relationship with writing management firmly on the agenda. Next, Part II recommends encouraging students to participate in wider writing-support networks, presented up-front in the book to implicitly argue that extending support options from the outset fosters students' efficacy and self-awareness and lessens their dependency, enabling supervisors to survive increasing pressures. Then, because writing inevitably raises issues of style, Part III tackles the stylistics of writing, the mechanics of language and the persuasion of rhetoric.

Advice throughout the book applies to all students, but we also recognize particular cohorts. Part IV explores how supervisors can best support students for whom English is an additional language (EAL). Part V looks at supervising shorter research projects: master's and honours dissertations. Writing support for thesis by publication and performance-led research is addressed in Part VI as these practices require specific awareness.

Part VII suggests ways to maintain momentum and sustain productivity in the face of students' tendencies towards procrastination and perfectionism. Part VIII unpicks what examiners are looking for in the thesis, so that students can be directed to defend their ideas *within their writing*—and to appreciate the importance of the reader. Part IX concludes by exploring how supervisors can help students develop their professional identity through writing, resulting in an independent researcher as well as a timely thesis.

Each part ends with bullet-pointed strategies as a reminder checklist for how to foster students' agency with writing skills development. Drawing on research, literature and experience, the book as a single entity offers well-theorized, yet hands-on advice conducive to good practices.

Part I

Starting a new supervision with writing in focus

John Bitchener; Vijay Kumar and Elke Stracke; Barbara M. Grant and Linlin Xu; Anne Lee

Edited by Susan Carter

> **Supervisor:** *Getting a candidate to start writing in the first year . . . has been challenging . . . I try to encourage students to start writing from day one by collating their notes into sections, which seems to help them get over their initial reluctance to start writing.*
>
> **Student:** *I felt nervous about submitting writing for the first time. I was unsure what state the writing should be in, how to name or label the document I was submitting or the email subject. I was uncertain around the level of writing skill expected.*

Part I covers the early supervision discussion that establishes writing expectations and practices. Writing sharpens thinking. It is inherent in academic culture; as a principle cultural artefact, writing has implicit protocols to be learned (Aitchison, Kamler and Lee, 2010). Students build their academic identity through writing (Kamler and Thomson, 2006), enabling their acceptance into discourse communities (Aitchison and Guerin, 2014; Guerin, 2013; Wenger, 1998). They need to write early and actively engage with writing skills development. Yet when our participant doctoral students [n=80] described the first time they gave their supervisor writing and received feedback, their responses showed that students are often not sure of what supervisors want, have different expectations to their supervisors, and are extremely anxious about the first exchange of writing.

Supervisors can pre-empt many later tensions by focusing on writing and establishing ground rules at the start.

As a professional skill (Murray, 2011), writing requires the attentive guidance given to apprentices (Golde et al., 2006). Supervisors can prompt thinking that results in purposeful prose by asking leading questions and setting exercises. The early phase is the place to enculturate students to the ethics of doctoral writing by initiating ethics approval application and ensuring awareness of copyright issues. It is also healthy to enfold students within writing communities that normalize the reiterative nature of doctoral writing, its drudgery, and the associated emotional highs and lows (Flaherty, 2004). While still in the honeymoon phase, supervisors can discuss protocols for handling emotion and disagreement around writing with the goal of open communication towards productivity.

In Chapter 1, John Bitchener looks practically at the first year of a doctorate, and suggests ways to help students orientate themselves during the initial literature review and full proposal writing stages. He provides exercises and templates that 'nudge' (Kiley and Wisker, 2008) students towards thinking critically rather than merely taking notes during these early stages. Vijay Kumar and Elke Stracke (Chapter 2) suggest ways to alert students to the textual and linguistic features of academic writing. They emphasize the good practice of establishing peer groups for supporting writing development. In Chapter 3, Barbara Grant and her candidate-at-time-of-writing, Linlin Xu, tease out the potential for miscommunication across cultures—and endorse the benefits of explicit talk about expectations. Anne Lee presents an overview of the thesis writing project in Chapter 4, suggesting that supervisors orient students to the different stages of development ahead of them, so that they develop self-efficacy and agency. Her overview map closes Part I.

Chapter 1

The relationship between reading, thinking and writing the literature review component of a doctoral confirmation proposal

John Bitchener

In many universities, the first year of doctoral study is a provisional year. Confirmation of candidature typically follows a Board of Doctoral Studies approving the candidate's research proposal by the end of the first year. During this year, students develop the initial research proposal submitted with their doctoral application. Sometimes, a number of changes may be made to the initial proposal as a result of further reading, thinking, discussion and writing, but by the time they are required to present their proposal (always as a written document and often as a seminar as well), students need to have confirmed the direction of their research. The role of the supervisor (and any other supervisory team members) in guiding students through the provisional year can vary from institution to institution and from supervisor to supervisor. The aim of this chapter is to provide an overview of what I consider important in the first year so that students are well set up to produce a carefully considered and cogently defended research proposal. Essentially, the focus is on helping students understand the relationship between reading, thinking, discussing and writing about the proposed research topic.

STARTING WITH THE APPLICATION PROPOSAL

The application research proposal is typically less than 1000 words. It provides (1) a skeletal overview of the problem/issues that they want to investigate; (2) some form of literature contextualization and justification of the problem; and (3) an outline of the likely design and methodology of the project. Often, the proposal focus at this stage is more empirical than theoretical; any gaps in the literature that students have identified as worthy of investigation are presented as potential research questions. Proposals like these are not necessarily an indication of how widely students have read or thought about the literature in the field. Thus, if I am unable to meet applicants in person, I exchange a number of emails so that I can (1) probe how well they know the subject area; (2) determine whether or not they are able to argue and support ideas; and (3) see whether they can write clearly and effectively. While some applicants may meet all the university's criteria for enrolment, there is no guarantee that they will meet the expectations of supervisors. After all, some applicants have been known to ask other students or academics to write their proposals.

THE FIRST FACE-TO-FACE MEETING WITH A NEW STUDENT

Apart from introductions and an overview of the university's key doctoral processes and procedures, the first meeting with new students is critical for establishing a clear understanding of (1) what is involved in doctoral study; (2) differences between doctoral study and other types of university study; (3) the purpose and aims of the provisional year; (4) their stance towards and commitment to the focus of their initial proposal; and (5) what needs to be done in the following weeks and months as they seek to create their confirmation research proposal.

The discussion about the student's stance and commitment to the application proposal is important because some students, since submitting their application many months earlier, find that their thinking has developed and a new direction needs to be considered. Thus, it is important to be on the same page as the students when establishing the plan for the following weeks and months. This discussion is also important because it is the first chance that students have to hear what I think about their proposal, and the extent to which I believe it is likely to produce a thesis that moves the field forward theoretically, empirically and methodologically. Following this discussion, an action plan is negotiated. Typically this involves setting the date for the next meeting (usually within a week) and deciding what will be done before that meeting. The day before the meeting, students are asked to email me some bullet-point answers to questions in the following 'Pre-proposal questionnaire' (see box below). In order to answer the questions, students are expected to have reflected on their application proposal and completed some further reading and thinking about their proposed research focus.

PRE-PROPOSAL QUESTIONNAIRE

As a supervisor, I can never be sure what students will present at the second meeting. Typically, however, I find that they need some clear guidance about how to manage their reading, thinking and writing. The following section of this chapter outlines some of the key guidelines and strategies I discuss at the second meeting to help them develop a strong argument for the literature review component of the confirmation proposal.

- What is the problem or issue you want to investigate?
- What literature (theoretical and empirical) underpins the problem/issue?
- What gaps are there in the literature (theory and research)?
- What rationale can you give for suggesting that the gap is worth investigating?
- What do you think your research questions might be?
- What research approach and methods do you think you would use and why?

Provide a list of 12–15 key references that support what you have written here.

GUIDELINES AND STRATEGIES FOR READING, THINKING AND WRITING THE PROPOSAL LITERATURE REVIEW

The most effective proposals are those in which students (1) reveal a clear understanding of the literature they have read; (2) have selected that which is relevant to the problem, issue or question they plan to investigate; and (3) have clearly and rhetorically organized an argument and justified each component of the argument (i.e. each proposition), using the literature they have selected. Each requires careful thinking about what is read. There are a number of strategies that can be employed to facilitate the reading, thinking and planning-to-write stages so that the argument starts to be created from the reading of, and thinking about, the very first piece of literature.

Strategy 1: keeping a record of the focus or foci of each piece of literature

A spreadsheet can be used to record key information about each piece of literature. Table 1.1 illustrates what this may look like. The value of this type of record is that it enables students to see similarities and differences at a glance as well as providing them with a concise overview of the literature. Some students also like to record elsewhere other details about the literature (e.g. definitions of constructs and terms, key quotes and cross-references to other literature).

Strategy 2: creating a mind-map to show relationships between topics/headings

Table 1.1 shows how key topics or themes have been identified and recorded. These can then be included in a mind-map as the reading and thinking progress, and be moved about on the mind-map as new relationships between

Table 1.1 Sample key information on each piece of literature

Author/date	*Bitchener (2012)*	*Next author/ date . . .*
Key topics or themes	Types of written corrective feedback (CF) Effectiveness of different types Item-based vs rule-based linguistic error categories	
Key theories	Attention Noticing with awareness vs understanding	
Research questions	Are some types of written CF more effective than others for L2* development?	
Methodology and design	Pre-test/treatment/post-test Four groups (three treatment and one control) Linguistic focus: articles; simple past tense; prepositions	
Context and participants	ESL learners (mixed L1†) 75 low intermediate level	
Data sources	Three writing tasks Same genre	
Data analysis	Error analysis ANOVA testing of effectiveness of different groups	
Key findings	Direct error correction plus oral and written meta-linguistic explanation more effective than direct error correction alone for articles and past simple tense	
Limitations	Linguistic categories do not distinguish between sub-categories Treatment groups are sometimes more than one type of written CF	

*L2 = second language; †L1 = first language or mother tongue.

topics are understood. Thinking about relationships in this way means that students can start to focus on which ideas will be included in their proposal argument, and about the order in which the ideas will be included so that the argument is as logical and cohesive as possible. This approach means that the 'brain work' is done 'en route' rather than being left to a later stage in the reading process when some of the detail may have been forgotten. Mind-maps can become cluttered over time, so separate mind-maps can be created for certain topics/headings. During the reading process, some initial headings may be subdivided into two or more additional headings, while others may be collapsed into fewer headings. As Figure 1.1 illustrates, arrows can be used to show the relationship between topics/headings. Horizontal arrows can be used to signal whether a certain topic would make logical sense if it were to be discussed before a certain other topic. Sometimes, it

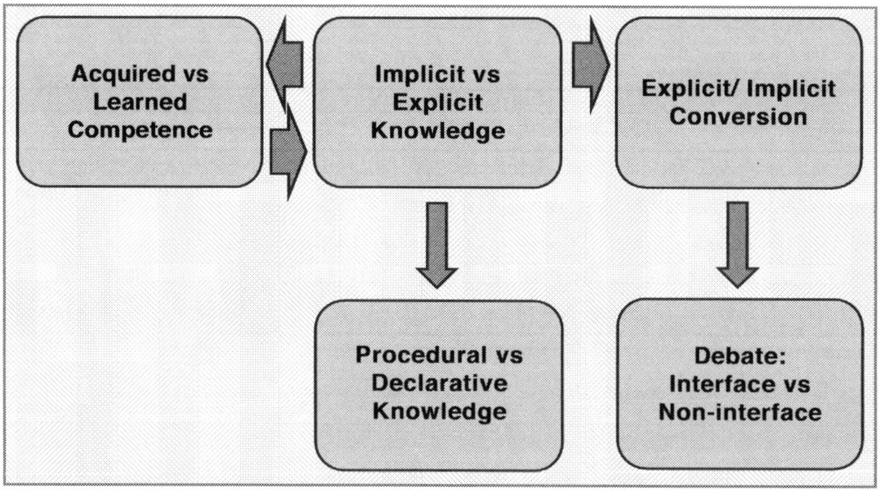

Figure 1.1 One section of a mind-map, showing relationships between topics

may not matter which of two topics/headings is discussed first. In this case, horizontal arrows pointing in both directions can be used to signal this possibility. On other occasions, students may want to create a new heading to signal that a topic needs to be expanded into a number of parts. For example, this may occur if there are several ways of defining a construct or term. This expansion of ideas/headings might be placed under the original topic/heading, with vertical arrows signalling the relationship.

Strategy 3: scoping the macro structure of the argument using a Table of Contents and/or PowerPoint slides

Creating a Table of Contents from mind-map relationships can help students to create a skeletal outline of the macro structure of their argument. As this is created, it is easy to see where the argument is heading and whether or not there are irrelevant topics or gaps in the argument. It can also reveal more easily whether certain topics or units need to be moved to a different position in the macro argument. Once students have created a Table of Contents like that shown in Figure 1.2, I ask them to talk me through the argument. This step reveals the extent to which they understand what they have written, and whether or not they can articulate the relationship between the ideas represented by the various headings and sub-headings. Students who experience some difficulty with this task may develop their Table of Contents more fully by creating PowerPoint slides (one for each major heading). The process of providing more information about each heading/ topic can help them to see the relationship between topics/headings more clearly and enable them to articulate the argument more effectively when they are asked to explain it again.

1.0 Goal of L2 learning: native/near-native competence
  1.1 Two types of competence: learned and acquired
2.0 Two types of knowledge: explicit and implicit
  2.1 Relationship between knowledge and competence types
  2.2 Explicit–implicit conversion debate
  2.2.1 *Interface position vs non-interface position*
3.0 Explicit information processing
  3.1 Skill acquisition theories
  3.1.1 *Anderson*
  3.1.2 *McLaughlin*
  3.1.3 *DeKeyser*
  3.2 Information-processing stages

Figure 1.2 Sample Table of Contents for a key heading

Strategy 4: writing an argument overview

This strategy asks the student to use the Table of Contents or the PowerPoint slides to write an argument overview (300–350 words) for a major section of the review and finally for an overview of the whole literature review. Having completed strategy 3, most students are able to create a reasonable first draft of the argument. Some students find it helpful if sample overviews are read and discussed first. The argument in the box below (for the theoretical justification of one research question in a doctoral dissertation) illustrates the type of overview that might be expected for one unit or section of the review. A deconstruction and discussion of this overview can also help students see how they can signal the relationship between the various components of the argument. Discourse markers and meta-text can be seen to be effectively signalling the connections between propositions.

CONCLUDING REMARKS ON THE ADVANTAGES OF THIS APPROACH

This approach has the advantage of helping students consider the direction of their argument as soon as they have read their first piece of literature. It asks them to think about the relationship between various topics and ideas across many pieces of literature and shape the direction of the argument as they read each item. The diagrammatic representation of the student's thinking makes it easier to see gaps or flaws in the argument than may be the case if one has to read many pages of text. This approach tends to reduce

EXAMPLE OF AN ARGUMENT OVERVIEW

- The aim of this section is to present a case that supports a role for written corrective feedback (CF) in L2 development, drawing upon theoretical perspectives that have something to say about the cognitive processing of L2 information and the potential of written CF as explicit L2 input to facilitate such processing.
- I begin by explaining that the central goal of L2 learning is the acquisition of native or near-native speaker competence.
- In doing so, I argue that acquired competence which draws upon implicit knowledge can be developed from learned competence that draws upon explicit knowledge such as that provided by written CF.
- Explaining this process, I refer to the skill acquisition models of Anderson and McLaughlin to show how explicit, declarative L2 knowledge can be proceduralized through meaningful, contextualized practice over time to a point where it may be converted to implicit, acquired knowledge.
- Then, I describe the specific information-processing stages identified by cognitive theorists like Tomlin and Villa, Schmidt and Swain, for example, that have been represented in frameworks such as the one designed by Gass (1997).
- In processing written CF as input, Gass's framework explains that learners need to attend to written CF as input if they are to progress through the other stages that will enable them to produce modified accurate output and ongoing accurate output in new written texts over time.
- The other stages include an understanding (comprehended input), an internalization and an integration of written CF as input.
- Producing accurate output as a result of this conscious processing is the beginning of a longer consolidation process during which practice is believed to facilitate acquired competence.
- I acknowledge that this linear route towards acquisition may be both facilitated and interrupted as a result of the type of written CF a learner is provided with, and as a result of intervening individual internal (cognitive and motivational/affective) factors and individual external factors.

The extent to which these theoretical proposals are valid explanations of the acquisition route is something that only empirical research can investigate. This will be the focus of the next section.

the number of iterations required to make the argument effective. Finally, because the thinking is done 'en route', it is less likely that students will experience 'a writing block'. This approach can also be employed when thinking about and writing other part-genres or chapters of a dissertation.

Chapter 2

Settling students into a community of practice

Vijay Kumar and Elke Stracke

Writing feedback intends to close a gap between an actual level of performance and an expected level of performance. There is often a gap between what supervisors perceive as useful feedback and what students really need. Our conversations with colleagues and analysis of written feedback on thesis drafts (Kumar and Stracke, 2007; Stracke and Kumar, 2010) indicate that many supervisors focus on error correction rather than providing feed forward to enable graduate students to move ahead with their writing. Yet students must develop writing skills, learning sophisticated writing conventions and practices that range from sustaining an argument to revising regularly and writing for subject specialists. The supervisor's role is to prompt the writer's development of writing skill. Feedback needs to provide a clear sense of direction forward for growth rather than merely feeding back on error.

When they engage with their students' work through feedback, supervisors usually prefer to focus on content-related matters. After all, they became the supervisor because of their shared interest in the student's topic area. However, if the student's ability to write has not yet developed to the desired level—and this is often the case regardless of whether the student is from a non-English-speaking background or not—supervisors are challenged to also provide assistance so that students acquire the writing conventions and practices that they need to demonstrate in their thesis. Literacy teaching is a time-consuming exercise, even more so when the quality of the student's written work is poor. Supervisors can tackle this challenge of providing useful feedback to their students—with regard to content *and* language matters—through dialogic feedback from the early stages of the candidature onwards in their one-to-one supervision meetings where the focus would often be on content matters.

Based on our experience as supervisors and our research into peer support groups (Stracke, 2010; Stracke and Kumar, 2014) we suggest that, in addition to the individual consultations, supervisors should settle students, from the very beginning of their candidature, into a community of practice (Lave and Wenger, 1991) in which they will engage in dialogic feedback practices, not only with their supervisor, but also with their peers (and perhaps other academics). Supervisors could encourage the formation of peer-led mentoring groups, preferably teaming up with other academic colleagues and merging groups of students. These peer support groups have been reported to provide positive learning experiences to postgraduate students (Buissink-Smith, Hart and van der Meer, 2013; Stracke, 2010; Stracke and Kumar, 2014). The advantages are many: graduate students can motivate each other, routinely give and receive feedback, share between them a range of academic writing skills (Carter and Kumar, 2016), and find an immediate audience for their written work. An additional benefit is that learning does not take place only within the supervisor–student interactions, but also with other members of the community of practice.

These peer-led groups could take proactive initiatives to acquire academic writing skills and explore the writing expectations of supervisors and examiners. In order to learn academic writing, group members can pick topics such as grammar issues, academic vocabulary, cohesion, structuring effective paragraphs, or identifying argument patterns. They could research these topics and share what they have learnt with their colleagues. Then they learn about writing and about teaching. The group members can also study examiner reports or previous theses to identify essential components. All these activities within the community of practice will address low-level concerns in writing in the early stages so that supervisors can focus on providing higher-level content-related feedback in their one-to-one meetings with the student.

We present in the following sections five strategies that supervisors could consider when working with their students in a community of practice: develop writing and feedback as a thinking process; encourage 'noticing' (Kumar and Kumar, 2009) and acquisition of lexical bundles and academic vocabulary; provide a range of feedback; consider the emotional aspects of feedback; and, finally, pre-empt possible misunderstanding and tensions. Depending on the university's support services, these strategies should ideally be implemented and practised with the support of academic skills advisors.

WRITING AND FEEDBACK AS A THINKING PROCESS

In essence, writing is a highly recursive and interactive process: changes can be requested in draft after draft and multiple revisions are expected. Recursiveness also implies that knowledge is contestable and thus becomes interactive through various levels of engagement with a range of readers. It is through these 'contests' and subsequent feedback that abstraction in writing is developed. The peer support group provides the first prospective audience to which this level of abstraction could be explained. A writer needs to plan before writing, and discuss these plans in peer support groups and with the supervisors prior to writing. In our experience of supervising postgraduate students, discussions using visual representations of emerging ideas, structures, and argument allow for better interaction and engagement with feedback. Feedback at different stages of writing, right from the conceptualization to the actual writing, provides developmental opportunities for the writer. Recursive feedback can regularly endorse the idea that writing is a form of thinking, and revision is a process of discovering new connections in writing.

LEXICAL BUNDLES

In our experience of studying supervisory feedback on drafts, academic staff often lament that their students' writing does not seem to reflect disciplinary discourse. Often, supervisors have difficulty providing the right type of feedback to bring the level of discourse to that of the discipline. Our suggestion is for supervisors to take note of the contributions of linguistics and consider *lexical bundles* (Cortes, 2004; Hyland, 2008a), word combinations that co-occur frequently in a discipline. Some examples are *'in the presence of'*, *'in the present study'*, and *'on the other hand'*, which Hyland (2008a: 12) lists as the three most frequent 4-word bundles for Biology, whereas he found that in Business Studies, the three most frequently used 4-word bundles were *'on the other hand'*, *'in the case of'*, and *'at the same time'*. The data that Hyland provides for four disciplines (Biology, Electrical Engineering, Applied Linguistics, and Business Studies) suggest that despite some bundles being used by all four disciplines (such as *'on the other hand'* in the examples above), there is variation between disciplines.

The frequent use of these lexical bundles is a marker of proficient academic writing (Bamberg, 1983; McCulley, 1985). In addition, lexical bundles 'occur and behave in dissimilar ways in different disciplinary environments' (Hyland, 2008a: 20). Supervisors may be so familiar with typical lexical bundles in their discipline through their own reading and writing that they are unaware of them. Thus, they may expect that students would have a similar understanding. Yet one study of lexical bundles used in History and Biology (Cortes, 2004) reported that students rarely use these bundles. The study concluded by demonstrating that even though these bundles appear frequently in texts, exposure to them does not mean that they are acquired and used without overt instruction (Biber and Barbieri, 2007; Cortes, 2004). Supervisors cannot assume that students will master the lexical bundles unconsciously or acquire them naturally, and could assist students to 'notice' them by reading published work together and highlighting key bundles related to text organization, markers, connectors, and phrases. Systematic teaching and explicit feedback on the use of these bundles assist the creation of academic discourse (Hyland, 2008a).

Beside lexical bundles, supervisors could also draw candidates' attention to various online academic phrase banks (e.g. *Academic Phrasebank* from the

University of Manchester in the UK; www.phrasebank.manchester.ac.uk). Another strategy to support students' development of discipline-specific use of word combinations could be to ask students to record interesting academic phrases that they come across as they read in their subject area. These phrases will develop their academic lexicon and widen the range of discipline-appropriate words to use in their academic writing.

THE FUNCTIONS OF FEEDBACK

Supervisors could benefit from considering the pragmatic functions of feedback: feedback can be referential, directive, and expressive (Kumar and Stracke, 2007). Referential refers to utterances that provide information (for instance, *'this does not belong in the literature review'*; for more examples, please refer to Kumar and Stracke, 2007). Directive refers to utterances that ask the writer to do something (for instance, *'whose term is this?'*), and expressive refers to utterances that express the speaker's feelings (for example, *'I would be interested to explore what triggered this'*). In the referential category, there are three main sub-categories: editorial, organization, and content. Editorial refers to lexicon issues; organization focuses on the logical structure of the text; and content is a consideration of whether information is relevant. In the directive category there are also three main sub-categories: suggestion, question, and instruction. Suggestion asks the candidate to consider something; question probes the candidate to reflect and have a fresh look over something; and instruction tells the candidate to do something. In expressive, there are also three main sub-categories: praise, criticism, and opinion. Praise comments positively; criticism comments constructively (or negatively); and opinion tells one's point of view.

Supervisors should note that candidates favour the expressive type of feedback (Kumar and Stracke, 2007)—that includes the supervisor offering their opinion, praise, and also criticism intended to improve the writing quality. The use of both praise and criticism has also been called the sandwich technique of providing feedback (Hyland and Hyland, 2001): feedback should begin with praise, followed by well-directed feed forward that ends with more praise. Supervisors could encourage the candidates they supervise to use the sandwich technique when providing peer feedback and to value the impact of praise in feedback.

EMOTIONAL ASPECTS OF FEEDBACK

An important aspect in supervision is the emotions involved when giving and receiving feedback (Boud and Molloy, 2013). The right kind of feedback will encourage learning and motivate students, while the wrong types can be counterproductive. We recommend as a caveat that if you can't think of a constructive purpose of giving feedback, don't give it at all. Empirical insights into emotional aspects of feedback (Boud and Molloy, 2013; Falchikov and Boud, 2007; Kumar and Stracke, 2007) indicate that long-lasting consequences of feedback could range from career choices to new learning initiatives. For example, comments such as *'irrelevant'*, *'rewrite'*, *'this is not of PhD standard'* (Carter and Kumar, 2016) may shatter students' confidence in writing, especially if the writer is only beginning to venture into academic writing at the postgraduate level. Indeed, such comments do not provide information that helps the writer to close the gap between their actual level of performance and the expected level of performance, our opening definition of feedback. Expressing the frustration of the feedback provider in summative negative assessment can ultimately have negative implications for the learner.

Two useful strategies that supervisors can use are:

- After writing the feedback, take a break, come back and read as if you were the candidate. Would you be emotionally affected by what has been written?
- Is there enough well-directed information to move the candidate forward with the revision? Have you provided feedback (and not assessment)?

PRE-EMPTING MISUNDERSTANDINGS AND TENSIONS

Misunderstandings and tensions do occur as a result of feedback. One way to overcome this is to establish good ground rules, especially in regard to what the expectations are when feedback is provided. Supervisors expect students to take on board the feedback that has been given; however, empirical research (Carter and Kumar, 2016) has implied that, at times, students ignore feedback. Supervisors are happy if students *decide* not to agree with the feedback and explain why, but fume when failure to respond seems due to laziness. Students could be asked to prepare a list showing changes they have made, and notes if they chose not to act on some feedback. Such practice is excellent preparation for the often-required candidate's response to examiners' reports and, ultimately, future submission of revisions to peer-reviewed journals.

Another possible area of tension is when supervisors overwrite the student's voice. Supervisors should mentor students to make revisions and guide them in the revision process—guiding involves discussions, pointing to the right directions, and perhaps writing together. They might model how they, as expert writers, would attend to the feedback. A final area of tension could arise if expectations are not clear. Some students may not be familiar with the kind and types of feedback that are given at the postgraduate level. Supervisors could discuss their strategies of providing feedback, and their expectations in subsequent drafts.

WHY IT MATTERS

Feedback plays a fundamental role in the development not only of a postgraduate writer, but also of an emerging researcher. Supervisors can enhance dialogic feedback practices by considering the value of communities of practice in the early stages of the candidature. They can help their candidates understand that writing is a thinking process while encouraging them to 'notice' appropriate academic and discipline-specific vocabulary. Supervisors need to provide a wide range of feedback, thus going beyond the often dominantly provided referential type of feedback. The emotive aspects of feedback need to be recognized, and supervisors need to be fully aware of the potentially damaging impact of negative, summative assessment if restraint is not exercised. Tensions and misunderstandings can be avoided by, on the one hand, making expectations clear and transparent; and, on the other, inviting the student to respond to such expectations. Based on our research into feedback practices, our writing experience in learning writing, and our experience as supervisors now, we acknowledge that the life of a writer is one of permanent insecurity. Our students, with less experience, will certainly share these feelings.

ACKNOWLEDGEMENTS

The authors shared the work to prepare this chapter equally.

Chapter 3

Framing feedback expectations

A 'pedagogy of explicitness'

Barbara M. Grant and Linlin Xu

SEEKING A GROUND OF SHARED UNDERSTANDING

Feedback on research writing is an intriguing part of supervision. For some supervisors, and I am one of them, it is the sine qua non of our practice. It's also enormously time-consuming and always operates within the delicate and complex psycho-socio-cultural dynamics of supervision that I have written of elsewhere (Grant, 2003). There are many ways to respond to such complexity: in this chapter, I write about a supervision practice that I think of as a (small) 'pedagogy of explicitness'. I often invent (or poach) practices of this kind—in which I try to establish a clear ground of shared understanding—when I find myself on particularly uncertain, yet high-stakes, terrain in supervision.

THE EXPECTATIONS GAP IN SUPERVISION

For many years I worked with university supervisors and research students on strengthening and enriching supervision practice. When I first began, I had no experience except that of being supervised as a master's student. At the time, though, I was a reasonably experienced and adventurous academic developer and, for several years, I worked in partnership with another, more experienced, colleague, Adele Graham, from whom I learned so much in many merry hours.

One of the insights we garnered early on was the gap in expectations commonly lying between supervisor and student with respect to how supervision worked. Over time, more than one University Mediator described supervision breakdowns and how fraught situations often had the humblest beginnings—a misunderstanding, say, over how long it would take to get feedback on a draft chapter, or confusion over who was responsible for setting meetings, or an unspoken disagreement about whether or not it was okay for the supervisor to have a conversation on the phone during a supervision meeting. The difference in structural power and the consequences of failure meant that misunderstandings very quickly escalated in significance, especially for the student. Adele and I also experimented with a 1-day workshop for supervisor–student pairs that included some separate discussion exercises: we were surprised, as were they, at the scale of the gaps between supervisor and student viewpoints for some issues.

As a consequence of this insight, Adele and I wrote a draft 'supervision contract' with a series of questions for supervisor and student to work through together in an early meeting. We sent the first draft to the Mediator and to interested supervisor colleagues for feedback, on the basis of which we prepared a revised document, now entitled 'Postgraduate Supervision: Guidelines for Discussion'. The document was always controversial: some supervisors refused to use it because it felt too legalistic, and most students felt that they could not suggest its use—it felt too presumptuous, given the difference in structural positions. Despite that, the 'Guidelines' live on in various forms: at the time of writing, a later edition can be found on the University of Auckland's website (University of Auckland, n.d.) and an adapted version is a resource for the on-line course on doctoral supervision offered by Epigeum in the UK. Adele and I also wrote about the document and its rationale (Grant and Graham, 1994); subsequently, research supervision became an enduring research interest for me.

Many years later, when my own supervision load suddenly began to increase, I thought again about that structural—and thus inevitable—gap between supervisor and student expectations. I decided to experiment with another pedagogy of explicitness, and drafted a 600-word document called 'Guidelines for Feedback on Writing in Supervision'.

CLARIFYING EXPECTATIONS ABOUT FEEDBACK ON WRITING: A ROCKY START

'Guidelines for Feedback' differed in style from the earlier document: rather than being a series of questions for discussion, it was a series of statements about my practice. The gist of the statements (in the order that I wrote them) was that:

- I was only prepared to read full proposal or chapter drafts twice.
- In between, I was happy to look at shorter pieces of writing that build towards full pieces.
- I expected draft work to accord to certain listed conventions.
- The return date would be set when I received the work.
- My 'fundamental feedback practice' had a predictable form.
- My practice in pointing out proofreading-level error had clear limits.

I also gave information about a doctoral writing group that students could join, which is organized by other doctoral students, but facilitated by me.

Having polished the draft carefully, I emailed it out to my students (five doctoral and two master's), my five co-supervisors, and two academic friends, with an invitation to give me 'critical feedback'. I described the guidelines as 'experimental' and said, 'I want to work with them for six months or so and then review them' (email, 11 January, 2012).

From my notes, three students (two doctoral, one master's) gave feedback as did one co-supervisor and both academic friends. Here, I explore some of those responses and the changes I made as a consequence. All quotations are included with permission.

Students responded with the following comments:

> [T]hank you for preparing these guidelines. I have read them through and printed out a copy so I have a copy at my desk before I send off writing to you. I don't have any feedback, other than they look helpful, but I'll read them again before I send you my standpoint piece and before our next meeting on Feb 10th, just in case there's anything I want to ask you about.
>
> (Doctoral student's email, 31 January, 2012)

This response is appreciative, but also guarded, which is not surprising given the structural inequality in power between supervisor and student. Interestingly, when I asked the student for her permission to include the quotation in this chapter, she wrote further about her reaction:

> Guidelines via email/text seem stripped of lots of communication clues and, although I found them a bit tough, I wasn't really sure how to voice that in a way that was respectful and because of course they were essentially reasonable, but also they felt quite fixed. I guess that's one of the contexts when tone can become especially important, when you're talking about borders, boundaries and responsibilities.
>
> (Doctoral student's email, 27 January, 2016)

Four years later, she offers a more analytical and *critical* view, which may be a function of having read the draft chapter, but also she has now worked with me for several years and we know each other better.

The other two student responses were verbal: the master's student thought the guidelines were clear, but a bit confronting. After we talked further in a supervision meeting, she wrote '. . . and thank you for putting my mind at ease yesterday' (24 January, 2012), which suggests she was quite worried about the implications of the guidelines. The doctoral student, who was an international student writing in English as an additional language, told me he thought the two-draft limit was a bit 'harsh', given his language skills. So the limits were worrying, for at least two students, who both preferred to talk to me about their concerns rather than write them in an email.

The responses from academic colleagues were encouraging, but some warning notes sounded as well:

> Thanks for this—it is so useful to see these processes and expectations being articulated and evolved, and I concur with all of your recommendations. It would be really good for us to also discuss our expectations of co-supervision . . .
>
> (Co-supervisor's email, 13 January, 2012)

The co-supervisor had no criticism to offer, but proceeded to build on the exchange by talking about how good it would be for him and me to talk about how our co-supervision would work. So the explicitness of the guidelines invited further explicitness, which was a valuable outcome for us both.

My friends, people whom I trust for their critical responses to my work, wrote:

> I think these are excellent and give students a clear sense of what your expectations are and what they can expect to get from you in return. . . . The one other thing that I found interesting was the tone of the guidelines. It is very crisp and matter of fact as it should be for guidelines, but *I wonder how students will hear that tone?*
>
> (Friend 1's email, 14 February, 2012; emphasis added)

> Thanks for these. They look really great. They really signal to students that they are in charge of their thesis project and need to take responsibility for their own writing. *The idea of saying you will only look at a draft chapter twice sounds a bit scary*, but I realize it's not set in stone for those who need more iterations and you have the other guidelines about looking at various forms of shorter work, outlines etc. And it should certainly encourage them to think carefully about whether or not they have got it into the best state before they send it off. *Might be a bit daunting for less confident students maybe?*
>
> (Friend 2's email, 11 February 2012; emphasis added)

Both friends sounded warnings thoughtfully couched as questions. I found their comments on tone interesting: it had not occurred to me until then that crispness and matter-of-factness can be experienced as uncompromising and scary, especially when it comes from a supervisor to a student. In the drafting process, I was overwhelmingly focused on getting practice guidelines clearly structured and expressed.

The friends' questions also echoed the expressed feedback of the two concerned students—and possibly those of students who did not give feedback. Silence always poses questions, but in New Zealand culture—from both Pākehā (descendants of British settlers) and Polynesian sides—silence towards authority quite often indicates disagreement.

TAKING TONE SERIOUSLY: REWORKING THE DRAFT

As a consequence of the feedback, I made quite a few amendments to the 'Guidelines for Feedback', although the substantive description of my practice remains unchanged. I continue to believe that it is helpful to use guidelines in an effort to make supervision expectations explicit from the outset. The second version of the document was expanded in scope to include a first page called 'My doctoral supervision practice', my 'womanifesto' of supervision. In this section, hoping to provide a softer ambience for the feedback guidelines to be read within, I tried to capture the ethos and values that underpin my practice. Here are the first four (of nine) statements:

> I am committed to helping students produce the best academic work they can under the circumstances in which they do their doctorates.
>
> I don't want my doctoral students' work to look like an imitation of the academic work I produce.
>
> I want to be kind: doing a doctorate is hard and many students work under difficult personal circumstances.
>
> I also want to be moderate in what I will do for the work. It is the student's work: their question, their reading, their research, their thinking, their writing that needs to happen. I want the student to finish knowing the work belongs to her or him, even though it was encouraged, influenced, sparked even, by others (which is the nature of academic work).

In the feedback guidelines document, I made a series of changes. At the suggestion of a friend who annotated the draft, I added a quotation from Laurel Richardson at the beginning about the deeper significance of writing, about why it's worth struggling with: "I consider writing as a method of inquiry, a way of finding out about yourself and your topic" (Richardson, 2000: 923).

In a similar vein, I moved the statement about my hopes for students' writing from the end of the document to the beginning:

> By the time you have finished your doctoral thesis, I want you to be able to write good scholarly prose and to have found a writing voice that you enjoy. Through giving feedback on your writing, I'll give you advice and materials to assist with this goal.

In the list of guidelines, I moved the one about responding to short pieces up to the beginning of the list so that it started on a positive note of what I *will* do, rather than on a negative one of what I *won't*. The first guideline now reads:

> I like to get writing from students as soon as possible and regularly. This can include responses to reading, outlines, short sections of chapters, or agreed writing exercises. In this way, you can get into the habit of writing, which is essential for getting finished. You can also test out samples of certain kinds of writing, such as critical literature review, theoretical explanation, data analysis etc., and get feedback to help you strengthen them.

I also tweaked some guidelines to be more positive. For example, I replaced 'make sure this is not a raw draft' with 'ensure it is a good draft', and 'I don't see my job as being a proof-reader' with 'over time, you need to learn to be your own proof-reader'. I added 'sometimes I use comments' after the earlier statement that 'I never use track-changes'. And I modified the most forbidding guideline (the limit of two readings for full drafts of chapters, etc.) by adding a note about setting up peer exchanges with other doctoral students.

REFLECTIONS: AN UNSETTLED TEXT

Nowadays I give my guidelines on supervision practice and feedback to any student who approaches me for supervision to inform their thinking about whether I might be a suitable supervisor or not. From long and wide experience, I suggest that some kind of clarity about student and supervisor expectations of supervision be a central aim for the discussion that occurs as the supervision is established. More specifically, clarity about the all-important but ticklish work of giving feedback on writing may help to pre-empt those supervision breakdowns our Mediators reported.

I also continually tweak my guidelines. To date, I haven't taken up the suggestion made by one of the friends to negotiate feedback on writing guidelines individually with each student, partly because the purpose of the document is to establish a transparent baseline for all students. In practice, though, I do vary my approach in the light of various factors.

To close this chapter, I asked Linlin Xu, one of my doctoral students, to respond to the latest version of the guidelines in terms of how she thinks they are likely to be read by other international, especially EAL, students. Linlin is researching written feedback from non-Chinese supervisors on draft proposals written by Chinese international doctoral students—her research expertise makes her an astute co-author. Linlin picks up the story with her thoughtful response:

> The supervision practice and feedback guidelines are very helpful in making clear what is expected of doctoral students and what they can expect from the supervisor. Such clarity is of especial importance to newly arrived international students who, like myself, come from countries with different academic and supervision cultures. The guidelines can save them the troubles of experimenting. I can still remember the stressful days of exploring the right codes for being the right student when I was new here. With these documents, the students can figure out the 'gaps' and either adjust themselves to meet the new rules, or initiate communication with the supervisor to bridge the gaps, or take action somewhere in between.
>
> However, as a Chinese international student from a high power-distance culture where teachers stand far above students, I feel very reluctant to challenge the supervisor's authority, let alone situate myself as a so-called equal to communicate any differences or disagreements. Particularly, I sense an assertive tone all through the document, such as 'I want to', 'I only want to',

> 'I don't want to', 'I like to', and so on. Those phrases give me the impression of non-negotiation, which scares me far away from communication.
>
> In addition, I think further clarifications on certain requirements would facilitate students' understanding. For example, both documents mentioned 'writing from the students as soon as possible'. This sounds a bit scary, to be honest, and what is meant by 'as soon as possible'? One week or one month? The item about independence is also frightening and ambiguous. In my home country, I received a differing style of education, in which students are highly dependent on their teachers. Therefore, I also have difficulties in understanding the implications of 'your work: your question, your reading, your research, your thinking, and your writing'. Does this mean I have to do all these things on my own? I think some examples of help and scaffolding from the supervisor could elucidate this point and calm students down.
>
> Lastly, the idea of 'seeing the whole piece of writing twice' makes me so anxious. Being a second-language learner poses extra difficulties for my academic writing, apart from the subject knowledge. I really don't have the confidence to complete quality writing with only two rounds of feedback. Although there is a mention of 'good reason to bend', I may not be able to give these reasons as, in my culture, this would indicate my incompetency and give extra workload to the supervisor, which may be threatening to the harmonious supervision relationship.
>
> Overall, this document is valuable for making supervision and learning visible and communicable. However, further consideration of the students' cultural background may increase the document's effectiveness when students are not used to communicating and negotiating with their teachers, but to following and obeying.

Linlin's thoughtful and informed reflections challenge me as supervisor to think further about my document's pedagogy, about how it might be read by students from a variety of places and about how I *want it to be read*. I can see another version on the near horizon. To me, such documents are only worth creating and using as unsettled texts—as living expressions of the tensions that arise when trying to clarify complex but substantive elements within the work of supervision.

For a copy of the current document, 'Supervision Practice and Feedback Guidelines 2017', please contact the main author.

Chapter 4

Setting up frameworks

Anne Lee

In this chapter, I deconstruct the process of student research writing in two ways: first, by analysing from the student or candidate's perspective the stages of understanding what academic writing is; and second, by looking at the many ways the supervisor or advisor could help the novice researcher move through these stages. I use the terms *candidate, researcher* or *student* interchangeably to refer to the student who is aiming to write at a doctoral level. Internationally, the debate around nomenclature is influenced by local practices. In some countries and departments, the phrase 'student' is firmly used where enabling learning is seen as central; in other countries, the emphasis is on creating academic colleagues, so 'early career researcher' is preferred, with 'doctoral candidate' emphasizing the fact that assessment and a rite of passage are looming. As we will see throughout this chapter, these hints about the envisaged identity of our researchers will also affect how we supervise and how they expect to respond to our advice and mentoring. The terms *supervisor, advisor, coach* and *mentor* are also used interchangeably. However, their meanings vary across nations. We do need to know what is meant by them in the context in which they are used. More importantly, the doctoral candidate needs to understand what we mean by them.

I work with both doctoral students (in short courses entitled 'Managing your supervisor' or 'Getting the best out of your supervision') and with supervisors and advisors in many countries and across many disciplines. Sometimes this takes place in the context of longer, assessed and accredited supervisor development programmes, and sometimes in a shorter workshop or course. In advance of these sessions, I might ask participants to describe their main challenges either in writing or in small discussion groups. Of 380 people surveyed by questionnaire (comprising 332 research supervisors and 48 doctoral candidates), over 25% of the supervisors raised concerns directly related to doctoral candidates and their writing. Comments included:

> My student finds it difficult to write concisely and clearly, keeping to the main point and sticking to the topic.
>
> My main concern is how to get the student to learn the right 'mind set' for writing scientific papers.
>
> They need to realize that analyzing data and writing up take time.
>
> My research students are insecure about whether what they are writing is 'good enough'.
>
> They find it difficult to structure their ideas and adopt the right tone or register.

From the supervisor or advisor's perspective, there are management and ethical concerns as well:

> I am worried about the sheer amount of time involved in reading drafts, often when new material is combined with older material that I have read before.
>
> I have difficulties with students for whom English is not their first language—feeling as though I have to correct drafts as I read through them.
>
> I am concerned about knowing when to push them to begin writing versus giving them the space to explore ideas and read widely.
>
> Can I trust them not to cheat/plagiarize?
>
> And the plaintive cry: 'Just how do I get them writing?'

The student voice also echoes this concern but in a slightly different way. There was concern about their ability to write, and about feedback, particularly where there is a perceived absence of it or where what is provided is not clear to them. Further research would be fruitful.

HOW DO WE COME TO UNDERSTAND WHAT ACADEMIC WRITING IS?

This section identifies some of the key stages in the academic writing journey. I have put them in a flow chart to try for some chronological order. This is necessarily generic and these issues will not necessarily be experienced by every researcher or in this order.

Figure 4.1 below identifies some key elements in academic writing. These may be altered to suit particular disciplines or genres or even individual supervisors' preferences, but the aim of producing such a flow chart is to give supervisors and advisors a toolkit for identifying areas where more detailed supervision is necessary.

If we explore these headings in a little more detail, their use may become self-evident.

Words on a page: this refers to an early and naïve conception of academic writing. There is little understanding of plagiarism, rigor or verifiability and

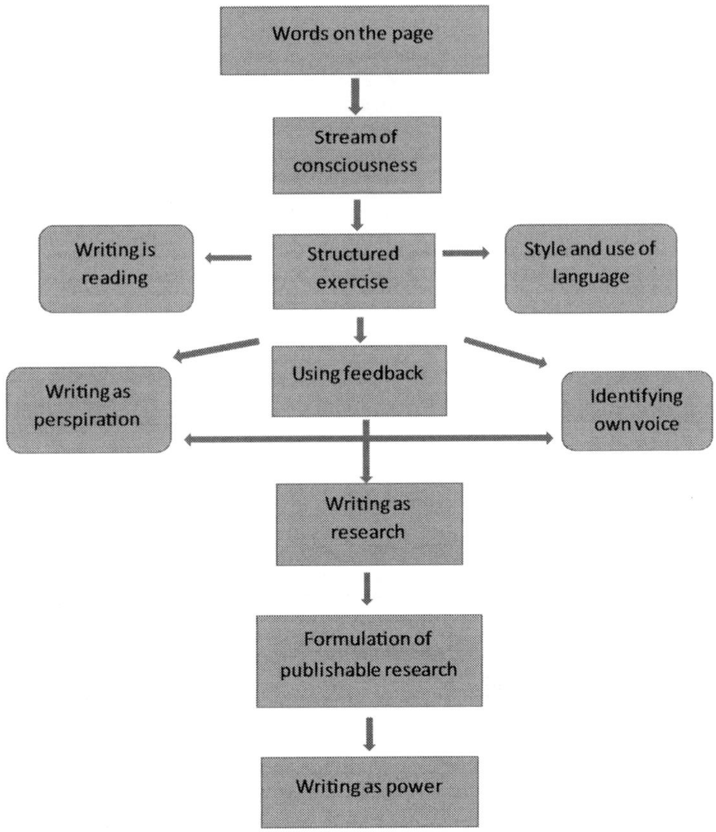

Figure 4.1 A chronological approach to elements of academic writing

anyone's words that are relevant to the topic can be included in roughly any order. There may be an understanding of the need for a beginning, middle and a conclusion, but even that might be a cultural demand that is foreign to some.

Stream of consciousness: here I have borrowed the phrase used to describe the approach of early twentieth-century authors, such as Virginia Woolf. There is an increased introspection and self-awareness about writing at this stage (as well as a desire to have agency, 'a room of one's own' [Woolf, 2002]). There is a tendency to be highly self-critical, which can mean students find it difficult to write anything because they feel inadequate. It also marks the beginning of a later stage which is about 'finding your voice'.

A structured exercise: there is a growing understanding of the need for structure. It might be to understand the Anglo-American idea of how an essay is expected to be written, or recognize that another form of skeleton is needed. At this stage, a supervisor or advisor might identify sub-headings, chapter headings or key themes for each paragraph. They will also need to emphasize the importance of keeping a file of references and some form of reference management system.

Writing is reading: there are two main reasons for encouraging reading. First, candidates need to master the research knowledge base, and conceptualize the literature survey. In some countries and in some professional doctorates, this first 'mastery of knowledge' phase is examined before the candidate is allowed to proceed. The second reason is cultural: encouraging students to understand how writing is undertaken within a particular discipline (or disciplines) and in different countries—with regard to the language that the thesis is to be written in (see Kumar and Stracke's 'noticing' in Chapter 2 in this book).

Style and use of language: some supervisors struggle with their own writing when it comes to grammar or even word choice. A heavy reliance on the grammar and spell checkers available within computerized systems does not deal comprehensively with inadequate or incorrect terminology or use of language. Some textbooks such as Swales and Feak (2004), Strunk and White (2011) or the classic by Fowler (Burchfield, 1996) can help both advisors and doctoral candidates identify and work on problem areas.

Using feedback: as many have observed, writing is usually a social (as well as a socialized) process. Doctoral students need to understand the art of encouraging and using critical feedback. It is part of the academic endeavour to seek out criticism, preferably before publisher rejection or examiner rebuttal. A dialogue between supervisors and researchers to manage expectations about how much feedback is given, and when it can be expected, is important. Equally, opening up researchers' awareness of other sources of feedback is important (for example, can they engage in journal clubs or peer groups?).

Writing as perspiration: closely linked to the idea of getting feedback is the understanding that academic writing is about rewriting, rewriting and rewriting. Sometimes this notion helps overcome the fears associated with writer's block, because knowing that what is first put on the page is never going to be good enough can free people up to start writing. Rowena Murray has published many ideas around generative writing (Murray, 2011) and the implicit requirement for constant editing.

Identifying your voice: this stage links the formulation of the researcher's identity (possibly, their identity as an academic) with an understanding of their own perspective within their field, and their relationship with the audience. As Kamler and Thomson argue, identity is both plural (we have many and evolving identities) and a performance (2006: 16–17). As the writer begins to embrace an ontological perspective, so their voice becomes clearer. The supervisor will be asking, 'Who are you writing for?', 'What do you want them to believe?' and 'What do you want them to believe about you?'

Writing as research: the accumulation of all the above elements is leading to a comprehension of how to formulate original knowledge: whether the author believes original knowledge is an incremental step in understanding or a major reformulation and reframing of an idea will be becoming apparent.

Inherent in the idea of writing as research is the proposition that research is only valuable if it is communicated in some way. There will need to be discussions about intellectual property, patents, copyright, and creative commons licensing at this stage.

Formulation of publishable research: at doctoral level, there are many definitions of 'publishable'. The reality of publication is that it is difficult. The threads of writing as a social activity are picked up again here when discussions about co-publishing and co-authorship need to happen. The medical profession has promoted the Vancouver Protocol (www.research.mq.edu.au/documents/policies/Vancouver.pdf) and many others have used it as a lever for negotiation over authorship. It states:

> All persons designated as authors should qualify for authorship. Each author should have participated sufficiently in the work to take public responsibility for the content. Authorship credit should be based only on substantial contributions to
>
> 1) conception and design, or analysis and interpretation of data; and to
> 2) drafting the article or revising it critically for important intellectual content; and on
> 3) final approval of the version to be published.
>
> Conditions 1, 2, and 3 must all be met. Participation solely in the acquisition of funding or the collection of data does not justify authorship. General supervision of the research group is not sufficient for authorship.

Different disciplines have very different protocols in their publications: in some cases, authors are always cited in alphabetical order; in others, the first and last named authors are recognized as having made the most substantive input; and in other cases, it might be the first and second named authors who are most prominent. Understanding these, sometimes implicit, rules is an important part of learning to negotiate (and renegotiate) one's place in the authorial hierarchy. It becomes even more complex when interdisciplinary teams publish together.

Writing as power: publishing research is in itself an insufficient objective. As many research councils and ethics committees are now demanding, there has to be some awareness of the potential use and impact of the research. Here the opportunity for research to change the world needs to be explored. Assuming that the message has been ethically and rigorously arrived at, how it is conveyed and to whom (finding authorial voice and adapting it to write for different cultures, disciplines and audiences) becomes the key objective.

COMBINING TWO FRAMEWORKS

Some readers will be familiar with an established framework used for different approaches to supervising research (e.g., Lee, 2008; Lee, 2012; Lee and Murray, 2015). The framework I am using below integrates five main approaches to supervision. They intertwine in a complex manner and although they are disentangled here for clarity, in practice they are inter-dependent.

- Functional: where students' projects are managed;
- Enculturation: where students are encouraged to become a member of the disciplinary community;
- Critical thinking: where students are encouraged to question and analyse their work;
- Emancipation: where students are encouraged to question and develop themselves;
- Developing a quality relationship: where students are enthused, inspired and cared for.

The purpose of the framework is to prompt supervisors to think of different ways of supervising students so that they can adapt to meet the differing needs of different students at different stages in the research process.

Table 4.1 describes what students may be seeking from supervisors and advisors through the doctoral process. They might be seeking any combination of these factors at any time during the process, which makes supervision an interesting and challenging process.

A researcher operating from a *functional* position will be focusing on the project timetable, whether or not deadlines are being met, the assessment and prevention of risks that could lead to failure, the number of words they need to write and the interim assessment procedures they need to navigate through. A student focusing more on *enculturation* will be looking to be part of the research or academic community, and wanting to be invited to the research seminars, journal clubs and conferences. They will be keen to steep themselves in the literature that is relevant to their topic and important in the department. Feedback on their writing from peers and colleagues will be eagerly sought. This is different to the candidate who is operating from the *critical thinking* approach, for whom inquiry becomes almost an obsession. They will be constantly asking themselves the question 'in how many ways could I be wrong?' They will be looking for fallacious assertions hidden in the written word, and wanting to see a strong thread uniting a coherent argument in any piece of work. Enculturation contrasts particularly strongly with *emancipation*. The student seeking an emancipated approach from their supervisor may react strongly against the imposition of what they may see as artificial deadlines, rigid disciplinary conventions and forced attendance at various events. The difficulty in supervising this student's academic writing is in judging whether they are formulating an innovative project with new ways of expressing themselves, or are timewasting and filibustering. It is the brave and perhaps foolhardy supervisor who does not require some evidence of the ability to write early on.

There is some evidence to suggest that candidates value the fifth approach, *relationship development*, more than their advisors do (Löfström and Pyhältö, 2015). In this approach, the student wants to feel that their writing is

Table 4.1 What do students want? Identifying student motivation, objectives and needs

	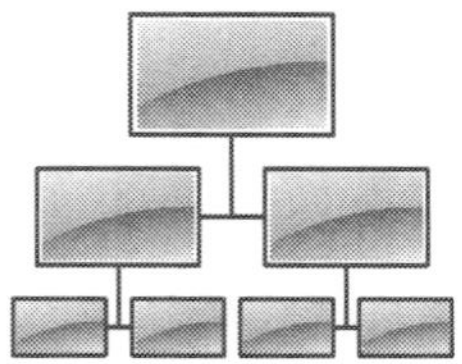				
	Functional	*Enculturation*	*Critical thinking*	*Emancipation*	*Relationship development*
What students might be seeking	Certainty Clear signposts Evidence of progress	Belonging Direction Career opportunities Role models	Ability to think in new way Ability to analyse, recognize flaws in arguments	Self-awareness Autonomy Self-actualization	Friendship Nurturing Equality

Table 4.2 A chronological approach to elements of academic writing extended by analysis through the framework of five approaches to research supervision

	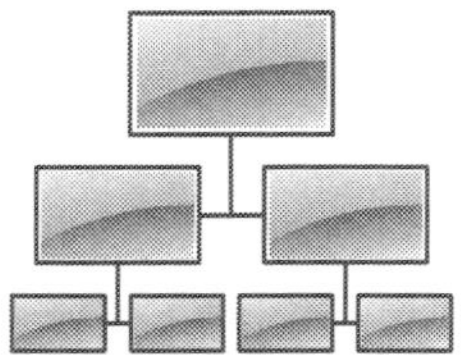				
	Functional	*Enculturation*	*Critical thinking*	*Emancipation*	*Relationship development*
Words on the page	Short writing task in response to prompts	Explore the difference between popular and academic articles	Discuss the 'chronological elements' as appropriate	Encourage generative writing on the topic	Share your passion for the topic or research methods
Stream of consciousness	Write anything on given topic for 5 minutes	Look at popular writers on the topic	Encourage reflective writing (theorizing from experience)	Freewriting (see Elbow, 1989; Murray, 2011)	Discuss own use of academic reflection
Structured exercises	Set a series of headings to write to	Look at headings in other theses and journal articles. Share referees' reports	Analyse the purpose of structure. Encourage precision	Compare writing with and without structure	Take a piece of your own writing and reveal its inner structure
Writing is reading	Give a series of journal articles to read	Look at good examples of literature reviews	Look at how literature reviews are structured	Set reading about students' doctoral journeys	Share your own reading and note-taking strategies
Style and use of language	Encourage the student to go to generic writing courses	Enable peer review of writing style	Analyse the style of great writers, e.g. Bertrand Russell	Encourage reading widely	Share reading work out loud so that you can stop and discuss key points

Using feedback	Establish a protocol for feedback; keep records of feedback	Encourage attendance at journal clubs, presenting work at seminars and conferences, etc.	Explore the role of feedback in developing critical thinking	Discuss whether your feedback is having impact and what the student wants	Share how you have dealt with difficult feedback; give feedback verbally (face to face) and in writing
Writing as perspiration	Discuss time management of writing and rewriting	Look at the careers of successful academics in your field	Analyse the processes involved in getting to a completed piece of work	Discuss how to cope with tiredness, boredom and failure	Share your own writing and rewriting experiences
Identifying your voice	Explain any important academic conventions	Identify who the critical readers are and what is most likely to influence them	Discuss ways to identify the likely audience for any given piece of work	Help the doctoral candidate identify when they are 'in flow' writing.	Describe how your own inner voice works when you are writing
Writing as research	Setting a project plan and timetable	Chart the evolution of thought through key articles in your subject	Look at what can be accepted as original knowledge	Explore how the student formulates their ideas	Share first and final drafts of articles you have written
Formulation of publishable research	Set or negotiate a publications plan	Discuss authorship policies. Look at key journals in which to seek publication	Formulate a strategy for publishing work	Discuss whether or not publication is important to the student	Reveal the impact that publishing your work has had
Writing as power	Discuss what you mean by power. Set objectives and create a plan to realize them	Look at careers successful researchers in your field have subsequently undertaken	Probe the values that are important to the researcher	Look at the role of autonomy in research	Share any ethical concerns that you have

personally valued and to exchange ideas about how to cope with writing challenges. These approaches are summarized in Table 4.1 below.

This framework plays out against the chronological elements of doctoral students' understanding of the academic writing process as described above. So, if the advisor believes that the candidate is at stage 1 (just about getting the words down on the page), they might use any of the five approaches described above (or any combination of them) to move them on to the next stage. For example, in an early discussion, they might ask the student to bring in a popular magazine article on the topic and contrast it with an academic journal's article (enculturation), or reveal the chronological stages described in Figure 4.1 and ask the student what he or she thinks about such a process (critical thinking).

Table 4.2 is intended to show how the framework of five approaches can create new ways of looking at supervising writing. There is more information on this framework, and suggestions for more writing tasks in Chapter 13 (see also Lee and Murray, 2015).

Enabling writing at this most advanced level is an essential part of supervision. For many academics, words are the central tool of their trade, and focusing on how to craft them and what they mean both epistemologically and ontologically is both an exciting and central part of advising on original research projects.

* * *

Establishing focus on writing—things to do

- Jointly develop 'things to think about' checklist.
- Talk about writing practices, its many forms and stages, the drudgery of reiteration, and the emotions involved.
- Develop a document of your own expectations for writing and feedback, share with the students, remaining aware of cultural and power ratio differences.
- Set manageable tasks from the outset.
- Establish templates for responding to literature, mind-mapping, etc.
- Recommend exemplars of written text (theses and experts in the field).
- Encourage students to 'notice' language use when reading and consciously acquire relevant lexical bundles and academic vocabulary.
- Re-read feedback from students' point of view: rephrase negatives as positives, observations as 'action points', vague statements as clear concrete ones that enable development.
- Explain protocols around writing and feedback deadlines.

Part II

Making use of other resources along the way

Deborah Laurs; E. Marcia Johnson and Andrea Haines; Cally Guerin and Claire Aitchison; Inger Mewburn and Pat Thomson

Edited by Deborah Laurs

> ***Supervisor:*** *In my experience, candidates value having an extra pair of support hands [in a process] which is fairly labour intensive.*
>
> ***Student:*** *Resist saying 'just do . . .'; show how. If you don't have time to show how, acknowledge this and direct your student to someone who can.*

Sometimes students expect feedback at the very moment supervisors are tied up with other commitments. Once supervisors have responded to a draft, the resubmitted version may come back largely unchanged—or so completely reworked that the feedback process must begin all over again. Alternatively, students may have nothing to show on paper even after months of apparent 'writing', creating tension about how to get them producing. At times, it can feel as though supervisor and student are working at cross-purposes, neither truly certain what the other one wants.

Moreover, underpinning students' production of written text are implicit skills—grammar, stylistics, critical thinking, paraphrasing, structure, referencing, data analysis—whose mastery only becomes apparent in their absence. Readers know what works and what doesn't, but, as noted in other chapters, supervisors are often less able to articulate concerns. Vague feedback such as *'what are you trying to say here?'* puzzles a student author for whom the meaning is perfectly clear. Making the shift from writing for oneself to writing for an audience is crucial within the thesis-writing process, a developmental transition that is aided by feedback and discussion in multiple spheres; that is, beyond the supervision meetings.

The growing awareness of the interrelation between research and *writing* about research (Boote and Beile, 2005) has led to a call for supervisors to model effective academic writing (Lavelle and Bushrow, 2007) and/or for institutionally-based writing courses (Rose and McClafferty, 2011). However, as shown by a recent New Zealand study (Bitchener et al., 2011: 22), many supervisors remain ambivalent about the extent of their responsibility for developing students' linguistic and stylistic skills. Similarly, our data identify that supervisors' greatest frustration is the amount of time they devote to feedback, time they perceive as under-valued institutionally. Accordingly, this Part makes the case that supervisors need to actively encourage doctoral students to take up all available avenues of feedback and support with writing—academic learning centres, online resources and peer-writing groups—in order to complement supervisory input and enhance the doctoral writing feedback process.

Contributors draw upon literature and a wealth of personal experience: in Chapter 5, Deborah Laurs argues for the involvement of academic learning advisors at all stages of the doctoral journey; E. Marcia Johnson and Andrea Haines (Chapter 6) describe a generic writing workshop programme showing the benefits of talk across disciplines; Cally Guerin and Claire Aitchison (Chapter 7) demonstrate the value of peer writing groups in supporting students' production and critical evaluation of written text; and in Chapter 8, Inger Mewburn and Pat Thomson evaluate the growing array of writing resources available online. Encouraging students to take advantage of any or all of these additional resources constitutes good-quality supervision.

Chapter 5

The role of tertiary learning advisors in successful doctoral completion

Deborah Laurs

Together with library and IT-related support, many institutions offer adjunct academic support to help students develop skills for success. Often, learning centres are assumed to primarily focus on undergraduates' transition into tertiary studies and/or on developing EAL students' academic literacy (Chanock, 2007; Percy, 2011). However, in response to the world-wide growth in postgraduate enrolments, academic learning advisors also work closely with higher-degree students on all aspects of postgraduate skills development, including thesis writing.

Rather than expecting supervisors to possess—or somehow acquire—proficiency in grammar and academic literacy over and above their research-specific expertise, institutions commonly have learning advisors who p ossess these skills already. Well-versed in the thesis as a genre, its moves and components (Paltridge and Starfield, 2007), learning advisors see many more instances of postgraduate writing than any one supervisor. Referring students to a learning centre not only frees supervisors to concentrate on more research-specific matters, it also affords student access to a wide range of writing-related expertise, both academic and technical (Picard and Guerin, 2011). At the most fundamental level, this may entail attending 'research skills' workshops and seminars on generic topics such as research proposals, literature reviews and ethical approval. In more targeted cases (instigated by either student or supervisor), learning advisors can work with students one-on-one. Learning advisors provide formative guidance at each stage of the writing process and can also support distance students through digital channels (Larsson and Hansson, 2011; Picard and Guerin, 2011). For many students, the very act of explaining the situation to a learning advisor—*'My supervisor says my writing isn't critical enough'*, *'I'm not sure how to re-work this section, but I think I should probably . . .'* or *'I want to conduct five case studies but I suspect that's too many'*—is an ideal first step towards figuring out the solution. Operating outside the formal student–supervisor relationship (Carter and Laurs, 2014), learning advisors play a valuable role in helping students refine their thoughts—developing audience awareness in the process.

In practical terms, learning advisors help to address supervisors' requirements by translating feedback into actions. Depending on the student and stage of writing, learning advisors can help with any or all of the following: grammar and syntax; the reader-centric, deductive nature of (Anglo-) thesis structure; rhetorical devices such as signposting and hedging; and editing and proofreading techniques. For students with English as an Additional Language, the merits of such professional input are obvious. Similarly, supervisors may know native speakers who would also benefit from writing support. Ideally, students should be encouraged to seek advice early, tackling writing-related issues from the first, rather than the penultimate, draft.

As well as improving written expression, learning advisors help students to hone their thinking, by acting as intelligent readers and impartial sounding boards (Carter and Laurs, 2014). Having to explain your research to a third party is always valuable, even more so if that someone is familiar with the thesis genre as a whole. A simple prompt from a learning advisor often effectively triggers the student's self-reflection about what to do next. In the process, implicit assumptions often come to light. For example, a student may mention that, in her home country, it may be that antibiotics are freely available in the local markets, whereas in another, teachers are appointed for life and promoted on seniority: contexts that make health or educational reforms even more challenging than academic readers might otherwise expect. Contextualizing such details within the thesis not only addresses readers' concerns, it also promotes students' confidence in their own voice. Similarly, working with students to unpack supervisory comments such as *'meaning unclear'* normalizes the dialogic nature of the feedback relationship, as well as highlighting the importance of attending to audience needs. If the supervisor and the learning advisor find a passage difficult to follow, examiners are likely to react similarly. Better to address such matters earlier, rather than later.

Learning advisors' status as 'outsiders' removes them from the perceived power dynamics (Grant, 2003) often associated with the formal supervisory relationship. Meetings between student and learning advisor are confidential and 'low-stakes', potentially allowing students greater freedom to voice uncertainties or half-formed ideas than more formal supervisory meetings. In some instances, students view a meeting with the learning advisor as similar to a coaching session, an opportunity to take stock of where they are. Some schedule regular appointments as a way of staying on track, sometimes bringing written work, at other times simply talking about why they haven't written anything—as a prelude to getting started again. By encouraging students to explain where they are, why (if that's the case) they are stuck, 'what I really mean is . . .' (WIRMI, see Flower, 1989), and what they plan to do next, informal sessions with a learning advisor can generate valuable grist for students (as in, 'Now go and tell your supervisor') to build on.

However, having multiple actors working towards the same goal requires careful negotiation of boundaries. In many institutions, learning centres operate under the same confidentiality constraints as health and counselling services, meaning that interaction between learning advisor and supervisor needs to be initiated by the supervisor or the student. Students working independently with a learning advisor may be reluctant to let supervisors know they are seeking additional support, whereas those referred by their supervisor are likely to feel aggrieved (if not dismayed) that their writing is apparently not considered up to standard. Students may misconstrue advice: telling a learning advisor their supervisor wants them to work on *x* when they should in fact be addressing *y*, or reporting resultant suggestions (as in *'the learning advisor said . . .'*) in a manner that appears to challenge supervisors' primacy. In order to work, student–supervisor–advisor communication channels should be transparent and clearly delineated (Carter and Laurs, 2014). Negotiation may require diplomacy, with supervisors emphasizing, for example, that seeking additional guidance is a normal part of the thesis-writing process, rather than some form of remediation (even if—*particularly* when—it is exactly that). In this way, the specialist writing support offered by academic learning advisors, in the form of research skills workshops and seminars and one-to-one consultations, has potential to complement the supervisory relationship, addressing the needs of all concerned.

Chapter 6

Making the implicit explicit

Generic writing workshops

E. Marcia Johnson and Andrea Haines

RATIONALE

Our main focus as academic learning developers has been to design and implement generic writing development opportunities for doctoral students. Recent research (Johnson, 2013) with supervisors and students into doctoral writing threshold concepts (TCs) identified that students can lack an understanding of what doctoral 'writing' actually requires. They also lack confidence to structure and present ideas at the doctoral level. From these findings, two TCs emerged—'talking to think' and 'developing self-efficacy' (Johnson, 2013).

Academic writing involves much more than the mechanics of putting words on the page, although clearly that is a crucial starting point. Only through a process of reflection and discussion (internally with the self and with others) can intellectual and written clarity of expression emerge. Self-efficacy is closely linked, but includes more than self-confidence and independence. To become a competent doctoral writer, one must also possess the ability to

> understand research practices, extract meaning from data, clearly articulate ideas (talk), and then present, shape, and reshape text on the page (write). Completing a written thesis requires resilience and also includes the belief that understanding will emerge as new ideas are discussed, clarified, written, and refined.
>
> (Johnson, 2014: 74)

Along the way, students can become lost in 'liminal space' (Meyer and Land, 2005), unable to determine what needs to be done next or what steps to follow. This can be demotivating.

Our approach to helping doctoral students across intellectual thresholds and into self-efficacy as doctoral writers has been guided by activity theory.

The concept of activity derives from sociocultural theory (Lantolf, 2005), which recognizes that virtually all human endeavours are embedded within, and mediated by, a social matrix of people and artefacts (tools). Mediation of doctoral writing development includes language, text, and shared activities. Further, the interactions between tools and tasks are not one-way; the tool affects how and why learning emerges, and the learners use the tool in 'unexpected and creative ways in order to make sense of their own learning activity' (Lantolf, 2005: 348). This recognition that social dialogic activity can lead to writing success underpins a generic doctoral writing development programme at the University of Waikato.

THE DOCTORAL WRITING CONVERSATION (DWC)

The DWC is a pan-university, cross-disciplinary writing discussion forum for doctoral students, which runs for 2 hours every Friday morning from March to November. As the DWC attracts students from all Faculties across the institution, any writing activity offered must have general relevance and usefulness.

The DWC primarily disaggregates implicit aspects of expert academic writing and makes them explicit. It helps students understand that high-quality academic writing is neither straightforward nor quick to achieve, but that expertise can be developed through discursive practices both within and outside the supervisory relationship. Another DWC feature has been its inclusion of supervisors in some panel discussions of writing topics. Over time, this has served to raise supervisor awareness of the DWC as a legitimate, deep-level source of knowledge about literacy and an effective support for student writing development. What follows are three practical examples of interactive workshops that make the implicit explicit for doctoral students.

Workshop 1: Elicitation—talking to write

One structured dialogic workshop is a 'talking to write' activity. We call this the 'four by four' (4x4) as it includes four components. First, students (on their own) identify a problem in their writing. They articulate it (in lay terms) to a small group of workshop participants (peers) who ideally are outside their subject area. Collaboratively with the group, each student then develops a plan for addressing the writing issue. Finally, all groups reassemble and share both problems and the solution plans that have been devised. At this final stage, the learning developers also contribute comments and advice on the plans.

Talking through their obstacles to writing allows students to extend their thinking. Engaging in critical conversation in small groups and then reporting back to the entire group helps students clarify their ideas and plan what steps they need to take next. The dialogic process is strengthened by the cross-disciplinary nature of the DWC, as each participant must be very clear, for example, when describing the complex chemical properties of concrete to an applied linguist. Students report that the dialogic activity has enabled them to close conceptual gaps, improve planning processes for writing, write more effectively, and use supervisory sessions more productively. In addition, the collegiality of the discussions has created a physical network of social and learning support for higher-degree students. They are aware that they can draw on this when needed.

Workshop 2: Developing academic voice

In this workshop, students begin by discussing, in small groups, their understanding of the concept 'academic voice'. Frequently they think that academic voice is their overall contribution to the research literature, or else they have no idea at all. Students often do not understand that planning, structuring, and shaping text all contribute to the development of academic voice.

The workshop involves a discussion of three levels of thesis writing—the macro, meso, and micro. At the macro (whole document) level, the organizational structure of the thesis must be visually clear to a reader. Although there are discipline-specific conventions for presenting a thesis, they are not rigid. To develop creative ways of structuring an argument, students are advised to print a table of contents, which becomes the physical tool to mediate discussion with their supervisor. The point here is to help students develop confidence, not only to discuss thesis structure, but also to push the boundaries of writing conventions.

The meso level includes paragraphs and sections within chapters. This involves the idea of 'flow'—the language used to guide the reader through an argument. Strategies such as appropriate word choice and the use of short summaries and clear conclusions are illustrated. Students work through example texts and identify and discuss with peers the appropriateness of particular language structures. They need to develop understanding of how much repetition is actually required to maintain flow, and at what point text becomes redundant.

At the micro level, fine-tuning of grammar, punctuation, and elimination of wordiness contribute to coherence and cohesion. Here we use the expression 'cut the fat' to defuse the emotions of revising critically by making the editing process more objective (Carter and Pitcher, 2010). Students are also reminded that whatever they write must be underpinned by their research questions.

The main focus throughout the workshop is to help students become aware that stylistic language choice plays a critical role in conveying ideas. Students need to understand epistemic stance and its role in expressing degrees of certainty and uncertainty, which can be considered essential aspects of academic voice.

Workshop 3: Preparing conference abstracts

Part of becoming a successful academic is establishing relationships (networking) with others in the field by attending and presenting research at conferences. This workshop helps students interpret conference 'calls', make choices, and prepare an abstract accordingly. Here, technology guides the discussion, as we visit a range of conference websites, across different disciplines, and within various countries. Structured group discussion of the formats and types of information at each site guides students on how to evaluate and choose the most appropriate conference for their needs. Choices will also be affected by the stage of their research.

The final phase focuses on abstract writing, which is often formulaic. A 'locus, focus, significance' format provides a robust model for what to include and how to structure an abstract. 'Locus' refers to locating the content in the broader research context or in a physical environment (and could include aspects of both). The 'focus' sets the scope of the study within that locus. The 'significance' then highlights the potential relevance and importance of the research. Significance could also include what a participant might learn in the session. Throughout the session, the workshop focuses on the need for clarity and adherence to specified details in order to meet acceptance requirements.

SOUNDS GREAT—BUT IS THE WORKSHOP APPROACH EFFECTIVE?

The main point of this section is to endorse Part II's message that students' writing momentum is often sustained outside supervision meetings. The activity theory framework, with its blend of talking, working with texts, and social interaction raises student awareness of academic writing requirements. Some supervisors are able to establish writing support groups within their schools or departments, because they have enough supervisees of their own. Those who do not should consider whether a generic writing conversation group could be established to help students maintain momentum, especially when they recognize student demotivation. One of the key advantages of the DWC is that it makes explicit many aspects of the internalized writing knowledge that academic supervisors may not always explain. Thus, the generic programme complements supervisory work, does not intrude into supervisory relationships, and provides rounded, sustainable writing support.

Student feedback indicates that the DWC provides them with the skills to engage more productively with their supervisors. Alerting students to important aspects of not only *what* to discuss with supervisors, but *how* to structure their discussions, can lead to more productive supervisory meetings. In addition, better understanding of academic writing requirements can lead to increased confidence. Another interesting outcome is that the dialogic approach of the DWC raises awareness that ambiguity is normal during the research process. Students realize that they are not alone in feeling lost in their project; everyone at some point feels intellectually inadequate and unable to write. Writing together and talking about writing help students to live with uncertainty and manoeuvre through liminal space to make writing progress. Students report that the DWC is *their* place; they find strength and acceptance within the group, which helps them to continue writing even when they are unclear about what they are discovering in their research.

The pan-university nature of the workshops also contributes to writing development, as students learn about academic approaches and paradigms from disciplines outside their own. Awareness of the commonalities across research extends students' knowledge of methodologies, which in turn helps them to write from a more widely informed perspective.

Generic doctoral writing programmes function to make the implicit explicit. A key strength of a generic writing programme is that it can disrupt the hierarchical nature of supervision in engaging and positive ways. Somehow, this productive disruption boosts students' confidence in their writing ability and can help maintain productivity, as part of the supervisory process.

Chapter 7

Peer writing groups

Cally Guerin and Claire Aitchison

Stand-alone writing groups for doctoral candidates have become increasingly popular—even fashionable. Anthony Paré (2014) credits Peter Elbow (1973) and Anne Ruggles Gere (1987) as key players in the evolution of the practice and theory of writing groups. Twenty-first century renditions come in myriad forms (Haas, 2014), including technology-mediated, asynchronous and globally networked hybridized events.

The rise of writing groups might be explained by the rapid growth and diversification of doctoral research students and programmes globally, in turn requiring new responses from institutions and supervisors. Increasingly, institutions centrally fund such writing support via learning or writing centres, research offices and faculty resourcing. Perhaps the simultaneous and independent movement for self-help and community-building by doctoral students, often via online technology, may be a contributing factor. (See more on this latter aspect in Chapter 8 by Mewburn and Thomson.) Whether these groups are self-organizing arrangements between peers, centrally provided, or run by supervisors, there is a burgeoning interest in writing groups for doctoral education.

In this chapter we describe different kinds of writing groups and the roles they play in supplementing the feedback cycles between student and supervisors. We propose that both critique-focused and productivity-focused writing groups provide rich and diverse opportunities for doctoral students to learn key academic practices through participating in authentic scholarly networks of exchange over writing.

CRITIQUE-FOCUSED GROUPS: DISCUSSING WRITING TOGETHER

Critique-focused writing groups can be facilitated by institutional representatives, such as language experts and supervisors, or by peers. When they are facilitated by language and literacy advisors or writing teachers, participants are more likely to build advanced academic writing and language skills and knowledge—for example, form and style, genre, argumentation and grammar are commonly addressed. Having such facilitator expertise may be particularly useful for researchers for whom English is not a first language, but its utility is by no means confined to this group; those who enter doctoral studies from industry or other non-traditional pathways may be equally inexperienced with the complex requirements of advanced academic research genres. Alternatively, critique-focused groups may be run by discipline-specific departments or centres, or by supervisors or advisors for their own students, thereby bringing different areas of expertise to feedback and discussion. These kinds of writing groups usually have institutional support, thus gaining credibility with students and perhaps a sense of obligation to attend regularly. Commonly, the work of authoring, reading and constructing feedback occurs *prior* to group meetings so that time together can be devoted to sharing and discussing peers' texts. Often, too, the facilitator needs to take on an organizing role, ensuring regular group communication, meeting and writing schedules, and timely circulation of texts to be critiqued.

Critique-focused groups require significant commitment, since members need to commit to regular participation (e.g. fortnightly meetings) and invest additional time for reading and reviewing peers' work. The processes of giving and receiving feedback in this situation can generate extra advantages. The feedback sometimes adopts the qualities of a 'gift', and draws participants into the mutual obligation of reciprocal gift exchange (Guerin, 2014). Thus, membership in a writing group can develop ties of mutual responsibility, reciprocity and trust, contributing the valuable sense of belonging to a scholarly community, and building confidence in their academic and researcher identities as a result.

While there is a relative lack of in-depth research into the exact nature of the feedback exchanged in these groups, there are many smaller studies and participant accounts of highly successful groups (Aitchison and Guerin, 2014; Guerin et al., 2013; Wegener, Meier and Ingerslev, 2016). Studies have indicated that critique-focused writing groups help participants improve their own writing by receiving constructive feedback, and, importantly, from giving critique and participating in discussions on writing (Aitchison, 2009). Participants have also reflected on the value of writing groups for building agency, communities of practice and skills related to scholarly and publication writing (Aitchison and Guerin, 2014). One study showed how students use these groups as a confidence-building strategy, 'a good first step before taking it to the supervisor' (Aitchison, 2014: 60), with members working together through discussion to make meaning and co-construct texts.

The feedback generated in writing groups facilitated by language experts is aimed at aiding participants' understanding of the generic and discipline-specific conventions of thesis writing. Issues discussed are likely to include the organization of the document and its structure, the use of headings and subheadings, the use of topic sentences and paragraphing, and the logic of the argument being presented. Feedback can also focus on the mechanics of grammar and nuances of vocabulary. In these environments, rather than simply seeking 'correctness' of sentence form, punctuation, grammar and word choice, support is provided for a more in-depth understanding of how language works.

Critique-focused groups can also be led by supervisors, who are usually experienced academic writers and publishers and have particular disciplinary or methodological expertise to offer. Supervisor facilitators are also closely aligned to current expectations of the discipline in which students are working, and hence able to provide up-to-date advice.

When peers form writing groups, they bring different areas of interest and expertise to the group, reflecting their unique research studies, approaches and stages of candidature. Peripheral learning occurs in mixed-discipline groups as newer researchers learn from more senior and experienced candidates.

PRODUCTIVITY-FOCUSED GROUPS: DOING WRITING TOGETHER

Productivity-focused groups are a relatively new, and increasingly popular, model of writing group in which participants get together to write rather than to discuss their writing. Common forms of productivity-focused gatherings include regular café-style meetings through to larger, more resource-intensive events such as boot camps or residential retreats.

In Australia, at least, the café meet-ups known as 'Shut up and write!' have become widely adopted by doctoral students (Mewburn, Osborne and Caldwell, 2014). These groups generally meet in public cafés, on or off campus, or in institutional spaces such as libraries or cafeterias. The Pomodoro technique (Cirillo n.d.) is commonly used, with 25 minutes of intense silent writing interspersed with brief periods of conversation. The café environment is convenient (no booking required!) and conducive to socializing before and after the formal meet-ups.

More extended productivity-focused writing groups, such as retreats, boot camps or Academic Writing Month (AcWriMo), bring people together for extended periods. Writing retreats (see, for example, Murray, 2015a) are often more collegial and supportive; they may include aspects such as writing workshops and opportunities to talk about one's writing; they frequently have institutional backing, especially when held off campus (see, for example, Grant, 2006). Boot camps generally involve long and intense days of writing, prioritize the attainment of writing goals, and may include gamified elements such as soft competition and 'rewards' for achievement (Freestone and Connell, 2014, 15 October). AcWriMo is an international online month-long writing marathon with an emphasis on setting personal targets (e.g. pages or word counts). It uses social media for mutual support and for sharing writing-related resources.

'Feedback' in productivity-focused writing groups is mostly focused on performance. Participants learn from observing the routines of others working alongside them, or by sharing tips and resources for making writing more efficient and avoiding procrastination. Productivity groups feed back a sense of accomplishment in the number of words produced or number of sections completed (or at least begun), or a longer time devoted to writing without distraction; participants are more likely to learn about writing practices and processes, and how to develop more disciplined approaches to increasing output. Feedback can also be experienced as a measurement of the self in relation to the achievements of others, and whether or not one is meeting the norms of expectation in this emerging scholarly identity: Am I producing as much writing as others at the same stage of their doctorate? Am I keeping up? Am I approaching the writing tasks in the same way as my peers, or are there ways I could adjust my process to be more productive or effective? These are valuable insights in the world of doctoral writing, where much of the process is highly individualistic and often swathed in mystery.

WHAT'S IN IT FOR SUPERVISORS?

From the supervisor's perspective, there are a number of benefits in having students participate in the various kinds of writing groups we have outlined here. These include the reduced pressure on supervisors, better developed drafts submitted to supervisors for feedback, and the integration of doctoral candidates into research communities. We note that students who participate in writing groups have a better understanding of the iterative nature of writing and the highs and lows of the reviewing process, which empowers and extends authentic scholarly skills and practices.

A key advantage for supervisors of having students involved in critique-focused writing groups is the reduced reliance on them to provide all the feedback for every student under their supervision. Academics are under greater pressure with ever-growing teaching, research and administrative workloads, and higher student numbers than ever before (Carrigan, 2015, 7 April). Meanwhile, research indicates a high level of student dissatisfaction with supervisor feedback (Can and Walker, 2011). By endorsing writing group members to read and respond to each other's drafts, supervisors can facilitate their students receiving feedback sooner and more often than they themselves might be able to provide.

In addition, feedback from writing groups can also reduce the burden of responsibility on a supervisor as the sole evaluator of PhD candidates' writing, particularly in institutions where team or joint supervision is not the norm. Supervisors sometimes facilitate the formation of writing groups, and may even seek out the views of writing group members to confirm or challenge their own opinions (Aitchison, 2014). Supervisors whose students participate in critique-focused groups will generally receive better-quality drafts, thus alleviating the need to deal with poor grammar and expression in the early stages. Having already acted on the suggestions provided by the writing group, students are likely to present writing with greater clarity, improved expression, refined argument and logical flow.

For supervisors whose students belong to productivity-focused writing groups, the main benefit is that their candidates are generating text. Sometimes this preempts or cures writer's block (Aitchison and Lee, 2006). While it might not be carefully refined work, once the ideas are on paper, supervisors are then able to work with students on these ideas. The feedback on their performance that students gain from belonging to productivity-focused groups can reinforce the supervisor's feedback on whether students are maintaining an appropriate level of output and progress. Importantly, writing groups draw students into the research community, thus reducing the isolation that many doctoral candidates report as they move through their highly specialized studies. The 'feedback' students receive in this way affirms their sense of belonging to a community of scholars and their own emerging identity as a researcher.

We acknowledge too that supervisors also need to be aware of potential downsides. It is possible for writing groups, particularly peer-to-peer groups, to become spaces in which students focus on the negative aspects of doctoral candidature. Mutually reinforcing 'whinging' can be harmful, setting up a feedback loop that is discouraging and unproductive, although some 'troubles talk' can be beneficial at times (Mewburn, 2011).

Just as conflicting feedback from members of the supervisory team can unsettle candidates (Guerin and Green, 2015), feedback from writing groups that conflicts with that from supervisors can also pose problems. Contradictory views within the writing group can be similarly challenging for research writers. It may be that sometimes feedback, however well-intentioned, is simply wrong. Learning to manage and integrate multiple perspectives is valuable preparation for novice scholars. Having an open and engaged approach to students' participation in writing groups means that supervisors can use such occurrences for teaching their students how to handle the very common challenge of conflicting reviews. Nonetheless, the learning opportunities that accrue from participation in writing groups benefit both supervisors and students, and far outweigh any potential problems arising from occasional inappropriate writing group feedback. It is clear from our experience and the literature that students who join writing groups find them a useful accompaniment to the work of supervision.

Chapter 8

Online thesis-writing resources

Inger Mewburn and Pat Thomson

Research students can now access vast amounts of information about their PhD journey in general, and thesis writing in particular, on the Internet. Whether they are experiencing trouble or merely curious, doctoral researchers can simply Google for answers, or crowdsource advice from social media sites such as Facebook and Twitter. While there is a lot of high-quality advice on the Internet, there is also much that is of questionable value, and doctoral researchers may not be well equipped to know the difference. In this chapter, we discuss the destabilization of supervisory authority, the types of advice available online and the pressing need for savvy information use—a key digital literacy. We argue that supervisors have a role in helping students to navigate, choose and apply advice they find outside the supervisory relationship.

THE DESTABILIZATION OF SUPERVISOR AUTHORITY

Doctoral researchers have probably always looked beyond their supervisors, to friends, family and their peers. More recently, their universities have also offered a range of support and training through graduate schools, reading groups, formal mentoring and internship schemes, writing groups and individual tutoring. And the development of online doctoral support, available day and night, and from all parts of the globe, means that supervision, while still a primary relationship with one person or a small group of people, is now irrevocably distributed.

Perhaps the most serious problem with online advice is not simply that distributed supervision can destabilize supervisory authority. The claim of supervisors to know more than their students is one of the central tenets of research education. Supervisors are assumed, by virtue of having already completed their own doctorates, to have knowledge that those just beginning doctorates lack. This is increasingly a problematic way of thinking about the

PhD. The doctoral cohort is much more diverse than it used to be, and many doctoral researchers come into their degree after long periods as professionals. The widespread access to learning resources about doctoral education on the Internet further challenges these conventional learning hierarchies. The online learning landscape is constantly diversifying and proliferating; new resources and ways to communicate are always emerging.

We suggest that the Internet can be thought of as a 'shadow supervisor', ever present, ubiquitous and available on demand. This shadow supervisor has many potential effects on students, even if the interaction is never explicitly visible. We can compare this situation with that faced by medical doctors who are increasingly presented with information sourced from 'Dr Google'. Hartzband and Groopman (2010) suggest that access to a wider range of views on treatment options can be helpful when patients are making difficult treatment decisions. Likewise for doctoral candidates, having access to other opinions about issues such as writing, method and project management can be advantageous because it enlarges the repertoire of approaches that might be offered by their supervisors.

However, Hartzband and Groopman also point out that patients can experience high levels of health anxiety when faced with copious advice. Likewise, students might 'self-diagnose' problems they do not necessarily have, or contemplate solutions and approaches that they are not equipped to properly assess. In her blog post 'Social media and expertise' (2013, 22 August), Rachael Cayley, a writing instructor at the University of Toronto, argues that social media enable a more flexible way of engaging research students with appropriate and timely expertise, unless offered with universalizing claims. Advice that claims to be 'correct', no matter the circumstance, fails to take into account disciplinary cultures and norms—the layer at which a supervisor should operate to help students negotiate the emergence of an effective and appropriate 'textwork/identitywork' (Kamler and Thomson, 2006).

Access to self-diagnosis tools is a mixed blessing, but may at least encourage patients to seek help earlier than they might otherwise. For doctoral students, social media and blogs break down what Lovitts (2006: 9) calls 'pluralistic ignorance in the doctoral cohort'. Doctoral students encountering difficulties with their writing or their supervisor often blame themselves for a situation that is structural, rather than a matter of individual level of competence. Lovitts suggests that this self-blame is why so many doctoral students 'leave in silence', experience a sense of 'anomie', a kind of 'placelessness' and/or feelings of marginalization, without thinking to ask for help with their difficulties. But Lovitts' analysis assumes that communities are geographically placed and contingent on discipline. Social media services such as Twitter and Facebook enable like-minded and situated individuals to make extra-institutional connections and build community. Students who are connected with others via services like Twitter, or membership in Facebook groups such as 'Older, wiser learners' (www.facebook.com/groups/708019069302386/) and 'Mums who study' (www.facebook.com/

groups/mumswhostudy/) have access to sources of community and support they might not otherwise experience on campus.

While access to tools for self-diagnosis has obvious advantages, there are some key drawbacks. General Practitioners know well the problems of communicating with patients who have read unsubstantiated claims for the benefits or drawbacks of any treatment option and opinion-based medical ratings systems; these can lead to doctor shopping or refusing treatment. Supervisors need to avoid these kinds of situations. But, unlike patients, students may not think to tell supervisors about the information they have accessed online, as it might not seem relevant to the discussions at hand. If the supervisor has expressed disdain for sources like blogs and Twitter, the student may be too ashamed to admit they are engaging with this material. Similarly, online communities offer students forums for privately discussing supervisor behaviour and seeking feedback, some of which they may not want to share. However, such comments are likely to be from fellow novice members of the scholarly community and, thus, of varying degrees of use/importance. It is therefore crucial that supervisors ask their students what online sources they are using and make themselves knowledgeable about the potential information and advice that might be circulating.

Just as the 'vast imbalance' of knowledge between doctor and patient is somewhat redressed by the Internet, so it is too for students. However, as Hartzband and Groopman (2010) maintain, the doctor still plays a vital role in mediating information and providing accurate diagnoses. Clearly, supervisors who are pragmatic about the sources that students are exposed to, and are better informed about the plethora of advice available on the Internet, are well placed to provide a critical filter and accurate diagnosis.

CHANGING DEVELOPMENTS IN ONLINE DOCTORAL SUPPORT AND ADVICE

While supervisors might be concerned about the advice that students can consume, there are far more interesting developments just around the corner. The robots have arrived—but they don't look like we expected. We thought they would be shiny and human-shaped, but instead robots are largely immaterial, taking the form of clever, adaptive 'assistive software' and hardware that make our existing machines work better. These new algorithm-driven tools can display what is labelled as 'narrow band artificial intelligence', delivered via the Internet, as 'bots': bits of software that act in semi-autonomous ways. Most of us don't understand these new forms of robots very well and underestimate them, mostly because we tend to think of human activities as irreplaceable. This is the exciting—and possibly frightening—new frontier of the non-human 'shadow supervisor'.

Talking about emergent software is always problematic because by the time this book is published, it's likely to have changed. We will briefly turn our attention to two of these tools, *Writefull* and *Grammarly*, as good examples of what is coming next in terms of assistive software for researchers and writers. We will briefly describe this software and reflect on the possibilities—and dangers—it might present.

A 'bot' is simply an algorithm, a procedure or a formula for solving a problem. The ever-increasing processing speed of computers enables algorithms to become fast, flexible tools that adapt themselves to user need. An example of a simple algorithm-driven scholarly tool is *Writefull*, an app designed by doctoral researcher Juan Castro who codified his own writing practice in order to help non-English speakers check their scholarly idiom. Computer scientist Castro, like many other non-native speakers, used Google to 'sanity check' his sentences—if he pasted a sentence in the search bar and found there weren't many hits, he could conclude that the sentence was somehow 'wrong'. His *Writefull* app sits 'over' all other open writing applications and, when specific text is highlighted, scans the Internet, specifically Google Books, to find matching text. The algorithm tells the user how often a particular phrase is used. If the frequency is low, it's more likely the original sentence is somehow 'wrong'. *Writefull* is a great example of peer-to-peer assistance enabled by a globalized communications system. Without the Internet to distribute his app, Juan would merely be automating his own practice—but the Internet shadow supervisor enables him to share and influence the practices of peers.

Of course, a good teacher does much more than point out if sentences are 'normal' or not; a good teacher corrects and provides formative feedback that helps a student learn how to write a better sentence. A teacher is steeped in the norms and text practices of their discipline(s) and can direct the student to align with these (often unstated) guidelines. It's tempting to think that this steerage is a uniquely human quality that cannot be replicated, but, before we jump to this conclusion, it is worth taking a closer look at other available software that can automate this aspect of supervisor practice. The most popular is *Grammarly*.

Similar to *Writefull*, *Grammarly* is assistive software for correcting text in alignment with English conventions. After text is uploaded into the *Grammarly* cloud, the software analyzes it using a number of different algorithms, and can identify a surprising range of both grammar and style issues. The software also has a built-in plagiarism detector. Before the student starts working on a text, they can adjust *Grammarly* and 'dial up' the style of writing they are attempting (the software has an 'academic' setting). The user can then scroll through to see which problematic text is highlighted, together with possible solutions. The software teaches as well as correcting the student's mistakes; if the user responds incorrectly to an error, *Grammarly* notifies the user, providing a short explanation of their mistake. If the user finds the explanation inadequate, they can ask for more information and examples. The software can be set to 'vocabulary enhancement', so that it will offer more words. If it notices that you over-use a certain word, it will suggest alternatives. *Grammarly* doesn't just correct and give feedback—like any good teacher, it extends the student at the same time so they can learn new skills.

Writefull and *Grammarly* are not the only academic bots out there, and there is no doubt that they will soon be joined by others, then superseded. So does the advent of the advice 'bot' mean that the supervisor is becoming superfluous?

THE RESOURCE-FUL SUPERVISOR

Many supervisors may be unaware of what their students are doing 'after school'. They themselves may not engage with social media or in any systematic survey of what is currently available and on the horizon. This, we suggest, is no longer tenable. Supervisors need to find out *where* their supervisees are getting their advice and support, not to police behaviour, but to verify that such resources are appropriate and helpful. They/we need to approach this task positively, not defensively. Online advice and support are not a substitute for pedagogical interaction, but may be a helpful addition. However, both supervisors and supervisees need to determine the quality and applicability of the advice on offer. This is a task that can usefully be done together.

While many of the online resources students can access are produced by professional educators or academic publishing companies, a significant and growing number of sites are run either by for-profit companies specializing in selling help to students, or by fellow doctoral researchers motivated to share what they know with their peers. To complicate the picture, not all professionally-maintained sites are of high quality, and not all amateur sites are of low quality. Doctoral researchers need to assess what advice to use and what to ignore—with the potential for obvious problems to develop. Early in candidature, the supervisor needs to take an active role in helping students develop what Howard Rheingold (2013) calls 'crap detection'. As Rheingold suggests, all advice must be considered critically; the value of any piece of information is always contingent on the specific circumstances of the student and the project they are seeking to undertake.

'Crap detection' is now a key digital literacy, and learning how to tell what advice is good, and what is bad, is a task that supervisors should be well-placed to teach to their students. But first they must educate themselves—an ongoing task. Our previous research on academic blogging (Mewburn and Thomson, 2013) suggests that many sites maintained by working academics, while not specifically directed at students, contain useful advice for their colleagues. Some academics do specialize in writing about their experience of writing and studying, but these tend to be from a singular point of view and not based on research and practice experience. Provenance matters. The blogs that are most useful for students and supervisors tend to be run by academics with a special interest in learning support and writing instruction. If the academic has a convincing CV in this area, their blog is most likely a good source of information.

Supervisors need support in order to keep up with the online advice on offer. The provision of such support is a potential new role for university libraries. Working with graduate schools and writing instructors, university librarians should provide regular updates about interesting software developments, indicate sound sources of online advice and support, and issue alerts about dodgy online doctoral dealers. In addition to providing information about predatory publishers and their own versions of online writing advice, university libraries could become key partners in distributed supervision, offering expertise in both crap detection and the identification of high-benefit services.

Supervisors should welcome such support. The work of keeping up with alternative avenues of support is time-consuming, but should be seen as augmenting, rather than taking time away from, the primary role of nurturing the education of the next generation of researchers.

* * *

Making use of other resources—things to do

- Encourage students to familiarize themselves with all available avenues of support.
- Do the same yourself.
- Suggest that students conduct a self-audit, identifying areas they need to develop.
- Recommend that students (not just those with English as an Additional Language) seek linguistic advice early in their writing process.
- Promote research skills workshops: critical thinking, developing argument, meeting audience needs, genre-specific requirements (conference papers, abstracts, literature reviews, etc.).
- Take advantage of learning advisors' expertise to help students address 'matters arising' from your feedback.
- Encourage participation in peer writing groups, as a way to foster students' audience awareness and regular production of written text.
- Encourage students to explore the plethora of online resources—and to share their merits (or otherwise) with you and fellow students.

Part III

Encouraging style through control of language

Helen Sword; Rachael Cayley; George D. Gopen

Edited by Susan Carter

> ***Supervisor:*** *Almost all students initially experience problems with expressing themselves in an appropriately academic manner . . . I make extensive comments and corrections as to style, grammar and spelling on every piece of draft writing.*
>
> ***Student:*** *My supervisor doesn't like to read unpolished writing, whereas I don't like to waste time polishing my writing before I've had my supervisor's input on the ideas it contains and the way it is structured. I've submitted rough writing seeking broad feedback on the direction I'm heading in, only to receive angry comments about missing punctuation and typos.*

Part III looks at feedback that shows students the mechanics of language, the nuts and bolts of grammar and punctuation, syntax and word choice, for the achievement of clarity, voice and style. Many supervisors use the rules of grammar without knowing them, and find it hard to *teach* students rather than merely editing. Others do not write clearly themselves: advice here may improve supervisory writing as well as student writing. Doctoral students generally come from generations who were not overtly taught punctuation and grammar at school (recent contemporary teaching philosophy felt that it stifled creativity) and then find it hard to learn as adults. Many excellent guides exist on writing clarity, but students are unlikely to consult them without being directed to them. And the best way to improve style and clarity is through ongoing conversation about writing's mechanisms with others, including the supervisor.

We endorse Sword's (2009) declaration that readability matters in research writing. In some disciplines, accuracy in writing matters to research—NASA's Mccaskill (1990) offers an excellent handbook on grammar, punctuation and capitalization for Science's technical writing where clarity of written words may have implications for resultant actions. Those writing in highly theorized Social Sciences and Humanities find that grammar and syntax may betray bias—as Toni Morrison (1992) demonstrates by showing that syntax in the American literary canon conveys racist assumptions of whiteness. Researchers maximize their original contribution through clear stylish writing, which makes it more likely that they have engaged readers. Doctoral students are likely to find themselves in a competitive environment on graduation (Austin, 2002). Skill in marketing themselves and their work through accessible writing gives them a greater chance of landing the research career they want. For many disciplines, writing is the principal marketing medium: hiring committees pay heed to publication. Precision is powerful; supervisors are in the business of empowerment.

Three chapters establish excellent principles for writing style and clarity. Helen Sword opens (Chapter 9), addressing the attitudes to foster in students and pointing out the power of questions, while noting that students should also be encouraged to emulate good academic writing. Sword provides both questions to pose and practical exercises to set. In Chapter 10, Rachael Cayley focuses on supervising the reiterative toil that achieves style, flow and focus. She points out the need for openness about writing as thought progression: 'essential, conceptual and multifaceted'. George D. Gopen (Chapter 11) contributes the notion of the 'Reader Expectation Approach' and demonstrates, through a scripted interrogation of a sentence, that authorial control of syntax is vital for precise communication.

Chapter 9

Giving feedback on grammar and style

Helen Sword

Your PhD student has just sent you a draft chapter riddled with grammatical errors and misspelled words. Her sentences are at once over-egged and undercooked; apparently she holds an unfounded yet unshakable belief that 'serious' academic writing must be long-winded, wordy, and dull. Her paragraphs lack coherence and flow; her referencing is inconsistent and sloppy. How do you give constructive feedback on this mess? Where do you even begin?

PUT AWAY THE RED PENCIL

If you are a clear, confident writer yourself, your first impulse may be to submerge your student's paper in a sea of red ink or to festoon it with colorful Tracked Changes and comment balloons. While some writers respond with gratitude to this kind of detailed feedback, research on student learning suggests that excessive attention to surface errors can be a waste of time for the marker (Haswell, 1986) and counter-productive for the student (Smith, 1997). Even if you walk your student through your corrections line by line, she is unlikely to take most of them on board in a single session; all that chastising color may provoke feelings of shame and distress that will in turn trigger a defensive response (Sommers, 2006). Moreover, by making specific suggestions for revision, you risk creating a culture of dependency. Rewriting your student's prose for her is a bit like tying your child's shoes day after day rather than taking the time to teach him how to do it himself.

DON'T ACCEPT ROUGH DRAFTS

But let's take a step backwards. If your student tacitly believes (as many students do) that 'good' writers effortlessly produce elegant prose, she may not yet have learned the simple and powerful truth that writing well is hard work that requires multiple drafts. 'A line will take us hours maybe', as poet William Butler Yeats reminds us; 'Yet if it does not seem a moment's thought, / Our stitching and unstitching has been naught' (Yeats, 1956). It may be helpful to let your student know that you're not expecting a perfect piece of writing, because no piece of writing is ever perfect; no matter how polished her prose, you will still be making suggestions for improvement and prodding her to refine and revise. That's your job. Her job is to bring you her very best effort from the start, so that you can help her shift her writing from acceptable to excellent rather than from shoddy to acceptable.

FOSTER A 'GROWTH MINDSET'

Psychologist Carol Dweck (2012) draws a distinction between people with a 'fixed mindset', who believe that talent is doled out in finite qualities, and those with a 'growth mindset', who value effort as well as accomplishment. 'Fixed mindset' people regard difficulty as a sign of weakness and mistakes as a sign of failure, whereas 'growth mindset' people regard difficulty as a welcome challenge and mistakes as an opportunity to learn. If your student responds to your feedback with defensiveness or shame, she may be stuck in a fixed mindset that needs to be re-booted and re-routed before she can move forward as a self-sufficient and confident writer. Interestingly, the same goes for your most diligent students: those rare exemplars of efficiency and intelligence who write beautifully, submit only their best work to you, and expect unfettered approbation in return. Apprentice writers who have received copious praise all their lives may tacitly believe that all critical feedback is 'bad' and that being asked to revise is a sign of weakness. Cultivating a growth mindset is the first step toward teaching them to think like professional writers, who welcome rather than resist suggestions for lifting their game even higher.

MAKE YOUR OWN WRITING PROCESSES TRANSPARENT

One of the best ways of demystifying the writing process for your students is to discuss your own ways of working. How long does it normally take you to produce a publishable chapter or article: days, weeks, months? How many drafts do you typically go through by the time your research makes its way into print: two or three, a dozen, a hundred? There is no 'right' answer to these questions; I have interviewed successful academics at both ends of the time-and-effort spectrum as well as many in between (Sword, 2017). Generally speaking, however, the more elegant and persuasive a piece of writing, the longer and harder the author has labored to get it right. Some academics favor careful advance preparation (note-taking, outlining, conversations with co-authors); some plunge straight in and make frequent revisions en route (meanderings, cul-de-sacs, U-turns); some undertake meticulous editing afterwards (chopping and changing, rewriting, polishing); and some practice a messy but fertile combination of all these approaches.

By opening the curtains on your own writing practice, you validate your students' hard work and can help assuage their frustration when 'getting it right' takes a long time.

ENCOURAGE EMULATION

Imitation is said to be the sincerest form of flattery; however, emulation offers a surer route to learning. In *The Sense of Style*, Steven Pinker (2014) shows how any piece of good writing can be taken apart to reveal a set of transferable principles: 'Writers acquire their technique by spotting, savoring, and reverse-engineering examples of good prose' (Pinker, 2014: 12). The following emulation exercise may be undertaken one-on-one as part of an individual supervision meeting; however, it works best in a group setting, where participants can learn from each other's choices as well as their own.

Exercise: reverse-engineering exemplary prose

Choose an academic book or article that you especially admire and bring it with you to the session. Come prepared to describe at least one aspect of the writing that you aspire to emulate, for example: 'I like the way the author explains challenging theoretical material in clear and engaging language.'

Identify several *specific* techniques that the author has employed to achieve that result, for example:

- The author has made complex concepts accessible by using real-life examples.
- The author avoids gratuitous jargon and contextualizes crucial technical terms so that readers can easily work out their meaning.
- The author uses in-text citations sparingly and integrates quotations into the syntax of his or her own sentences.

In preparation for the next session, try applying each of these techniques to a few pages of your own work. In some cases, you will note an immediate improvement; in others, the exercise may help you and your supervisor identify a specific developmental need, such as a tenuous grasp of English grammar and punctuation or a clunky referencing style.

ASK QUESTIONS

Writing stylishly is a matter of making intelligent choices, not of slavishly adhering to disciplinary conventions or obeying rigid rules. A recent analysis of 500 articles from across the arts, sciences, and social sciences revealed that most peer-reviewed journals in most disciplines permit a surprisingly wide range of stylistic options (Sword, 2012). However, many graduate students (and sometimes their supervisors) still subscribe to the myth that academics are 'not allowed' to write anything other than stodgy, impersonal prose. The following questions and suggestions can help apprentice academics develop a more reflective and confident sense of their own style.

Exercise: ten questions about style

1. ***Thesis/argument:*** *Do you have a compelling central argument that you can express in a sentence or two?* (Often, though not always, your thesis statement will be the answer to your research question.)
2. ***Structure:*** *Do your sentences, paragraphs, and sections flow in a logical order? If not, why not?* (You can generate a 'reverse outline' by extracting the topic sentence of each paragraph or writing its main point in the margin; redundancies and logical gaps will immediately become apparent [Gray, 2015].)
3. ***Sentencing:*** *Are your sentences built around concrete nouns and vivid verbs, with no extraneous clutter?* (Run several samples of your writing through the free Writer's Diet test at www.writersdiet.com, then consult *The Writer's Diet: A Guide to Fit Prose* for hints on how to shape up your sentences, cut out verbal flab, and avoid the curse of 'zombie nouns' [Sword, 2016].)
4. ***Audience:*** *Do you know who are you writing for, and do you pitch your prose accordingly?* (Write down the names of five specific people whom you aspire to reach with your article or chapter, and keep them in mind as you write. Will each of them have the background necessary to understand your argument, the stomach to tolerate your disciplinary jargon, and the patience to follow the meandering path of your paragraphs? Are you aiming too high or too low?)
5. ***Voice and identity:*** *Have you made a conscious, informed, consistent choice either to employ first-person pronouns (I/we) or to write in an impersonal mode?* (Many academic writers mistakenly believe that they 'have to' produce passive, agentless prose: for example, 'The research was performed', rather than 'We performed the research'. However, most academic style guides encourage researchers to employ personal pronouns and an active voice, and peer-reviewed journals in most academic disciplines accept a range of stylistic choices [Sword, 2012].)
6. ***Title:*** *Is your title eye-catching? Memorable? Concrete? Packed with useful information?* (It's up to you to decide whether you want your title to be informative, engaging, or both. Each of these three choices is acceptable and defensible, depending on academic context.)
7. ***Opening hook:*** *Is your opening paragraph designed to capture and hold your reader's attention?* (Examples of effective opening hooks include quotations, questions, anecdotes, interesting facts, and real-life examples.)
8. ***Story:*** *What story or stories are you telling? Is that story evident to your readers?* (As a general rule, a *story* involves clearly drawn characters who interact with one another and undergo some kind of development and change. Effective storytellers use a range of narrative devices to engage their readers and make their main argument memorable.)

9 ***Examples and illustrations:*** *Do you use plenty of examples, illustrations, anecdotes, and metaphors?* (Stylish academic writers illustrate abstract ideas using concrete language and examples.)

10 ***Smart referencing:*** *When you cite other researchers, do you always make sure that the citation is relevant, useful, and elegantly integrated?* (To keep your references from dominating the text, you can cluster parenthetical citations at the ends of paragraphs and incorporate long, discursive footnotes into your main argument rather than letting them climb halfway up the page.)

CULTIVATE CRAFTSMANSHIP

Stylish academic writers regard writing as an artisanal activity, not merely a transactional exchange. They take pride in their craftsmanship and are constantly working to perfect their skills, acquire new techniques, and pass on their knowledge to others. A colleague of mine remembers the day when she devoted an entire supervision session to teaching a student how to convert agentless academic prose into short, sharp sentences composed of an identifiable subject followed by an active verb (see the 'Sentence transformation' exercise below). 'It's like magic!' the student declared at the end of the hour; instead of skating over the surface of his sentences with her red pen, the supervisor had helped to bring about a lasting transformation not only in his sentences, but in his attitude toward and respect for the craft of writing.

Exercise: sentence transformation

1 Choose a long, abstract sentence to work with, such as the following example:

> Together, these variables of team composition, range of collaboration, number of projects undertaken, and work climate constitute key elements in assessing and understanding the relationship between social and organizational characteristics of work and publication productivity among academic scientists in doctoral-granting departments.
>
> (Fox and Mohapatra, 2007: 545)

2 Identify the sentence's grammatical core: the central noun–verb pair upon which the entire edifice has been built. ('These variables constitute . . .')

3 Now find the sentence's human core; that is, who or what is the sentence really about? ('Academic researchers who are trying to understand how social and organizational factors can help create a more productive workplace for scientists.')

4 Rephrase the sentence as a series of pithy subject–verb clauses, each containing an **identifiable subject** paired with an ***active verb***:

> Some **scientists publish** more than others, and some academic **departments contain** more productive scientists than others. **We want** to know why.

> In this article **we examine** the many social and cultural **variables**—for example, team composition, range of collaboration, number of projects undertaken, and work climate—that ***help or hinder*** academic productivity in doctoral-granting science departments.

5 Play around with various ways of rephrasing the original sentence; for example:

> In this article we examine the many social and cultural variables—for example, team composition, range of collaboration, number of projects undertaken, and academic work climate—that make some doctoral-granting science departments more productive than others.

How many words can you cut out without sacrificing the conceptual complexity of the original?

SOW SELF-SUFFICIENCY

But you don't have to perform all that transformative magic yourself. There are many excellent writing guides available in libraries, bookstores, and online that can help your students get a better grip on grammar and style: for example, Lanham (1992); Pinker (2014); Strunk and White (2011); Truss (2003); Williams (2007); and Zinsser (1980), to name just a few. Consider asking each of your students to review and report back on a different writing guide every month for 2 or 3 months; eventually, you can encourage them to start doing their own digging and to pool resources with each other without any prompting from you. By teaching them to take charge of their own personal and professional development as writers, you will empower them to keep learning and growing long after they have left your supervision.

Chapter 10

Giving early feedback to doctoral writers

Rachael Cayley

Stylish research writing almost always relies upon waves of revision. Experienced academic writers can easily become inured to this reiterative process; doctoral writers, on the other hand, may struggle with the sense that their early drafts should be better than they are. Supervisory feedback on how to tackle early drafts can be invaluable. In this chapter, the focus is on how early supervisory feedback on broad writing issues—structure, focus, and flow—can help doctoral writers learn to manage the iterative nature of academic writing, thus supporting the eventual emergence of stylish academic prose.

If supervisors are to help doctoral writers with the actual writing process—as opposed to focusing on a broader research agenda or moving too quickly to proofreading—they will need to share what they themselves know as academic writers. Since many supervisors spend a great deal of time considering undergraduate writing, they may lose sight of the ways in which doctoral writing is more like the academic writing that they themselves do. Knowing how to do something is, obviously, different from being able to teach someone else how to do it; given how complicated and contested writing can be, expecting supervisors to have a pedagogically useful approach to writing at their fingertips seems unrealistic. In recent years, the notion of supporting supervisors in their work as supervisors of large-scale writing projects (Manathunga, 2010; McCulloch and Loeser, 2016) has grown in prominence, giving rise to the focus of this volume.

Teaching writing revision will not just benefit doctoral writers; supervisors can also benefit from deepening their ability to provide enhanced writing support because doing so can create more harmonious and efficient relationships, shorter times-to-completion, lower rates of attrition, and better drafts. To augment their attention to writing, supervisors will need to become more aware of their own expertise as writers (Paré, 2010) and more able to tap into their own writing struggles. Remembering how challenging writing is—and particularly was during doctoral studies—is crucial to providing meaningful writing support. It is equally important, however, to maintain a certain relativism about the ideal solution to those problems; being aware of a range of options rather than advocating a particular course of action can be valuable.

Drawing on our own struggles without privileging our own solutions can be a delicate balance. Students will benefit from knowing about strategies and techniques that supervisors employ in their writing process, as long as those approaches are presented as anecdotes and not axioms. In my experience, it is essential for doctoral writers to understand that others struggle with writing, and that writing success is more a matter of learning to overcome those struggles than a matter of inherent aptitude. Confronting what we have written and transforming it into a reader-friendly text is, for most of us, the central challenge of writing. Given the likelihood that an early thesis draft will require significant alteration, it is essential that supervisors be able to address the processes of revision with their doctoral writers. In what follows, I would like to suggest that supervisors could help their students by characterizing revision as essential, conceptual, and multifaceted.

The most important principle to be imparted to graduate students is that revision is essential for all writers. As I note in my *Explorations of Style: A Blog about Academic Writing*, students frequently believe that their early drafts are uniquely weak, either because they are comparing them with the polished prose found in published works or because their supervisors are disappointed with those early efforts (see Cayley, 2013, 18 December). If revision is framed as an essential part of all writing, weak early drafts start to seem much less significant. Ineffective first drafts cease to be inherently problematic; a problem only emerges if the writer is unable to work with an early draft and the supervisor is unable to provide the necessary guidance. While revision may be essential, we know that it is not necessarily done well. The ability to improve a text through revision is not a natural by-product of the research process: it is something that often needs to be taught.

Once novice academic writers accept that they must revise, they then need to think of the work of revision as fundamentally conceptual. When looking at our own early drafts, it can be incredibly difficult to see ongoing conceptual confusions; our deep familiarity with our own ideas so often blinds us to shifts in focus, flaws in argumentation, or slippages in terminology. While feedback that addresses these conceptual issues is crucial, it is also the most challenging to give. Early readers—including supervisors—may end up offering corrections, rather than suggestions for improvements, because it can be easier to see what is wrong than to articulate what ought to be there. When this conceptual feedback is lacking, however, doctoral writers may produce second drafts that do not yet address the problems in the first. When subsequent drafts are not moving in the right direction, frustration can start to afflict both sides of the relationship. On the other hand, if the supervisor does prioritize revision and provides the necessary insights, the doctoral writer can attend to broad conceptual tensions without allowing surface-level issues to act as a distraction.

Doctoral writers also need to understand that revision is a multifaceted process. In fact, revision is best thought of as an umbrella term for a range of different things that we may do to improve a text. Since revision often gets seen as an undifferentiated activity, it can be useful for supervisors to combat this misapprehension by stressing that revision must be recognized as iterative. In a deceptively simple formulation, Joseph Williams once said, 'We write the first draft for ourselves; the drafts thereafter increasingly for the reader' (1990: x). In other words, the first draft is likely to be weak in relation to its ultimate purpose, requiring an iterative approach to improving those early efforts (see Cayley, 2014, 18 December). To emphasize the importance of the early revision process, I will now discuss three crucial issues: structure, focus, and flow. Being able to target these issues in early drafts will support the development of stylish academic writers.

STRUCTURE

Most novice academic writers need to learn about the importance of tackling broad structural issues early. While this may make intuitive sense, it is frequently not how novice writers proceed. Since many writers tend to be fairly inexpert at revision, they are likely to rely heavily on revision skills involving grammar. When supervisors reinforce that sense by focusing on deviation from standard grammatical norms, they may further inspire students to address their attention to sentence-level writing issues. But starting with sentences can have deleterious consequences for the health of the whole text. As writers, we are necessarily preoccupied with sentences; as the fundamental unit of composition, we cannot help but direct our attention towards their correctness and efficacy. While attending to revision at the sentence level is crucial for enjoyable and readable prose, I would argue that most writers benefit from first paying attention to structural organization. Structural coherence is achieved through the arrangement of sentences into paragraphs and those paragraphs into sections and chapters. Readers then interpret the size and order of sections as signalling the content's degree of importance in relation to the overall argument (Carter, Kelly and Brailsford, 2012).

Recognizing the primacy of structural coherence is a crucial doctoral writing challenge. Thesis writers are often experiencing their first opportunity to engage in significant full-scale revision of a long text. They may have revised short texts, but have not likely undertaken the particular work of revising a complex text, one that is often written over a time frame in which the writer experiences significant shifts in identity (Kamler and Thomson, 2006; Thomson and Kamler, 2016). The length of the text and the duration of its composition mean that the revision challenges are both new and profound. Structural revision is a way to combat the fact that the act of reading tends to situate us in the local and thus obscures the demands of the global.

Drawing on their own experiences of working with long texts, supervisors need to encourage their students to resist the allure of making local changes until they have made the necessary global adjustments: drafting a maximally coherent text as early as possible means crafting an overall shape rather than refining specific prose. To find that optimal shape, doctoral writers should be made aware of the value of creating post-writing outlines. While writers will have divergent attitudes towards pre-writing outlines, most writers benefit from creating post-writing outlines that reflect what they have actually done in their text. When a supervisor encounters an early draft that still suffers from confusing organization and prioritization, recommending a post-writing outline can help the student to discern the nature of the problem and facilitate the writing of an improved draft (Cayley, 2011, 9 February).

FOCUS

One of the great benefits of the post-writing outline is the way it shows when writing includes superfluous elements while omitting elements that the reader may need. Since it is hard to let go of the material that we do not need and even harder to see what is missing, doctoral writers often need their supervisors to give feedback on the focus of the text. Supervisors can help by reminding their students of the value of writing, even if the writing itself ends up being discarded: there are things we need to write that do not need to be read. Most writers benefit from establishing whether they tend to say too much or too little. If a writer tends to say too little, what is it that they leave out? Some people leave out the examples; others leave out helpful elaborations; and others leave out crucial warrants. It is also common for doctoral writers to leave themselves out of their texts by prioritizing citations over a clarification of their own contribution, or by failing to provide enough insight into how the current text will work. Since it can be tricky to identify the habits of our own writing, supervisory feedback that either offers an explicit diagnosis of writing tendencies or suggests a way to develop that habit of self-reflection can be valuable.

FLOW

The third aspect of revision that supervisors should emphasize is the need to make sure that the text flows. One of the paradoxes of vigorous revision is that it almost always disrupts the original flow of the text, meaning that writers will ultimately need to create new cohesion within the revised text. Once the paragraphs themselves are solid and well-sequenced, we still need to make sure that the reader can see that structural integrity manifest in local transitions. Flow can also be managed by making sure that we as writers are sufficiently present in our texts through a range of metadiscoursal devices—for instance, signposting, hedging language, and use of the first person (Hyland and Tse, 2004)—in the text. Since supervisors often find that students are not employing enough of an authorial voice, directing them towards their use of metadiscourse can help to put a tangible face on that general concern (see Cayley, 2017, 31 January).

Focusing on revising an early draft for structure, focus, and flow will not, of course, obviate the need to attend to sentence-level issues (Pinker, 2014; Sword, 2012; Williams, 1990); once a text has been through the early phases of revision, it is crucial to attend to the style of the prose. However, even if a supervisor is unable to convey helpful feedback on style, they may still be able to offer meaningful insight into the broad imperatives of revision. Indeed, concentrating supervisory attention on the structure, focus, and flow of a document makes sense; those aspects of the text are often key indicators of the overall viability of a thesis as a contribution to a particular disciplinary conversation. Needless to say, the supervisor is uniquely suited to helping a writer to understand how a text can be revised to conform to the shared norms of writing within a given discipline.

If you listen to doctoral students talking about their writing process, you will naturally hear a great deal about their supervisors. Interestingly, even when students are satisfied with the supervisory relationship, I rarely hear them praising their supervisors for providing valuable feedback on writing. Often, when a student does report noteworthy supervisory attention to writing, this attention is characterized as sentence-level proofreading. As a writing instructor, I frequently see draft thesis chapters that clearly need structural revision and yet have supervisory margin notes that focus on small-bore mechanical problems. Moving away from an early emphasis on local writing problems might allow supervisors to focus instead on the broad revision process, and thus help doctoral writers to understand their own revision priorities and identify concrete revision strategies. Doing so could breed the sort of self-sufficiency that would support the overall health of the supervisory relationship. Supervisors are understandably cautious about exercising too much authority over the writing process and the resulting text; however, by adopting a stance that is pedagogical rather than editorial, the supervisor can draw on their own experience of writing in the discipline to support their students in developing those skills. Receiving feedback that stresses the revision process can help doctoral writers become attuned to the valuable notion of writing for a reader. One of the oddities of thesis writing is that audience as a beneficial construct often gets occluded. A doctoral writer who has an understanding of audience that goes beyond the needs of their particular committee is well placed to continue their development as an academic writer as they move past the thesis.

Suggesting that supervisors increase their commitment to teaching students about revision is part of a broader push to increase the pedagogical dimensions of thesis supervision. It is also part of a growing emphasis on the role of writing and writing instruction for doctoral students (Caffarella and Barnett, 2000; Micciche, 2011). Making writing a key aspect of graduate student training could lessen the existential angst and time-to-completion challenges that are such a prevalent part of the graduate student experience. Supervisors talking reflectively about the revision process could deepen the ability of their students to grasp the true nature of the thesis writing journey, and to get over the notion that academic writing is a technical skill that they should already have. Not all campuses have dedicated graduate student writing support, but where it exists, supervisors could partner with writing specialists to encourage students to develop their writing process. They could also routinely refer students to writing support units so that they develop their writing style rather than treating such referrals as a sign of an underlying problem. Doing so would benefit the student being referred, but also, over time, contribute to a more robust culture of graduate writing support. The growth of such a culture could meet the needs of both supervisors and doctoral writers, thus promoting a shared goal: doctoral students capable of strong and stylish academic writing.

Chapter 11

How to improve your advisees' writing permanently—in 30 minutes

George D. Gopen

Style is choice. One's writing style is the sum total of all the structural and rhetorical choices one tends to make on a consistent basis. We are all creatures of rhetorical habit. Recognizing and reforming the most troublesome of those habits can lead to permanent improvement.

It would be wonderful if advisors could help their advisees discover and correct their bad writing habits; but advisors, while they may and ought to be experts in their own fields, are almost never experts in the teaching or analyzing of writing. They tend to comment as they have formerly been commented upon, concentrating on error, semantics, and brevity.

Advisors can be of far greater help by focusing on their advisee's habitual style—not just on the details of a particular manuscript. This chapter offers a way for advisors to do just that, using a slow-motion, one-on-one, analytical process that need take no more than 30 minutes.

Once the advisee's bad habits have been eliminated, subsequent writing products will be submitted in a much clearer, better reasoned, and far more readable form, saving the advisor many hours of future editorial or advisory effort. The method described here actually works: I have used it successfully for many thousands of consulting clients. It has never failed me.

BACKGROUND: THE READER EXPECTATION APPROACH

I have developed this advisory technique as an outgrowth of a new approach to analyzing and controlling the written English language, which I call the Reader Expectation Approach (REA). All of REA is based on a single concept: Readers take the great majority of their clues for the interpretive process not from word choice, nor from word meaning, but rather from the structural location of words. Readers have relatively fixed expectations of where in the structure of an English sentence to look for the arrival of certain kinds of substance (Gopen and Swan, 1990). More colloquially stated: Readers of English know *where* to look for *what*. Knowing these Reader Expectations is the key to success in controlling your own writing and in overseeing the writing of others. You can explore REA without cost at www.GeorgeGopen.com; click on the 'Publications' link, and scroll down to find 'The Litigation Articles.' See too 'The Science of Scientific Writing' there amongst other lengthier works.

There are four questions for which a reader must instantly discover the right answers if the sentence being read is to convey what the writer intended:

1 What action is happening here?
2 Whose story is this?
3 How does this sentence logically link backwards and forwards to its neighbors?
4 What are the most important words here that should be read with extra emphasis?

If the reader gets even one of these wrong, the reader will fail to perceive the author's intended meaning.

The REA offers structurally-based answers to these questions. Here are the somewhat oversimplified but still powerfully useful answers:

1 Readers expect that the *action* of a sentence will be articulated by its verb.
2 Readers read a sentence as being the *story* of whoever or whatever appears as the grammatical subject of the main clause.
3 Readers will *link* a new sentence backwards to its predecessor with the first piece of information in the new sentence capable of being so backwards linked.
4 Readers wish to give extra *emphasis* to material that appears at any moment of full syntactic closure—i.e., at any moment when the grammatical structure of the sentence comes to a full halt. I call this a Stress position. It occurs at every properly used colon, semi-colon, or period. It can never occur at a comma.

The most important of these four questions is the last one, which will command our attention for the rest of this chapter: Which words should a reader be emphasizing the most to duplicate what the writer would have emphasized vocally if reading the sentence aloud? For anyone who uses the written English language daily in a professional setting, putting the stress-worthy information in a sentence elsewhere than in a Stress position is without question the Number 1 writing problem affecting almost everyone. In the last 12 years of dealing one-on-one with thousands of my professional clients, I have encountered only two who had intuitively figured out the Stress position for themselves.

The universality of this problem can be turned to an advisor's advantage: Instead of struggling to edit or 'correct' a given document, the advisor can lead advisees to perceive their Stress position problem—and other expectational problems stemming from the four questions above. This can be accomplished by a slow-motion, highly detailed exploration of only a single paragraph. Once the advisees can see the bad habit and learn how to deal with it, they can apply this new knowledge to the rest of the document by themselves—with difficulty at first, but with increasing success over the next two or three documents. The revised version will require far less effort from the advisor.

Readers—and especially supervisors—constantly trick themselves into believing they have understood the intended meaning of a sentence even when what they have perceived turns out not to be what the writer intended to convey. As long as they recognize all the words used, and there are no grammatical errors, it can seem to them a successful sentence. After all, it looks and sounds like a successful sentence. As long as a sentence makes *some* sense, a reader can easily believe that is *the* sense the writer intended. But if the stress-worthy words are not located in Stress positions, the readers are just guessing. Give a sentence to ten readers. Ask them to underline the words they think were intended to be stressed. You are likely to wind up with between five and eight different responses; and it is not unlikely you will wind up with ten.

If I am working with someone who already understands the main principles of REA, it takes me an average of only 22 minutes to explore a single paragraph closely enough to demonstrate convincingly to the writer what rhetorical habits are functioning.

The following example is intended to show you the process I have developed over the years. This sample sentence will probably not strike you as particularly interesting nor particularly in need of revision. That is part of the point: Unexceptional looking/sounding sentences can seem harmless, but can still demonstrate the imbedded power of the writer's structural choices. You may well be surprised by what subtle but significant ambiguities arise from this exploration. The discovery of a bad habit in a single sentence can help that writer avoid it in all other sentences.

THE EXAMPLE AND THE SLOW-MOTION TECHNIQUE

A few notes on this example are important to understand in advance:

- I have space here to sample only a single sentence. It usually takes a whole paragraph to convince advisor and advisee that what they find will recur often enough to be considered a habit.
- To describe this process actually takes longer than to do it in practice. Reading the following dialogue will require some patience from you—not because it is opaque, but because it is not the kind of passage one would expect to find in an academic article. Understanding how

expectation functions requires (1) pausing a moment before the expected arrival and then (2) retroactively considering the effect of the expectation's fulfillment or violation.

- I use the somewhat unusual form of dialogue here to suggest ways in which this interactive process can be made less oppressive to the advisee, who might well be highly anxious. That load of anxiety can be lightened significantly by the use of kindness, humor, or even a comically hyperbolic reaction. This dialogue attempts to suggest, without comment, how such moments might function. Its nature and procedure are as important as its substance. Example: The word 'oops' (below) indicates not only that the writer has done something wrong but also that the reader has stumbled. It indicates that the reader thinks it may have been a reading error, not a writing error. The humanity of this advisor–advisee interaction allows the linguistic/rhetorical advice to take root.
- I spent no time choosing this example. It was simply the first sentence of the first document at the top of a pile on my desk. My point: The technique can be used on any sentence. I am often, as I was here, surprised by finding important reading misperceptions that I could not have spotted on a quick, first reading looking just for substance.

Here is the example sentence: 'Tick-borne relapsing Fever (RF) Borrelia are global pathogens and a leading cause of morbidity and mortality in regions of Africa.'

Please take a moment to re-read this sentence, underlining any words you think were probably meant for emphasis.

Would intended emphasis not be crystal clear if, in this day of cheap color printing, we could print the words we want the reader to stress in red? Then no one, except for a few color-blind males, would ever mistake our emphatic intentions. Readers would see the red words approaching; they would effect an inner crescendo, building toward the climactic red words; and then they would, with elegance, read less and less emphatically until they reached the period. But such a use of color print is unlikely to be adopted anytime soon. Fortunately, we have something equally effective: Put the important words in Stress positions. Your readers will then know what to stress.

Important note: Colons and semi-colons form Stress positions if, as the grammatical rules require, what precedes them can stand by itself as a sentence. A comma can never form a Stress position because, unlike all other marks of punctuation in English, it never announces its function at the moment of its arrival. There are so many different comma uses that we always have to proceed *beyond* a comma to find out what kind of comma it was trying to be. The comma can never be trusted to signal a moment of syntactic closure.

Let us call the advisee who wrote our sample sentence Pat. It might seem effective, in my role as advisor, simply to ask Pat to identify the important words and then place them in one or more Stress positions. But Pat would be unlikely to 'buy' it simply because I requested it. Pat must be led to see, for Pat's own self, that the non-placing of important material in important places is actually a recurring and debilitating habit. Only when that has been accomplished, will Pat be likely to take this seriously.

To accomplish this, I have developed the following foolproof technique. It is foolproof because I never assume I know what the writer means: I only ask questions. That allows the writer to piece together for me what meaning was intended. Asking what deserves the Stress position here leads the writer back into the thought process to discover those intentions.

The technique: I begin by saying I am going to create an opportunity for Pat to watch and hear someone read this text—in ultra-slow motion. Then I read just a few words, stop, and announce how I am doing the interpretive process—in accordance with the REA principles Pat has already heard me explain. Then I read a few more words, stop, and announce how they expand (or confuse) my interpretive process. If by the time I reach the end of the sentence, I either have not understood the sentence as intended or had trouble doing so, it is probably because something was structurally mis-located, since structural locations are controlling my reading process. If the structural problem I perceive in the first sentence reappears in other sentences in this paragraph, it indicates the possibility of a persistent and pervasive writing habit—a bad one for the readers.

Here is the dialogue that actually resulted from our investigation of this sample sentence.

GDG: Pat, you know I have never seen this text before, since you've just handed it to me. I will not at any time read ahead beyond the last word I have read aloud. I won't see what you've written next and then adjust my comments to suit it. Whenever I stop reading, I will be telling you about my interpretive process only for that portion of the sentence and the portions that preceded it. I may also guess what I expect to come next. You'll see and hear me trying to make sense of your sentence. Here we go.

'Tick-borne relapsing Fever (RF) . . .' Stop there. Whose story is this? It's the story of who or what shows up as the grammatical subject. So this is the story of 'RF.' What is 'RF' going to do? It will do whatever the verb says it's doing. On we go. 'Tick-borne relapsing Fever (RF) Borrelia . . .' Oops. 'Borrelia' is not a verb. I was expecting a verb. I had thought 'RF' was the subject because an acronym like that usually comes at the end of the noun phrase. OK. I've recovered. This is the story of RF Borrelia. What are they going to do? Whatever the verb tells us they are doing. 'Tick-borne relapsing Fever (RF) Borrelia are . . .'

Pat: Oh dear, my high school teacher told me to avoid the verb 'to be.' It's weak. Sorry.

GDG: Ah, but remember what I said about 'weak verbs' in my lectures. No verb is weak or strong by itself, but only in context. The term 'weak verb' should be used for a verb whose meaning has little or nothing to do with the action in the sentence in which it exists. Conversely, 'strong verb' should be used for a verb whose meaning is the focal point of the action in the sentence in which it exists. 'Are' can be a strong verb if one of its meanings (to exist, to equal, or to be characterized as) is what's going on in your sentence. I suspect, without having read more yet, that you are just trying to say 'Borrelia are characterized as X.' It is commonly the job of a text's first sentence to make the simple presentation 'Here is X.' If that's the case, 'are' is a strong verb. Not to worry. Think reader usage, not rules.

Pat: Oh, good. That is all I was trying to do here.

GDG: On I go. 'Tick-borne relapsing Fever (RF) Borrelia are global pathogens . . .' I'm drawing a vertical double-line here. Whenever I do that, it means that, if I put a full stop here, no one could deduct any points for grammatical errors. You've already given me enough for a full sentence. So I have a problem: You are sending me two conflicting reading instructions: (1) 'There is enough here for a full sentence. So something clearly must be worthy of stress. Stress something'; and (2) 'There is no colon, semi-colon, nor period here. Therefore there is no Stress position here. Don't stress anything.' Which of these instructions should I follow: 'Stress something' or 'Don't stress anything'? I guess it's up to me. Looking back at the seven words I have just read, if I was indeed supposed to stress something, let me see how I might 'perform' the seven words as a reader. I can see several possibilities:

Tick-borne relapsing Fever (RF) Borrelia are global PATHOGENS
Tick-borne relapsing Fever (RF) Borrelia are GLOBAL pathogens
TICK-BORNE RELAPSING FEVER (RF) BORRELIA are global pathogens
TICK-BORNE relapsing Fever (RF) Borrelia are global pathogens

Or, obeying your alternative, 'don't stress anything instruction,' it could be read without emphasis—'Tick-borne relapsing Fever (RF) Borrelia are global pathogens,' reserving emphasis for the important things that will surface later on.

So here are five different 'musical' readings of your first seven words, only one of which can be closest to your intentions. Maybe none of them correctly grasped what you were trying to get me to stress. Look how much work I'm having to do, trying to ferret out your meaning. And part of my mind is going *backwards*—while most of it is still hurtling *forwards* to make sense of your sentence as a whole. Once my mind turns backwards, you've lost a great deal of me.

Pat: Wow, I had no idea!

GDG: Onwards. 'Tick-borne relapsing Fever (RF) Borrelia are global pathogens and . . .' This 'and' raises a small problem for me as a reader. When you tell me 'and,' I know I should connect something in the immediate future to something in the recent past, but I don't yet know *what* is to be connected. Look at the multiple possibilities for what this 'and' might be connected to as it reaches backwards:

pathogens and *toxins*
global pathogens and *locally contained* pathogens
Borrelia *are* global pathogens and *pose* a serious problem
Tick-borne RF Borrelia and *non-tick acute* Borrelia

The further back from the 'and' I have to go, the harder the reading task becomes. Let's see what comes after the 'and':

'. . . (RF) Borrelia are global pathogens and a leading cause . . .'

I've got it now: These Borrelia are global pathogens AND they are also a leading cause of something. OK. Onwards.

'Tick-borne relapsing Fever (RF) Borrelia are global pathogens and a leading cause of morbidity . . .' Here I put another of my vertical double-lines. The sentence could have ended here. Now I am *convinced* I've already been given something that needs to be stressed; but I still have no Stress position to tell me *what* it is I should be stressing. I'd like to stop here, but I'm being required to press on.

'. . . (RF) Borrelia are global pathogens and a leading cause of morbidity and mortality . . .' Yet another 'and' here, though a rather easy one: The two four-syllable 'm' words—morbidity and mortality —fit nicely together as a pair. More importantly, though, I could draw yet another vertical double-line here. Surely *something* in this sentence up till now deserves Stress, yes?

Pat: Yes. At least I think so.

GDG: Ah, if you're not sure, how could you expect your reader to be sure? Onwards. I'm certainly hoping I don't get another 'and,' followed by another whole clause! Let's see. '. . . in regions of Africa.' Here, finally, is the full stop; but I am willing to bet big bucks that 'in regions of Africa' is *not* the sole piece of information you wish me to stress! [Laughter on both parts.] It might even be the sentence's least important piece of information. It is also possible, even likely, that this geographical information is contextual for everything else. Context belongs in the place where it does the most good—up front in the sentence. Then we would know, while we were processing everything else, that all of it related to certain regions of Africa.

Pat: I think I must do this a lot.

GDG: Actually, it's statistically likely we will find a Stress position problem in more than 85% of your sentences. This problem afflicts almost everyone some of the time and a majority of us most of the time. We'll see. We only need to finish this paragraph for us to become convinced of it.

Pat: So, how do we fix this?

GDG: We figure out what you wanted the reader to stress; then we create a Stress position for it—or for each of them.

I then circled all the words I thought might reasonably have invited stress, asking Pat which of them was or were stress-worthy. A crucial note: I didn't *tell* her; I *asked* her. Had I told her, I would have been guessing; and had I guessed, I might well have been wrong. As it turned out, even Pat couldn't come up with a quick answer.

Pat: I'm not sure. [Hesitation. Concern.] I'm just not sure now.

GDG: If the writer doesn't know, how will the reader?

Pat: Right. Well, I think 'morbidity and mortality' are the important ones.

GDG: Really? So 'global pathogens' didn't deserve stress? But when those pathogens appeared, they completed a whole main clause, enough to be a sentence. I was tempted to emphasize them, but became confused by the lack of punctuation to indicate a Stress position. So then, now we have to signal the reader *not* to emphasize 'global pathogens.' What role do 'global pathogens' play here?

Pat: Actually, that's whose story I wanted it to be.

GDG: Then we make the pathogens the grammatical subject of the sentence, since that's where readers expect the 'whose story' to appear: 'The global pathogens known as tick-borne relapsing Fever (RF) Borrelia are a leading cause . . .' Now let's get the contextualizing information up front: 'In regions of Africa, the global pathogens known as tick-borne relapsing Fever (RF) Borrelia are a leading cause . . .' Now how do we stress *two* things—morbidity and mortality—in *one* Stress position?

Pat: [Quizzical look.]

GDG: We tell the reader, 'there are going to be *two* things I want you to stress in this Stress position.' And we can do that quite simply by using the word 'both.' Your reader will know to emphasize each of them—as well as both of them as a pair. The result:

> 'In regions of Africa, the global pathogens known as tick-borne relapsing Fever (RF) Borrelia are a leading cause of both morbidity and mortality.'

Given this revision, ten readers of this sentence are likely to agree with each other on what you wanted us to stress—and they would be right.

(I ask my present readers if, when you underlined your choices, you guessed correctly. Fewer than a third of you are likely to have gotten it right—and this is a fairly simple, 19-word, single-clause sentence that does not advertise any of its reading difficulties. Just think what might happen when you are up against a 42-word, three-clause sentence with several candidates for the accolade 'stress-worthy.')

Pat: Question: What if I had wanted to stress the 'global pathogens'? I may be starting to change my mind about what I meant.

GDG: Then you should give that term its own Stress position as well. Since you clearly wanted all this information to be in a single sentence, we can manage to maintain that by providing a mid-sentence Stress position, courtesy of a semi-colon: 'In regions of Africa, tick-borne relapsing Fever (RF) Borrelia are global pathogens; they have become the leading causes of both morbidity and mortality.'

Do you see how forcing yourself to answer the major Reader Expectation questions, like 'what deserves a Stress position?', also forces you to re-enter your thought process to seek greater clarity?

Pat and I found this Stress position problem in every one of her sentences. I predict you will be astonished to find how pervasive the problem is in almost all or (more likely) all of your advisees' writing.

What has caused this pandemic problem? I think it began from our learning most of what we know about writing from teachers in school. There, we were writing for an audience that already knew everything we could find to say. As professionals, however, it is we who are the experts; and we write so that people who do not know what we have to say can come to know it. The term for this writer–audience relationship is 'communication.' But that was never the task for us when we were students: Rather than 'communication,' it was merely 'demonstration.' We wrote to demonstrate to our teacher that we had done enough work and had found enough relevant material to be worthy of an A. When we graduated from student to expert, no one was around to point out to us that merely downloading the information onto an error-free page of writing will no longer get the job done.

The authors of the books on writing advise us, 'To make it better, make it shorter.' I disagree: The lengthiness, or seeming lengthiness, of a sentence does not depend on any particular number of words. I could show you a 13-word sentence that is completely opaque without the slightest surface hint that it is so. Then I could show you a 130-word sentence that rings clear as a bell throughout. Here are my two new definitions, based on the expectations of readers:

- A sentence is too long when it contains more viable candidates for Stress positions than it has Stress positions.
- A sentence is too short when it contains no viable candidate for a Stress position.

Length has nothing to do with numbers.

Once you become familiar with the concept of the Stress position, you can do this above-demonstrated kind of slow-motion reading with your advisees for just a single, important paragraph. They can then apply their new understanding of old habits to their future writings. Working with them for 30 minutes on one paragraph may save endless amounts of time and energy. You'll no longer have to slog through pages that are not yet well enough written to clarify the writer's thought. Hard as it will be for your advisees to revise a whole document (catch them early on, before they've produced too much), what they resubmit to you will be better thought through and much better expressed. Instead of struggling with their prose, you will actually be able to deal with their mind. Your feedback task will not seem nearly such a chore; and their thinking processes will be improved, permanently.

* * *

Attending to stylistic matters—things to do

- Talk about the need for (and purpose of) ongoing revision.
- Be open about your own writing processes.
- Ask questions about student word choice, structure and style.
- Cultivate student awareness of the craft of writing.
- Set exercises looking at style when reading the work of others.
- Direct students to software such as the automated feedback tool, the *WritersDiet Test* (available at http://writersdiet.com) for immediate, non-human feedback 24/7.
- Remind students that revision puts the reader at the centre.
- Take a typical sentence and show where/why readers need more guidance to understand meaning.
- Discuss syntax—or direct students to the Gopen website or similar; then ask them to teach you (and fellow students) about ways to improve clarity.

Part IV

Writing feedback on English as an Additional Language (EAL) writing

John Bitchener; Anne Lee; Martin East

Edited by Susan Carter

> ***Supervisor:*** *Students for whom English is not their first language have particular difficulty with mechanical aspects of writing. It was time-consuming to edit students' writings when they were not native English writer[s but] ESL students with a good preparation seem to do fine with a bit of language help and work on their part.*
>
> ***Student:*** *Being a non-native English speaker, all the feedback in grammar and spelling is more than appreciated . . . so that I would . . . know how to describe certain things in a better way or in a way the native speakers do.*

Increasing internationalization means that supervision in most western universities entails working with writing from doctoral students whose first language is not English—English as an Additional Language (EAL) students. Like others, we've considered the multi-faceted challenges for students who choose to do a doctorate in an additional language and for the communities which support them (Carter and Laurs, 2014: 69–84; Wang and Li, 2011). We suggest that cross-cultural and cross-linguistic supervision is not just about language (Braine, 2002; Jaworski, 2015; Woodward-Kron, 2007); it requires helping the student adapt into a new academic community that can feel alien and isolating (Ali and Kohun, 2007), and often has conventions unfamiliar to those back home. Western ideas of rhetoric may vary from their own language's conventions, in which they excelled (Holmes and Riddiford,

2009; see also Zeegers and Barron, 2008). Internationalization has altered the academic landscape, with many domestic students also having EAL.

In our survey of doctoral supervisors (n=226), we did not ask about supervising EAL students, but 66 supervisors mentioned this as a factor affecting their experiences of supervising writing. Our data chime with other findings (Bitchener and Basturkmen, 2006); many supervisors feel under-equipped for supervising international EAL students, yet perceive the need for extensive feedback on correcting grammar. In our study, supervisors felt that extra time spent at the level of literacy meant they gave less time to the more significant content, structure and ideas. Lack of deep-level feedback is problematic; our data from 80 doctoral students show that they value 'big picture', structural and ideas-related comments that draw on their supervisor's expertise, and are frustrated to receive only superficial comments about proofreading.

International students arrive with a history of success that includes recognition of their English language skills. Many are high-achievers who taught English language back home. Supervisors play a significant role in helping these ambitious people to feel reasonably supported and comfortable, a challenging task in itself (Ali and Kohun, 2007; Cotterall, 2014; Manathunga, 2014; Zamel, 1995). Realizing that their language abilities are regarded as deficient in the new environment is likely to significantly dent students' confidence. Supervisors need to establish working habits that allow progress in writing to occur alongside research skills development. It's especially important for these students also to be enfolded within the writing communities suggested in other chapters.

Part IV suggests ways to scaffold international students into the western culture of academic writing, and into fluency in English language. In Chapter 12, John Bitchener tackles practical ideas for supporting students to meet academic expectations regarding voice, critical analysis, use of literature, argumentation and coherence. Anne Lee (Chapter 13) factors in how to teach with awareness of cultural difference to allow enculturation, emancipation and the building of academic relationships. In Chapter 14, Martin East offers findings which suggest that supervisors commonly prioritize specific parts of the thesis as needing the most revision and editing: those that are both troublesome and significant during the examination process.

Chapter 12

Written feedback typically provided on L2 students' chapter drafts

John Bitchener

The provision of written feedback on dissertation chapter drafts of both native (L1) and non-native (L2) writers is a well-established practice adopted by dissertation supervisors and others involved, like learning-support and writing-support advisors or instructors. From the literature published on what supervisors say they often need to provide feedback on, it would seem that while L1 and L2 students receive feedback on many similar areas of interest and concern to supervisors, L2 students sometimes receive feedback on additional areas if their earlier studies have not been in the L2, and if their linguistic knowledge and use are not as well developed as those of L1 students (Bitchener, Basturkmen and East, 2010; Kumar and Stracke, 2007). The focus of this chapter is on the type of feedback I frequently give to L2 dissertation students, especially when responding to early drafts of their chapters.

The chapter begins with a brief discussion of what is meant by the construct *feedback* and why it is important for both L1 and L2 dissertation writers. It then discusses feedback that is typically given to L2 students on the content they present in their chapters. Particular attention is given to content coverage, voice and stance in relation to the content, claims and conclusions presented, the extent to which critical engagement is evident and managed, and the use and misuse of citations. The final section focuses on feedback that may be given on how the content is organized. I discuss feedback on how to create an effective argument, and on the importance of coherent writing at both the local, sentence level and at the more global, discourse level where cohesion also forms an important component of the wider coherence of a student's writing.

DEFINITION AND IMPORTANCE OF FEEDBACK FOR DISSERTATION STUDENTS

The term *feedback* has been defined in a variety of ways in the literature because of the different contexts and purposes for which it has been provided (Basturkmen, East and Bitchener, 2014; Ferris, 2003; Hyland, 2007). The type of feedback given to dissertation writers in English-speaking/writing tertiary institutions is typically written comment on what students have done well and what they might need to consider doing next. The latter may involve adding to, deleting, modifying or amending what has been written so that the text more closely approximates the norms, values, expectations and requirements of the discipline in which the research is situated. The feedback may introduce new suggestions or ideas for the student to consider, or it may refer to guidance and advice given earlier in pre-writing meetings and discussions with the supervisor, but which needs to be further attended to.

It is well understood that, at doctoral level, feedback is particularly important because it is often the primary form of instruction (Benesch, 2000; Hyland and Tse, 2004; Kumar and Stracke, 2007). In countries like Australia and New Zealand where doctoral students are often not required to take pre-dissertation courses/classes like their counterparts in the United States, the instructional aspect of feedback is particularly important, even if students are able to attend seminars and workshops on doctoral research and dissertation writing. Feedback, unlike instruction that may be provided by these other generic means, is tailored to the specific needs of students at the point when they are most likely to benefit from it. Given that feedback is critically important for dissertation writers, it is not something that supervisors only provide their L2 students with: L1 students also need to understand what is expected of them because the dissertation genre is a form of writing that is as new to them as it is to L2 students. However, because L2 students may have additional needs as a result of their different language and educational/epistemological backgrounds, their particular needs should be identified and addressed.

FEEDBACK ON CONTENT

In this section, I consider the type of feedback that may be given to L2 dissertation writers if there are issues with (1) their content coverage; (2) their voice and stance in relation to the content presented; (3) the claims and conclusions they provide or fail to provide; (4) the extent to which critical engagement is evident and managed; and (5) their use and misuse of citations.

Content coverage

Supervisors will typically provide more feedback on gaps in their students' content coverage than on aspects that have been covered comprehensively and effectively (Bitchener, Basturkmen and East, 2010). While most students need guidance from time to time on topics or themes that they should consider including, L2 students sometimes need more feedback on the range of theoretical perspectives relevant to their focus. This includes how to demonstrate depth of understanding about the significance of different theoretical positions and any debates or counter-arguments that have been prominent in the literature. Anecdotal explanations suggest that a focus on theoretical perspectives may not have been a priority in the earlier education of some L2 students (Bitchener, Basturkmen and East, 2010).

A range of approaches may be considered by supervisors to address this issue. First, supervisors would do well to find out whether or not their students have a clear understanding of the *purpose* of theoretical explanations in a doctoral dissertation. By the end of this discussion, students need to see that a theory seeks to explain a phenomenon/issue (i.e. why and how X exists or occurs) and can predict what they might expect to find as a result of their research. Second, it may be helpful to discuss with students the types and range of theoretical perspectives relevant to their research questions (or hypotheses being tested) after the students have completed an initial programme of theoretically-focused reading. This discussion could focus on students explaining to their supervisor which theories may be relevant to their research and why. Then, in response to what the students say, the supervisor has an opportunity to provide feedback. Some of the questions that supervisors might usefully ask in order to stimulate their students' thinking about the relevance of particular theories include those listed in the following box.

- What does the theory state, claim or explain?
- In what ways does the theory relate to the focus of your research (e.g. your research questions)?
- What other theoretical perspectives support the theory?
- Are there any theories that present an opposing position? What are they and in what ways are they different?

What arguments can you present for selecting one of these theories and not others to guide your research?

Third, it would also seem important for supervisors to find out if their students know how to present a range of theories (both for and against the position or framework they have decided is most relevant to their research). Without this kind of discussion, students will often present a shopping list of theories and just say that the relevant one to their research is X, without explaining and justifying their choice(s).

Voice and stance in relation to claims and conclusions presented

Much has been written about the importance of researchers presenting their own voice and stance in relation to what they say about their own work as well as that of others (Barton, 1993; Hirvela and Belcher, 2001). It has been noted that L2 students may sometimes struggle to do this more than L1 students, especially if their earlier studies have been in an epistemological context that does not prioritize the opinions and assessments of novice researchers. Additionally, if a self-effacing belief system has characterized how they position their work relative to that of their superiors, they may not understand that they are expected to make claims and draw conclusions that are justified on the basis of the quality and robustness of their argument. This reluctance may mean that some L2 students struggle initially (1) to debate the merits and demerits of others' claims and conclusions in the literature they read; and (2) to comment confidently on the findings of their research in relation to the wider literature. Additionally, supervisors may need to explain to such students that sometimes it is appropriate to use boosters when commenting on one's own work or that of others, whereas at other times a more hedged assessment or claim may be relevant. A discourse analysis of sample texts that use these devices effectively can be one way of giving confidence to L2 students about their use. Not only does this type of approach show them how and why a particular use is appropriate and effective, it also brings to their attention a range of linguistic frames they may not be familiar with.

Extent to which critical engagement is evident and managed

The extent to which L2 students critically engage with the literature they read and make use of in their dissertation may also be determined by their prior teaching and learning experiences in earlier study (Cadman, 1997; Li and Seale, 2007; O'Connell and Jin, 2001). For such students, supervisors would do well to explain, first of all, what they mean by a critical response because this can be variously understood by different researchers and supervisors. Second, they could explain what students are expected to critically engage with (i.e. the theoretical claims and positions of others; the validity, reliability and robustness of findings reported in the research literature; and the claims and conclusions they make about their own research findings in relation to those of others and to existing theoretical explanations). Third, it may need to be pointed out by supervisors that a superficial statement is unlikely to be satisfactory when drawing conclusions from a critical engagement with the literature, and that any position advanced needs to be carefully and convincingly argued and justified.

The use and misuse of citations

There is an ever-growing literature on the role of citations in academic writing (Pecorari and Shaw, 2012; Swales, 1986), on issues to do with accurate use and a misuse of citations (Currie, 1998; Pecorari, 2003; Shi, 2004), and on reasons that lie behind misuses (Li and Casanave, 2012; Thompson and Tribble, 2001). Depending on their prior education, L2 students may sometimes have different understandings about the role or purpose of citations in academic writing. They may not always understand, for example, that reference to the ideas of others is important for contextualizing their own ideas and research and for giving readers access to those ideas. Sometimes L2 students are also unclear about what constitutes an appropriate use of citations so that acknowledgement is given to the original source of an idea, and to their own voice or stance in relation to that idea. If L2 students do not have these understandings, there needs to be a discussion of the importance of the conventions of citation use in academic writing and of the consequences of not adhering to them. Given their prior learning experiences, some L2 students who transgress such conventions do so unintentionally. However, others who deliberately misuse citations (including, for example, those who deliberately plagiarize in order to make the reader think that an idea from another source is their original idea) need to be made aware of what is acceptable academic practice. Because effective citation requires knowledge and skill, supervisors may not be able to invest the time needed on a one-to-one basis with their students to ensure that they are fit for purpose in this regard. Fortunately, most universities provide seminars and workshops on citation so L2 students in need of such training should be made aware of these opportunities.

FEEDBACK ON THE ORGANIZATION OF CONTENT

This section focuses on feedback that supervisors may give on how the content has been organized. In particular, attention is given to three aspects of feedback:

1 the relationship between the aims/purposes of a chapter, the discourse move options available and how they are presented;
2 what constitutes an effective academic argument and how to create it; and
3 the importance of coherent writing at both the local, sentence level and at the more global, discourse level where cohesion also forms an important component of the overall coherence of a text.

The relationship between chapter aims and discourse move options

The content presented in different chapters of a dissertation varies according to the aims and purposes of each chapter, and its effective organization is determined by the particular communicative aim that the content is being used for (Bitchener, 2010). Thus, it should not be surprising that some L2 students (as well as L1 students) have an incomplete understanding of what is expected, especially if the type of thesis or method of research-reporting they have completed in earlier studies was different to what is expected at doctoral level. One effective way of helping students understand, through feedback, what constitutes an effective organization of content is to discuss the *aims* of different chapters or sections of a dissertation. This can be followed up with a discussion of what it means to use the content to write an argument that builds a case or justification for the content's inclusion in the chapter.

Research on the typical discourse moves or units of content that one might expect to find in a particular chapter (e.g. a literature review chapter) has led to a range of generic options that students might consider employing as they scope the macro structure of a chapter. Two thesis/dissertation guides by Bitchener (2010) and Paltridge and Starfield (2007) have presented and discussed such moves as they are typically found in traditional, empirically-based dissertation chapters (e.g. introduction, literature review, methodology, findings, discussion and conclusion). These two books are empowering and students should be directed to consult them.

Creating an effective academic argument

Additionally, a supervisory discussion with students about what an academic argument is and how it can be created may minimize the frequency and amount of written feedback that supervisors need to give. In academic writing, students need to understand that the term *argument* can refer to individual claims or a whole text (or units/sections within the wider text). With individual claims, *argument* refers to a proposition that is supported with evidence and reasoning (e.g. why a particular theoretical claim is valid), but with the whole text, and major units or sections within the text, it refers to 'a connected series of statements intended to establish a position and implies a response to another (or more than one) position' (Andrews, 1995: 3) or to 'a sequence of interlinked claims and reasons that, between them, establish content and force of the position for which a particular speaker (writer) is arguing' (Toulmin, Reike and Janik, 1984: 14). Feedback on ineffective argumentation can be time-consuming, but one approach that has proven to be effective has been presented earlier in this volume (see Chapter 1). Additionally, a deconstruction of an effective argument across and within units of a chapter, followed by discussion of what is effective, can be a useful follow-up activity, especially if undertaken in groups.

Coherent writing

Coherent writing is essential if an argument is going to be clear, logically developed and soundly justified. Much has been written about the coherence difficulties that L2 students can encounter when developing an argument, but less has been written about how supervisors and others address the issue (Basturkmen and von Randow, 2014; Cooley and Lewkowicz, 1997; Dong, 1998). Reasons for the absence of such a discussion may be a lack of understanding about (1) what the term *coherence* means, (2) what constitutes coherent text and therefore (3) how to explicitly articulate what is expected. Dictionaries and books of terms and concepts (e.g. Finch, 2000) can provide a variety of guidelines on some of the constituents of a coherent argument: cohesion and clearly organized ideas, uninterrupted connection or unity of ideas, and comprehensible language or thought. While L1 students may sometimes reveal weaknesses in the quality of their arguments, L2 students may sometimes be more likely to struggle with what EAP (English for Academic Purposes) experts and supervisors understand to be a logical presentation of thought. Typically, we expect students to be able to reveal continuous thought patterns at the sentence level (i.e. from sentence to sentence) and at the wider discourse level (i.e. from paragraph to paragraph and from section to section). Thus, there is an expectation that there will be cohesion enabling an uninterrupted connection of ideas. However, L2 writers sometimes need to have it pointed out to them that in their prose there is an absence of connection between one sentence and the next, requiring the reader to supply the missing link between the two sentences. Sometimes L2 students will include an over-supply of discourse markers (e.g. moreover, furthermore, however) in the belief that they provide the necessary connection. However, an over-supply can interrupt the fluidity of ideas as much as the use of incorrect discourse markers (Gardezi and Nesi, 2009; Hinkel, 2003). Comprehensible language is critical to coherence at the sentence level.

Within a single chapter, it has not been possible to identify all the areas that supervisors often need to provide feedback on, but it is hoped that this overview of a number of recurrent areas of concern can alert readers to some of the common L2 issues and the ways in which they may be addressed.

Chapter 13

Five approaches to supporting students writing in English as an additional language

Anne Lee

Research at the doctoral level is increasingly an international and an interdisciplinary exercise. The use of any language other than one's mother tongue(s) requires a deep cultural understanding as well as a good memory and significant effort. To write in English at the highest academic level that we know of is not a task for the faint-hearted, whatever the author's first language. Supervising and advising candidates working at this level can bring a rich combination of challenges and joy.

There are three key points that I would like to make at the beginning of this chapter. First, good practice in supervising or advising on writing at a doctoral level is essential, and is not notably different for students working in English as an additional language (EAL) and local researchers. Second, EAL students will become more valuable citizens and possibly more valuable employees because of their mastery of different languages and cultures. Third, international students offer a wonderful opportunity for advisors and supervisors to learn more about other worlds.

However, there are some aspects of supervision that we particularly need to be sure are explicit when working with EAL students on their writing. These include:

- ways of articulating arguments;
- views about the construction of knowledge and validity;
- institutional practices and support in connection with plagiarism, literacy and proof reading;
- ways of presenting the thesis.

SUPERVISOR/ADVISOR IDENTITY

Before focusing specifically on writing, the supervisor can usefully address their conception of their own identity in this relationship. Barbara Grant has identified several relatively successful accounts of self in her research about Pākehā (i.e. non-Māori) supervisors of Māori students (Grant, 2016):

1 Treaty partner *(standing up for the other partner)* ['Treaty' refers to the Treaty of Waitangi, a foundational document in New Zealand]
2 Conscientious but ignorant *(if I am ignorant it is possible for someone else to know)*
3 Good gatekeeper *(keeping them western enough to get their PhD)*
4 Guardians of a sacred space *(recognizing culturally sensitive information)*
5 Member of a whānau-of-interest *(becoming part of the student's communal world-view).*

Significantly, Grant's work focuses on the role of the supervisor or advisor in a culturally sensitive way and enables conscious choices about how supervisors manage any cultural gap between the student and a western doctorate.

EXPLORING CULTURAL HERITAGES

Hofstede, G., Hofstede, G.J. and Minkov (2010) have described three levels of uniqueness in mental programming, and emphasize that the personality of the individual is as important as the culture from which they come. So understanding the culture from which the doctoral candidate originates will only give the supervisor part of the picture. Figure 13.1 shows how this can be portrayed.

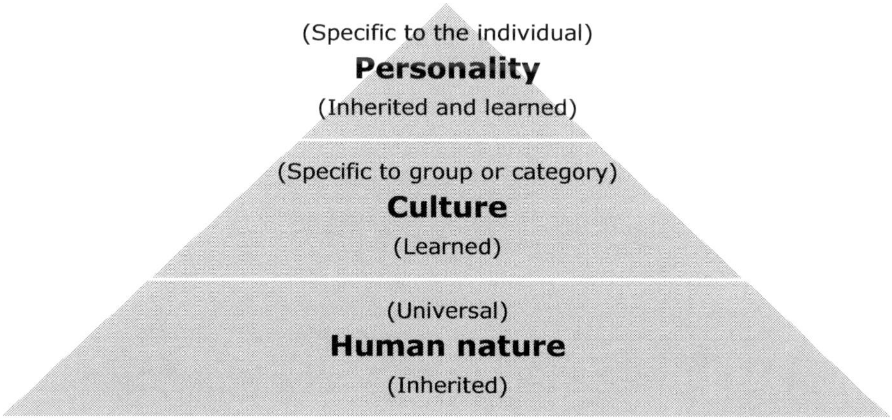

Figure 13.1 Three levels of uniqueness in mental programming

Hofstede et al. (2010) also pioneered a binary approach to identifying six key different dimensions of culture which we can use to try to understand what our doctoral candidates might be looking for in their studies. This binary approach can form a useful format for discussion if the supervisor(s) and candidate both mark their own cultural preferences and discuss areas where they have identified a significant difference (see Table 13.1).

Table 13.1 A tool for exploring different cultural dimensions in supervision

Six dimensions of culture (after Hofstede G., Hofstede, G.J. and Minkov)						
Mark an 'x' in the box that you think identifies your culture in relation to another						
More democratic						More autocratic
Collectivism						Individualism
Femininity (Person/relationship orientation)						Masculinity (Competitive task orientation)
Avoids uncertainty						Tolerates ambiguity
Long-term orientation						Short-term orientation
Indulgence						Restraint

Erin Meyer (2014a, 2014b) has produced a similar map with eight dimensions that are also worth exploring and concludes with the following advice for navigating the cultural minefield:

1 *Don't underestimate the challenge:* preferences stem from habits acquired over a lifetime and they can be hard to change.
2 *Foreground multiple perspectives:* in a multicultural team we need to understand each person's perspective.
3 *Find the positive in other approaches:* our initial negative reaction to a cultural preference may stem from ignorance of how it works.
4 *Adjust and readjust your position:* widen your comfort zones so you can move back and forward between differences fluidly on each dimension.

GOOD PRACTICE IN SUPERVISING WRITING AT A DOCTORAL LEVEL

Earlier, in Chapter 4, I introduced the idea of a framework of approaches to research supervision. Here I explore in more detail what doctoral candidates, particularly those working in English as an additional language, might be seeking when looking for feedback.

Common problems that research students face include writing in a circumlocutory manner, poor grammar and sentence structure, writer's block,

Table 13.2 A range of feedback needs that doctoral candidates need to make explicit

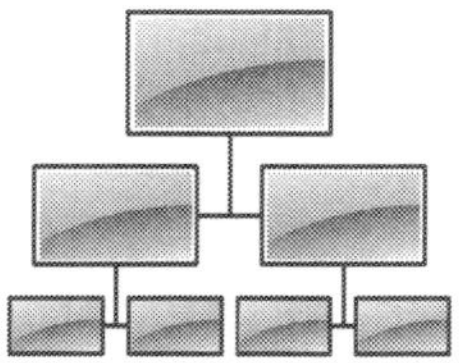				
Functional	*Enculturation*	*Critical thinking*	*Emancipation*	*Relationship development*
1. Timely and clear feedback 2. Help with structure and organization 3. Help with grammar, spelling and punctuation 4. Provide overview, then more detailed comments on the script	1. Supervisor to demonstrate genuine interest in their work 2. Consistent feedback 3. Help with finding literature 4. Help with appropriate expression, e.g. 'language is too informal here' 5. Help with appropriate methodology	1. Balance between critique and constructive comments 2. Guidance in identifying irrelevancies, or condensing material 3. Developing ability to critique own work	1. Recognition that the work is the student's responsibility 2. Suggestions that are not too directive	1. A partnership of equals, not a manager/employee relationship 2. Written feedback first, followed up by meeting to discuss face to face

Table 13.3 A range of approaches supervisors and advisors can use to offer feedback

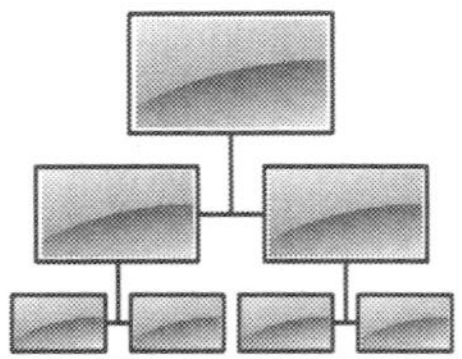				
Functional	*Enculturation*	*Critical thinking*	*Emancipation*	*Relationship development*
a. Advice on correct grammar b. Linguistic advice, e.g. correct 'bring the meaning of messages' to 'accurately reflect the meaning . . .' c. Summary sheet and/or track changes and/or hand-written comments d. Not to correct too much at once e. Keeping records of all feedback given	a. Referencing and genre-type advice, e.g. 'try to avoid using such colourful descriptions' b. Identifying theoretical gaps or omission of key points c. Noting where too much literature included; indicating when/where/how to include more	a. Focusing on cohesion: 'unfortunately "x" differs from "y"', and 'things are a bit jumbled in this chapter' b. Noting lack of conceptual depth c. Identifying theoretical gaps d. Signalling absence of transitions, e.g. 'unclear how this leads to your conclusion'	a. Highlighting absence/evidence of independent thinking b. Offering perspective: too narrow/too broad? c. Supporting student to find their own voice	a. Sending written comments to students before meeting b. Providing feedback promptly c. Discussing written feedback in person; checking student's understanding; clarifying reasons for feedback d. Meeting to agree what next stage should be

revising work as requested but not showing any further initiative, summarizing but not conceptualizing the literature, asking for excessive help with rewriting, and not submitting work to an agreed deadline. All of these problems can arise with either an EAL or a local candidate, and all of them can be managed through a combination of approaches (see Table 13.2).

These issues relate to what the supervisor needs to explore so that they can decide how expectations can be met. The supervisor might decide to be quite functional about the whole situation, and encourage the student to go on generic courses (if they are available), work with other colleagues or work through some of the texts that I recommended in Chapter 4. What matters is that the doctoral student is encouraged to express their requests, and all parties to the supervision session discuss how these can be met.

The same framework can be used to identify a number of approaches to offering feedback. Table 13.3 synthesizes the work of Lee (2012) with Bitchener et al. (2011). Bitchener et al. (2011) collected data in New Zealand from 35 supervisors and 53 students spread between Humanities, Sciences/Mathematics and Commerce. They issued questionnaires, carried out follow-up interviews and reviewed written scripts.

Common problems that research students face include writing in a circumlocutory manner, poor grammar and sentence structure, writer's block, revising work as requested but not showing any further initiative, summarizing but not conceptualizing the literature, asking for excessive help with rewriting, and not submitting work to an agreed deadline. All of these problems can arise with either an international or a local candidate, and all of them can be managed through a combination of approaches.

One frequent general comment, when working with EAL students, is that supervisors have given feedback, but it has not had the desired effect. The resulting frustration is understandable, but it is important to realize that learning to write at this level is an iterative process; the art of asking questions to ensure understanding is as important as giving information; feedback both in writing and face to face is helpful; and some repetition is likely to be necessary. Success from using a wide range of sources and services to support the student is shown when the candidate receives their hard-earned doctorate and the supervisor's life has been enriched by a greater understanding of both the topic and another culture.

Chapter 14

Feeding back on research writing

New Zealand supervisors' priorities with an L2 focus

Martin East

Writing a postgraduate thesis for the first time is a challenging enterprise. This is just as true for students whose first language (L1) is English as it is for those for whom English is a second or additional language (L2). Two dimensions of the struggle are limited understanding of the requirements of different sections of the thesis, and uncertainty about the expectations and requirements of their discipline-specific communities of practice (Bitchener, Basturkmen and East, 2010).

If postgraduate students are to have the greatest opportunities to succeed, they need to become acquainted with the new knowledge and skills they require, for which some form of instruction is necessary. For students writing a thesis, 'instruction' is most often provided in the form of written and/or oral supervisor feedback. Effective feedback is a critical step along the road to students becoming independent (Lantolf, 2000). Constructive and detailed feedback on students' written work has been noted as an important characteristic of effective research supervision (Benesch, 2000; Engebretson et al., 2008; Hyland and Tse, 2004), and plays a critical role in enculturating students into discipline-relevant literacy and knowledge (Hyland, 2009). As Kumar and Stracke (2007: 462) assert, 'it is through written feedback that the supervisor communicates and provides advanced academic training, particularly in writing, to the supervisee'.

For English as L2 students, who increasingly make up the composition of the postgraduate student population in Western universities, linguistic and cultural differences can become barriers to assimilating feedback. The effectiveness of feedback is influenced by the different expectations that both parties bring to the interaction. The supervisor 'requires the student to think again, to read more, to revise written drafts' (Grant, 2005: 76). However, 'at times these requests are likely to be delivered confusingly or inadequately by supervisors or misunderstood, resented and resisted by students (much more so by some for reasons of politics, biography, or temperament)' (Grant, 2005: 76). For L2 students, the problem is arguably exacerbated. A barrier to effective communication can be raised when cultural and linguistic differences exist between students and supervisors (Aspland and O'Donoghue, 1994; Li and Seale, 2007).

Given the above context, what do supervisors see as their priorities for feedback? Which sections of a thesis require more, or a different, focus than others? Answers to these questions provide some insight into the challenges and requirements of different sections of a thesis, particularly where L2 writers of English are concerned.

A STUDY INTO SUPERVISORS' PERSPECTIVES ON FEEDBACK

Observations here are built on the findings of a wide-ranging study into supervisors' and students' perspectives on effective feedback, and analyses of on-script examples of feedback, carried out across several discipline areas in six New Zealand universities (Bitchener et al., 2011). East, Bitchener and Basturkmen (2012) presented findings regarding what *students* reported they received by way of feedback from supervisors, and the kinds of feedback practices they perceived to be most effective. Findings suggested that having English as L1 or L2 did not lead to a differentiation in the type of written feedback students reported finding helpful, and linguistic feedback was required for some L1 as well as L2 students. A range of feedback was found to be more helpful than only one type of feedback. It was also seen as important to combine written feedback with oral feedback.

A follow-up study undertaken by Bitchener and East (2014) focused on the *supervisors'* perspective on feedback in one discipline area (applied linguistics) and several New Zealand and Australian universities. In this chapter, I present findings gleaned from a survey (n=16) carried out among applied linguistics/languages in education supervisors in eight university departments in New Zealand, and follow-up interviews with a subset of respondents (n=5), designed to probe survey findings more deeply.

FINDINGS

Of the 16 supervisors who responded to the survey, ten reported that at least three out of every four students they supervised had English as L2 (mean = 80.5%; mode = 75%). Years of experience in postgraduate supervision ranged from 3 to 25 years. Despite the small sample size, the findings presented here do make sense of those from the larger study, and seem likely to assist time-pressed supervisors in prioritizing which sections of the thesis need their most detailed attention.

Supervisors were asked to rank the different sections of a thesis in terms of their priorities for feedback (Table 14.1, where 1 designates the highest priority and 5 the lowest).

Table 14.1 Ranking of thesis sections in terms of priorities for feedback

Rank		*Section*
1	=	Literature review
2	=	Discussion
2	=	Methodology
4	=	Findings
5	=	Introduction
5	=	Conclusion
5	=	Abstract

It was apparent that the literature review ranked as the most crucial in terms of feedback, followed by the discussion and methodology sections. Although interviewees noted that it was difficult to determine which aspects of the thesis required the most focus when giving feedback, because the thesis, at the end of the day, needed to reach the required standard when judged holistically, data relating to the three highest-ranked sections are presented below, first with regard to survey data, and then with reference to the interviews.

LITERATURE REVIEW

A key issue for respondents to the survey was 'relevance'. The literature review required attention because it needed to provide *'a* clear *theoretical framework for the study'*. Reviews needed to be *'more than [a] sequenced description of studies'*. This required *'careful planning so the reviewer takes careful control of the review'*. In practice, reviews were often *'insufficiently probing or critical/not synthesized'*, with *'too much extraneous material'*. Feedback focused on the *'need for better synthesis to lead to student's study'* or *'[s]ynthesizing to achieve a coherent account of how the literature pertains specifically to the project in hand and reflects the writer's clear understanding (e.g. adequate paraphrasing rather than too much echoing)'*.

Interview data supported the above assertions from the survey. There was a sense that writing the literature review would be one of the toughest writing challenges of the whole thesis because it required students to write an argument to support the research. A common problem was that candidates merely described the existing literature, rather than constructing a good argument around the literature. In this section, therefore, supervisors' feedback focused particularly on the level of critical thinking shown by the students as they presented their argument. The literature needed to be relevant to the research and well-synthesized. There was, as Supervisor 1 put it, *'the need to be critical, to take a stance on the literature rather than just describe it'*. Feedback was required to help the writers *'to make the literature pointed towards the thesis, so you're making sure that the literature review is . . . an argument . . . something that identifies where the literature got to, in the sense [of] "where's the gap?".'*

DISCUSSION SECTIONS

The effectiveness of the discussion chapter was clearly linked to that of the literature review. According to survey respondents, since students *'often have the most difficulty connecting their research to the previous literature'*, feedback on the discussion section encouraged students *'not to forget the theoretical framework introduced in the literature chapter'*. A danger was that students *'often fail to adequately address the literature, or introduce a whole slew of new literature'*. There was also a need for *'[t]aking the discussion that step further—what do the findings mean in a broader context?'*, and for *'clarity and quality of the arguments'*. As one respondent put it, *'[e]ssentially I see the discussion chapter as very important to the thesis and I am always concerned about its clarity and the quality of the arguments involved'*.

Interviewed supervisors expected candidates to demonstrate a deeper level of critical thinking in interpreting the findings in the discussion section than was sometimes in evidence. A typical mistake in this section was that the students would not link the discussion back to the literature review very convincingly. Students needed to *'situate [their] research* within *[the] discussion'* (Supervisor 2, my emphasis). The supervisors challenged their students to go beyond merely *describing* the data. They also often found themselves reminding the candidates that they needed to be more conservative in their claims regarding the implication of the findings/results. Supervisor 3 explained, *'often there'll be a case here or there where people have stated beyond what they can ... they want to [do that] because they feel they should be saying something big'* in a research thesis. Supervisory feedback needed to encourage students to be more realistically conservative in presentation.

METHODOLOGY SECTIONS

Presentations of methodology were, according to survey responses, *'often vague and lacking detail'*, or including *'[t]oo much detail or too little!'*. Consequently, the chapter was *'[n]ot clear—someone else couldn't follow it'*. Feedback needed to focus on the *'clarity'* of *'the procedures described'* or *'process'*. This was *'generally best achieved by attention to the chronology of the decision-making'*. Students needed to be directed to pay attention to *'details and accuracy'*, showing *'[s]ophistication [and] thoroughness'*.

One of the most common problems for the methodology section, identified in the interviews, was clarity. It was noted that this could be because the students became too familiar with what they had done, and thus found it challenging to explain to an outsider how they had carried out the research. There was also an expectation that the student would provide some justification for methods chosen. As Supervisor 4 noted:

> *I find that [the] methodology chapter is a really difficult chapter for them, making sure that they've got everything. ... In their head they find it difficult to explain it clearly to another person, so that's something I work through a lot. ... It's not quite clear enough, so you have to actually put more detail here and justification.*

NEED FOR ORAL FEEDBACK

It was evident in the survey data that the key to successful written feedback was the developmental opportunity for post-feedback discussions. Eleven out of sixteen supervisors noted that they 'always' provided oral feedback in conjunction with written feedback, with the remaining five noting that this was most often the case. In other words, meetings provided opportunities to *'go through the written feedback'*, and *'after I've handed back my written feedback we will discuss my comments, for clarification, extension etc.'*. This was a procedure that one supervisor *'much prefer[red]'* because the candidate *'may wish to explain what they were trying to say'*. Talking through feedback is likely to be where students actually learn what the supervisor is trying to show them, so that feedback becomes effective in developing the independent research writer of the future, and not just in developing one thesis.

The usefulness of oral feedback was also highlighted in the interviews. Supervisors found it useful to discuss the written feedback because this provided the candidates with a better understanding of the feedback, and the supervisors with greater clarity around what their students intended when writing. Supervisor 1 summarized this point clearly:

> *They find it really, really useful. And when I say I go through it orally as well, I usually asterisk bits or I put a question mark because there are bits I want to discuss . . . It's a good discussion, often they help me understand things that I haven't understood before, so I find it an important part of the process to . . . talk it through.*

OTHER ISSUES EMERGING

The interviews revealed several dimensions that add to the survey data. With regard to feedback practices, there was evidence of eclecticism in practice. Each supervisor took contextual and relational dimensions into account, leading to different approaches and techniques depending on the circumstance. As Supervisor 1 noted: *'Every student, every chapter can be a different experience. With some students, you respond to a chapter without having seen much of the prior writing that goes into it. Other students, you're seeing bits of it coming through.'*

Importantly here, each candidate is different, and will work in different ways on their writing, and supervisors will need to adopt a flexible approach to feedback contingent on students' writing practices.

Several useful support mechanisms additional to feedback emerged. These included: (1) encouraging students to look at completed theses as examples, thereby providing a guide or benchmark for the students; and (2) alerting candidates to the various support systems offered by the universities for postgraduate students, recognizing that some students were not aware of them.

A significant finding arising from the interview data was that the supervisors did not tend to differentiate students on the basis of linguistic challenges. They noted that even L1 speakers of English faced linguistic problems in common with their L2 peers, especially with regard to grammar and appropriate register. They also encountered a number of L2 English speakers who experienced very few problems in the linguistic area. Nevertheless, it was common for L2 speakers to experience more linguistic challenges, and several supervisors did acknowledge providing more support for these candidates:

> *With English as a second language . . . I've always tried to duplicate that oral and written feedback so that they've got both . . . I like the students to have a copy in the meeting, so that they can see it, I can see it and it's kind of on record.*

The above presentation from the findings of a recent small-scale study (Bitchener and East, 2014) is necessarily brief, and I have chosen to focus on supervisors' priorities for feedback rather than instances of feedback. East, Bitchener and Basturkmen (2012) presented the students' perspective from a previous larger-scale study (Bitchener et al., 2011). The above consideration of supervisors' perspectives shows synergy with those from the students and provides clear priorities for feedback, and reasons for these. It is evident that no one formula of supervision can be applied to all candidates. Each has his or her own individualized practices. It is, however, crucial for supervisors to communicate their expectations for each section of the thesis to their students. The above presentation provides guidelines on those areas likely to require the most dedicated feedback, and what that feedback might need to focus on, particularly for students who come from divergent linguistic and cultural backgrounds.

* * *

Working with EAL writers—things to do

- Draw attention to western academic emphases on argument, critical analysis and coherent, cohesive, *deductive* thesis structure:
  - refer students to model texts as exemplars;
  - check that students understand that 'argument' differs from listing points, requires careful wording (using boosters, sign-posts and hedges), and needs to be supported by literature;
  - explain protocols around academic integrity, attribution of ideas, citations and referencing conventions, and techniques to demonstrate critical analysis.
- Be culturally sensitive, and explore cultural differences relating both to your own and your students' comfort zones:
  - acknowledge what is positive in other cultures' approaches; pay attention to your own, usually invisible, cultural assumptions;
  - appreciate how challenging cultural transition may be for students;
  - acknowledge that (mutual) learning will be cumulative, likely to require you asking questions as well as giving advice.
- Combine a range of feedback approaches:
  - establish balance between surface-level and ideas-level comments;
  - consider whether you agree with research prioritizing feedback on the literature review, discussion and methodology sections;
  - explain the need to link research questions, methods, literature and results to main argument or position;
  - make time to talk through feedback, as well as annotating drafts.
- Overtly encourage students to engage in academic community:
  - to partake of available peer-support communities;
  - to make use of library, language and learning centre courses and individualized support;
  - to read other theses, to become familiar with structural and linguistic patterns.

Part V

Master's and Honours smaller projects' writing feedback

Juliet Lum; Liz Beddoe and Jane Maidment; Sandra Nicol and Sarah C. Cornelius

Edited by Susan Carter

> ***Supervisor:*** *My experience with supervising master's students is that the quality varies greatly . . . I have found it challenging to get master's students to write . . . I have a lot of issues with [students' passivity or dependency] with honours and master's students.*
>
> ***Student:*** *During my Honours year, I received prompt and very helpful, constructive feedback from my advisor.*

Part V gives advice on how to manage the writing of a thesis or dissertation that is tightly time-bound and often undertaken by people in full-time employment. Most academics begin their supervision by taking on honours and master's students, who are making the tough transition from taught learning to research learning (Allan, 2011). At this level, usually an initiation into research writing (Healey et al., 2013), a high standard is demanded (Kiley et al., 2011). Advising novice researchers within the confines of strict time and external pressures is a tough entry-point to supervision.

Three chapters suggest ways to manage the project, develop independent writers and make use of communities of practice. Juliet Lum (Chapter 15) details how a project management approach can be applied to master's and honours supervision. In Chapter 16, Liz Beddoe and Jane Maidment highlight the fact that master's and honours students are often people with full-time jobs and other demands on their lives. Accordingly, they describe support which acknowledges that writing must be fitted in, recommending that supervisors set early writing chores that stimulate thinking and give prompt feedback, with a 'show and tell' approach. Sandra Nicol and Sarah C. Cornelius (Chapter 17) demonstrate a 'whole school' initiative, describing how a centralized course acts as the foundation for all master's and honours projects, interweaving supervision into a generic community of practice.

Chapter 15

Supervising master's/honours

A project management approach to researcher development

Juliet Lum

The most common pathway to admission to a PhD degree is by successfully completing a research master's degree or honours add-on year, both of which require conducting a research project and writing a thesis/dissertation. The duration of the master's/honours (hereafter M/H) project is rarely a full year, but is usually the equivalent of 8–9 months' full-time study, to allow time for the thesis to be examined, often externally, and for results to be finalized before the end of the academic year. While this tight timeframe limits the scope of inquiry and injects a degree of excitement and intensity into the research process, it also places pressure on the student and supervisor to manage the project and their relationship well.

An M/H project is characterized by firsts. It is usually students' first taste of conducting a research project from concept to dissemination: reviewing and keeping abreast of research on the topic, collecting and analysing data, and writing a thesis. Even if students have engaged in some of these activities as part of their previous coursework, the M/H year represents a new phase in their approach to learning: they are expected to move from being reactive students to pro-active researchers (Hunt, 2005). For supervisors, it can often be a first too, as it is not uncommon for new academics to be assigned supervision of M/H projects, as they are perceived as having fewer risks than doctoral projects. But although M/H projects are smaller in scale than PhD projects, they come with their own set of unique challenges.

While there are several resources available on the supervision of PhD research (e.g. Denholm and Evans, 2007; Kamler and Thomson, 2006; Paltridge and Starfield, 2007; Wisker, 2012), there is relatively little guidance or research that focuses on the unique challenges of supervising short-duration projects conducted by students with no research experience. Papers reporting on such challenges commonly comment on the fact that master's supervision is an under-researched area (e.g. Ginn 2014; Anderson, Day and

McLaughlin, 2006), due, among other things, to the 'chameleon-like status' of the master's dissertation (Pilcher, 2011). Nevertheless, there are a few resources that are written specifically for master's candidates, which cover thesis management and would be beneficial for new supervisors; these include Andy Hunt's (2005) *Your Research Project: How to Manage It* and Chris Hart's (2005) *Doing Your Master's Dissertation: Realizing Your Potential as a Social Scientist*. Additionally, new M/H supervisors would find Lynne Roberts' (2015) reports on best practice for honours and coursework dissertation supervision and her toolkits particularly valuable.

This chapter draws on the advice given in the resources mentioned above, as well as the author's own experience of teaching research communication and project management to research master's students. I suggest that within the tight timeframe of the M/H year, supervisors can take a staged approach to the type of feedback they offer, with the aim not only to enable the student to produce a polished thesis for examination, but moreover to foster independence in the emerging researcher, the M/H candidate.

DEVELOPING RESEARCHER INDEPENDENCE: POSSIBLE IN 9 MONTHS?

The M/H project is more than just a step up in scale from undergraduate study. Hunt (2005) underscores the significance of an identity transition by devoting two chapters to the topic. Hart (2005) also foregrounds the concept of 'independence' in his definitions of master's research and dissertations, and the word 'proactive' tops his list of the attitudes expected of master's graduates. The M/H research year often represents the student's first experience of learning in a one-to-one setting under the supervision of an experienced researcher in his/her field. How quickly and comfortably the student acculturates into this new mode of learning depends on several factors, including the student's age, life experience, cultural background, personality, prior relationship with that supervisor (e.g. as a former teacher), and the supervisor's own mentoring and interpersonal interaction style. Nevertheless, it is advisable for the supervisor not to assume that the student will be familiar with the protocols or conventions of research supervision. For instance, many M/H students will at least start the M/H year regarding the supervisor as a master who will issue instructions to be followed: unless explicitly told otherwise, they will assume that the supervisor will direct them in what they should be reading, doing, and submitting at each stage of the project, so that the dissertation is completed on time and to the level of quality required to pass examination. In other words, many students will start by transferring their reactive student mentality into a one-to-one setting.

While it is possible to supervise an M/H project in this highly controlled, didactic way, and some supervisors may prefer this directed approach as it guarantees that the project will be completed on time, if taken too far, there is a risk that the research can become the supervisor's project with the student acting more like a research assistant. This approach can deny the student opportunity to develop crucial skills and attributes, such as time- and self-management, adaptability and resilience, critical evaluation and reflexivity, thus suspending their development as independent researchers (Mantai, 2015; Sinclair, Barnacle and Cuthbert, 2014). So M/H supervisors are faced with the challenge of balancing the pressure to guide the student's project to completion within a very tight timeframe with the need to create conditions that foster in the student a degree of research independence and autonomy.

Admittedly, it is not realistic to expect a reactive, teacher-dependent student to transform into a completely autonomous, pro-active researcher within 9 months; the PhD is the time and context in which full transformation is most likely to be actualized. Yet M/H candidature allows the first step in the transformation, a transition year. And whatever level of autonomy that a supervisor may aim to develop, the thesis that goes to examination needs to demonstrate that an identity transition has taken place. The M/H thesis needs to be more than just a detailed and accurate report showing that the student has understood the research area; it needs to read as a sustained argument text, sensitive to disciplinary discourse conventions (Hyland, 2004), and must provide evidence of the writer's critical evaluation. Facilitating the transition will involve nurturing development in the following areas: autonomous learning, self-management, research literacy, and acculturation into the disciplinary community.

USING PROJECT MANAGEMENT TO FOSTER RESEARCHER INDEPENDENCE IN M/H STUDENTS

The term 'project management' is often associated with long-term, big-budget, multi-party manufacturing projects. There are Gantt sheets to produce, project sponsors to report to, budgets to track, and teams to manage. There may appear to be little need of or value in applying such concepts to M/H projects, which are usually run by a student on his/her own, using existing university resources. Nevertheless, the stages through which large-scale projects pass can be used to structure the management and supervision of small research projects (see Carson [2007] who elucidates this approach for doctoral supervisors). Table 15.1 maps typical project phases onto an M/H project.

Thesis manuals usually advise students to manage their candidature by breaking it down into stages, which may be associated with specific thesis chapters. Phillips and Pugh (2010: 72–73), for instance, suggest that students use the earlier stages of candidature to write the easiest chapters—for example, the Method or Literature Review—and reserve the Introduction chapter, for example, until a much later stage. Perry (2013) provides a numeric guide for planning candidature according to the percentage each chapter typically occupies of a traditional IMRD (Introduction, Method, Results, Discussion) thesis, based on the premise that the number of months one devotes to each chapter is proportional to its length. Applying Perry's guide to a 20,000-word M/H thesis to be completed within 8 months would lead to the thesis and candidature plan shown in Table 15.2.

Table 15.1 M/H candidature mapped onto traditional project phases

Phase	*Project management definition*	*Corresponding stage in M/H project*	*M/H period*
Planning	Project is scoped: milestones and deliverables; budget and deadlines	Project definition Outcome: research proposal and/or ethics application	0–2 months
Implementation and monitoring	Project tasks commence Regular team and stakeholder meetings to track progress (milestones and spending against time)	Research activities Regular supervision meetings	2–8 months
Completion and evaluation	Project concludes with the submission of final deliverables and report	Thesis submission and examination Outcome: M/H thesis Optional outcome: published paper(s)	8–12 months

Table 15.2 Perry's (2013) thesis formula applied to a typical M/H thesis and candidature

Chapter	*Topic*	*%*	*Pages*	*Months*
1	Introduction	6	4	1
2	Literature review	34	22	2
3	Methodology	18	12	1⅓
4	Data analysis	22	14	1⅔
5	Conclusion	20	12	2
Total		100	64	8

Dunleavy (2003) also connects candidature time management with the structure of the thesis, warning readers against following the common practice of devoting the bulk of their candidature and thesis to 'lead-in materials' at the expense of the value-added contribution of the research. Dunleavy emphasizes that thesis examiners are not impressed by a writer's detailed criticisms of others' work until the writer has established his/her own credentials as a solid researcher (2003: 58). So, rather than allowing it to consume half of the available time and word quota, students should compress the literature review and set-up to one or two short chapters, and devote the majority of time, effort, and pages to core materials and deeper discussions of their implications.

Dunleavy's emphasis on the value-added contribution of their research is sound, but it does presume that candidates have already developed a certain level of researcher autonomy and can adopt a confident authorial persona; M/H students may not have reached that level. However, supervisors can help students to develop a confident authorial persona and researcher identity by using the project management phases as a framework to pace the guidance and feedback they provide throughout the M/H year.

PLANNING PHASE (EARLY STAGE CANDIDATURE): MONTHS 0–1

The first month of candidature is a crucial time for setting expectations. Both students and supervisors will come to the supervision relationship with expectations of each other and assumptions about relative responsibilities. These assumptions often remain implicit until problems arise as a result of differing expectations. To avert these sorts of problems, supervisors and students are advised to discuss potential areas of misaligned expectations. Some thesis manuals even provide questionnaires to make explicit assumptions about relative responsibilities in the research process (e.g. the role perception scale in Paltridge and Starfield, 2007: 38, based on Moses, 1992: 25); students and supervisors compare responses and can negotiate ways forward if expectations differ. It is highly recommended that the M/H supervisor devote a proportion of the first meeting to discussing thesis project management, and agree with the student on who is considered the project manager. The statements in Paltridge and Starfield's questionnaire concerning initiating meetings and tracking progress will reveal whether the supervisor or the student is assumed to be the project manager (see Figure 15.1).

Hunt (2005) strongly advocates the 'Student as Project Manager' model, and provides reasons and strategies for master's students to assume this role. Roberts (2015), on the other hand, recognizes that there are several supervision styles, ranging from what she calls the 'hands off' approach, where the student is almost solely responsible for all processes in the project, up to a 'high involvement' approach, where the supervisor does as much as could be possible without overstepping academic integrity boundaries such as writing the thesis for the student. Involvement level need not be constant

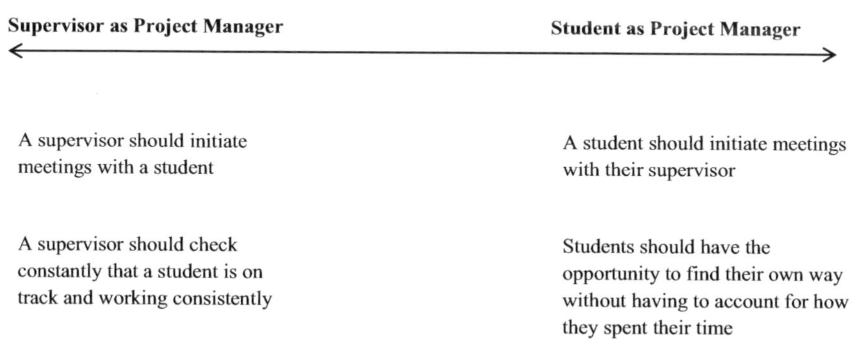

Figure 15.1 Prompts to help clarify who is 'project manager'

throughout the life of a project; M/H supervisors should consider strategically decreasing involvement over the course of candidature. Making this strategy explicit in the planning phase is important, so that the student will expect to assume increasingly greater responsibility for managing the project, including initiating meetings and keeping track of progress.

The planning phase is also the time to define the project and draw up a timeline. In contrast to doctoral candidates, M/H students do not have the luxury of time to scope, plan, and produce an extended research proposal for assessment before commencing. In some disciplines, students may not have the freedom to propose their own project. Rather, the department may publish a list of feasible projects which can be supported by their staff and resources, and students can select one of these. Nevertheless, most M/H students can be encouraged to take ownership of their project by proposing a few project ideas, each of which can be presented to the supervisor in the form of a written paragraph articulating the research question and methodology (good examples can be found in Mauch and Park, 2003: 74–79). Feedback can then involve discussing the relative merits, risks, and feasibility of these potential projects. Once a project has been selected, the supervisor can help the student refine the research questions/hypotheses and methodology, and plan a realistic project schedule.

IMPLEMENTATION PHASE (MONTHS 2–8)

In the implementation stage, M/H students will engage in different sorts of research activities depending on their discipline. For all M/H research projects, regardless of discipline, implementation also involves research writing; in other words, thesis writing should not be part of the completion phase. As Kamler and Thomson (2006: 4) strongly argue, writing 'is a vital part of the research process'.

In the implementation phase, supervisors can help to develop students' research literacy by encouraging 'noticing skills' as they review literature (Kamler and Thomson, 2006: 128–131; Murray, 2011: 22–29). Rather than simply reading for methods and content, students can be encouraged to observe how such texts are structured and their positions are argued. Some students may benefit from discussing a well-written paper or thesis with their supervisor during a session early in candidature, in which elements of argumentation can be highlighted; for example, how contribution is signalled, how other literature is integrated as evidence, how limitations and counter arguments are acknowledged and minimized, how unexpected findings are handled, how different sections are structured internally, and how the author uses metadiscourse, such as signposting, to enhance their authorial voice and help the reader to navigate through the paper. Noticing and discussing these features together early in candidature will facilitate the uptake of feedback on written drafts later, as the student develops his/her own voice.

Master's/honours students should be encouraged to share drafts of their work as early as possible so that feedback can be provided on their writing to identify developmental areas. Roberts (2015: 23) summarizes that quality writing feedback is direct, actionable, and motivating; that is, when it is clear, specific, detailed, descriptive (not judgemental), and addressing the work (rather than the individual). Some M/H students may be reluctant to show less-than-perfect texts to an academic, so Roberts suggests that feedback on early drafts should focus on structure, content, coverage, and relevance, with feedback on language flow and grammar saved for later drafts. Similarly, feedback on authorial voice can be saved until later in candidature, when the student has a firmer grasp of his/her stance and contribution.

Since the duration of an M/H project is much shorter than that of a PhD, regular fortnightly or even weekly meetings are advisable. Regular face-to-face discussion will keep students committed to their project even when things seem to be progressing more slowly than was originally planned (Hart 2005: 22). A shift may be observed in meeting interactions as the student progresses from a high level of dependence to a degree of learner autonomy: in the early stage, the student may ask lots of questions and the supervisor provide explicit instruction; and in the final stage, many students will have reached a level of expertise in the area and will be able to confidently articulate both what they have discovered or demonstrated and why it is significant. Supervisors can encourage this shift around the middle of candidature by refraining from immediately supplying answers to students' questions or solving their problems, and instead encouraging them to identify and evaluate a range of options and then settle on a course of action to try. The shift to independence can also be facilitated by providing opportunities for students to talk about their project regularly with other candidates; this may be in the context of group supervision sessions with students who have the same supervisor (Conrad, 2007), or in a regular peer accountability group (Fisher, 2012) or research writing group (e.g. Aitchison and Guerin, 2014) consisting of M/H students from the same or related discipline(s). Research has suggested that this sort of regular, meaningful contact with peers not only increases research students' self-efficacy, but can also socialize them into a disciplinary community and contribute to their identity as inter-dependent researchers (Gardner, 2008; Kozar, Lum and Benson, 2015; Sinclair, Barnacle and Cuthbert, 2014).

COMPLETION AND EVALUATION PHASE (MONTHS 9–12)

The final phases in a project are inevitably a time of intense activity. While completing the thesis is a cause for celebration and the student should be allowed time to rest and recover, it is not actually the final activity in the project and need not mark the end of the supervision–student relationship, especially if the goal is not merely to produce a thesis but to develop a researcher. The supervisor can invite the student to a meeting of joint reflection and planning; feedback from examiners may suggest further change for publication.

While publishing the research may seem an obvious step to the supervisor, many M/H students may view submitting their work to an academic journal as an unattainable goal, or at least an intimidating enterprise. Students will benefit from mentorship through the publication processes, including selecting a journal, researching its coverage and target readership, conforming to author guidelines, communicating with editors, and responding to reviewers' comments. Demystifying the process and walking alongside the student through it contribute to supervisors' broader goal of acculturating the emerging researcher into the disciplinary community.

A SHARED TRANSFORMATIVE EXPERIENCE

Guiding students through their first independent research project may seem formidable, particularly for those with limited experience as a research supervisor. The short timeframe in which M/H projects need to be conceived and completed allows little room for error. However, supervising fledgling researchers can also be a very exciting and rewarding experience for the opportunity it affords to oversee a student's first steps in their transformation from a passive, reactive, teacher-dependent learner to a pro-active, self-managed, and intrinsically motivated researcher.

Chapter 16

Directive feedback in honours or master's degree research

Liz Beddoe and Jane Maidment

The honours and master's students we deal with in the field of social work are probably typical of many: practice-focused workers wanting to improve the areas in which they work. Our students typically have a 1–2-year timeframe to carry out the essential tasks, often while in a concurrent clinical placement or, in the case of fully fledged practitioners, contiguous with a busy practice. Practitioners will inevitably be carrying out research activities in the evenings and at weekends. Few will have significant support from employers.

As a consequence, these students are time poor and understandably distracted by the demands of clinical practice. Carrying out the research is intellectually and emotionally demanding. For such students, the thesis-completion timeline is viewed across a busy calendar of paid work, the day job and personal commitments. 'Writing up' comes at the end in this task-dominated view and so, in the early stages, writing is not in the forefront of the students' thinking.

Their dissertation or thesis comes at the end of a professional qualification or is undertaken as professional development. The research may be clearly located in practice problems; for example, a qualitative study of the experiences of women who have reported to health professionals instances of violence by their intimate partner; or an examination of the barriers to social inclusion in a community welfare organization. The broad aim of such projects is to explore a phenomenon in a practice setting, identify factors of success or failure through exploration of actions or narratives and to make recommendations for change at the level of practice. D'Cruz and Jones (2014: 9) suggest that an impact of social work research is its 'capacity to invigorate and inform' professional practice. Practitioners undertaking research for professional development are highly motivated, but may be 'rusty' in their writing and need to rediscover their academic voice. Writing is something they also may believe they have mastered, having generally met accepted standards in their previous academic work. And yet, in our experience, it is the writing that is often a major challenge of master's and honours research. In this chapter we offer some ideas for addressing feedback and support for this academic writing.

In our role as supervisors we begin our work with a new student project from a place of experience. We know that seeking ethics approval takes several months. We expect recruitment and data collection will pose challenges and that transcription is time-consuming. Because we anticipate problems that will challenge the students' ambitious and often rose-tinted timeline, we urge students to complete good early drafts.

We typically ask for a literature review before ethics approval is sought, while writing a methodology chapter sits well alongside preparing the ethics application. The process of seeking ethical approval entails decision making. How many participants and how will they be recruited? Precisely what questions need to be asked and in what sequence? What are the risks? What might arise as 'incidental findings' and what steps might be taken? The ethics application is important writing under the pressure of agenda deadlines. It courts prompt directive feedback and starts students writing productively. Thus three separate pieces of writing begin the research project and are linked to thinking. Supervisors must balance three factors: the timeliness of task completion, ethical yet rigorous data collection and the production of a well-argued thesis. All require attention to writing, feedback and some degree of direction. Our stance is that feedback starts from receipt of the research proposal, as by the time a thesis is in a full draft, it is too late to address writing clarity.

Clarity about the purpose of our feedback on writing is part of relationship building with students. Adcroft (2011: 406) argues that feedback is 'a social process, where the fundamental points of analysis are the human relationships involved', rather than merely a technical process where the focus is on tasks and technique. While our feedback is by necessity framed by the task focus of the project, our aim is still to enhance learning.

Here we address this challenge in terms of three main features of feedback on writing: a writing focus from the beginning, prescriptive feedback, and support that encourages the development of an academic voice.

STEP 1: KEEPING WRITING IN FOCUS

Setting expectations from the start

From the outset of discussions with a potential thesis student, we outline our approach to supervision, providing a framework for the diverse tasks involved in researching and writing a thesis; the deadlines of the research process; and how feedback will be provided along the way. Most importantly, we are clear that the writing must start from the beginning of the research journey. Most postgraduate programmes expect potential students to develop a short version of a full research proposal prior to enrolling and this submission will be discussed with the student, providing the first opportunity to experience specific feedback from their potential supervisor/s.

At this point it is important to also discuss the process of giving and receiving feedback. It can be helpful to disclose a little about what your feedback style is like:

> As a supervisor I can often come across as a bit blunt, without necessarily attending to the convention of the 'feedback sandwich', a technique of noting a strength in the writing, then adding a constructive criticism, followed by another compliment.

An invitational conversation enables the student to get to know what they might expect from your feedback. It is equally important to ask the student how they respond to feedback. Naturally, given the power dynamics, a student can feel obliged to respond to this question by saying what they think we want to hear, rather than revealing their true feelings about how they react to critical feedback. We break the ice in this conversation by sharing our own experiences of receiving negative and overly critical feedback. The purpose of this early conversation is to acknowledge that we all have reactions to feedback, and to firmly locate the process of receiving both oral and written feedback as an integral part of the supervision landscape. Students need to understand how to work with and integrate the ideas from feedback to strengthen their thesis writing by the time they graduate: the writing feedback process is an additional learning opportunity the student encounters within the postgraduate space.

We find it helpful if thesis writing can be conceptualized from the start as an integral part of the research dissemination process. Writing up is an ethical responsibility as is communicating about the process and ideas associated with the development of the research. So we encourage students to begin research writing with a number of different audiences in mind: the research participants, the ethics committee, the examiners, journal reviewers, conference attendees and us as supervisors. To reap the benefit of multiple forms and sources of feedback before submitting the thesis for examination, we encourage candidates to find opportunities to write for different audiences throughout.

There are different forms of directive feedback that the student can receive. As supervisors we use both electronic tracked changes on documents, and handwritten comments on 'hard copy' drafts. There are pros and cons for each system. Electronic copies include legible feedback that can be tracked in terms of revision document control. One temptation of providing electronic feedback is to include ongoing document editing which is the student's work to do, or more worryingly, to effectively change the discourse of the document through insertions or deletions that are easy to do electronically.

Writing for the ethics application

The ethics application requires significant writing effort in the first part of the master's or honours project. As noted above, the process of ethics application can happen alongside the production of the methodology chapter. Discussion of the ethical dimensions of research informs writing crucial to the success of the thesis and occurs in two significant texts during the research process—the ethics application, which must be brief, clear and in plain English; and the methodology chapter which can be more substantive, being grounded in the research literature.

The ethics application functions as an important communication of the research intentions. It requires plain, jargon-free English which enables the ethics committee readers (who come from a diverse group of academic disciplines) to understand the research focus, questions and procedure. Research ethics calls for honest, scrupulous and careful writing of documentation, such as a consent form and participant information that provide clarity and safety for research participants and gatekeepers. In our experience, writing this documentation is more than just writing: it begins the iterative process that underpins many small but significant decisions about how the research will be carried out.

We spend a great deal of time discussing and providing feedback on writing about research ethics and indeed the methodological decisions which underpin the thesis project. In this particular writing, the student makes the thesis their own, unique and very specific to their research question and design. While it will be informed by literature, the decision making and judgements are the students', and we often find ourselves making comments like 'whatever you decide, take careful notes as you will need to write a rationale or justification for your decisions'. At this stage, the writing is clearly at the developmental edge of the students' skills. For some, highly prescriptive or directive feedback may not be necessary. For others, it will be needed to safeguard the project.

STEP 2: PRESCRIPTIVE FEEDBACK

A rationale for prescriptive feedback

We aim to strike a balance between doing detailed edits and giving examples. In the 'show and tell' tradition, we find it easier to write small passages to demonstrate what is needed. For example, a student's draft literature review may contain a list of previous research, with numerous paragraphs starting with 'Smith and Jones (2006) argue/report/assert that . . .'. The beginning student has gathered their sources and systematically worked through them, taking careful notes in a linear manner. As a consequence, their writing privileges the authors, not the ideas or findings that have emerged from the reading. We find it helpful often to rewrite a paragraph by way of an exemplar, setting out clearly how to introduce the topic or theme of the paragraph and weave in references to sources, demonstrating how to build the thematic map of the extant literature. We will then ask the student to rewrite the literature review in this manner.

We will also be directive about using a thesaurus to combat repeated words or phrases. The chosen referencing style may not be negotiable, and this will require us to be prescriptive about such matters as the hierarchy of headings, captions and formats for tables and figures and the referencing style.

Addressing procrastination

Many tasks can get in the way of actually writing the chapters. At the outset there is much reading to do, and talking with others about the topic. Students often cite lack of uninterrupted blocks of time and competing demands as reasons for not writing consistently. We have struggled with students who have had little writing to show after quite some time. With this in mind, we reiterate the importance of writing from the beginning of the thesis, with supervisors setting a target word or page length to be achieved between supervision sessions. While this course of action may seem overly prescriptive for this level of study, students do respond positively to such concrete expectations.

We aim to provide the student with feedback within a week of their having submitted the work. This turnaround time models for the student that their writing is important to us and that we will contribute to the successful progression of the thesis by meeting our own deadlines. This level of organization is reflected in the supervision session, where we set a clear agenda on how to expand on the written feedback given in the chapter, and discuss practical strategies for progressing and examining conceptual challenges that arise. At the end of each session, we make a plan for what work will be submitted before the next supervision session. Students may also email short pieces of work between formal sessions to demonstrate how they have addressed the feedback about writing, a practice which enables students to actively work on their writing and receive frequent feedback along the way. This process also signals further to students that continuous writing towards the thesis is expected. The iterative process of providing comment helps to generate a strong collaborative supervisory relationship between supervisors and students.

STEP 3: DEVELOPING ACADEMIC VOICE IN A SHORT TIMEFRAME

One of the suggestions we often make to students is to read a completed thesis. At the beginning of the research process, this can helpfully demonstrate the structure and 'feel' of a thesis or dissertation. As the student begins to write up their findings, they are faced with another challenge: a very new form of writing, generated by them alone. Their previous reliance on a good engagement with the literature is insufficient here. The challenge is to support them to create a strong narrative reporting of the findings and significance of their research in their own voice.

Sword (2012: 24) has noted that our intentions in shaping students' writing are often conservative: academics 'typically preach stylistic caution; they want their students to demonstrate mastery of disciplinary norms, not to push against disciplinary boundaries'. This does not mean, of course, that we don't encourage flair and style, but at master's and honours level, we do need to teach the basic conventions of research writing, which is often by necessity descriptive and explanatory rather than expansive.

Guidance is needed about disciplinary norms. There are many competing ideas about such matters and Sword (2012: 28) found that nearly half the writing guides she analysed were positive about creative forms of expression, but some from each major disciplinary category warned against creativity in academic writing. By way of an example, the majority advocated the use of personal pronouns, but in each discipline, some cautioned against this. And indeed our preferences as supervisors offer guidance close to our sociological roots, valuing both precise and transparent writing for the description of the method, while also encouraging students to recognize and write about their own positioning in the research process.

Locating the writing process with an eye to time management is essential when supervising students completing honours projects and master's theses. Setting clear expectations from the outset about quality and quantity of writing outputs is integral to moving ahead to timely and successful completion. For us as supervisors, providing constructive directive feedback is central to enabling the student to find and nurture her own academic voice.

Chapter 17

Effective supervision of master's researchers in professional contexts

Sandra Nicol and Sarah C. Cornelius

This chapter discusses the supervision of master's-level researchers in professional settings. The focus is on research writing for master's dissertations or Work Based Projects where students are concurrently engaged in professional activity, as in education, health, law, business and related areas. In our context (a Scottish School of Education), students work on independent research or development projects relevant to their professional role. They are diverse and globally distributed. Support takes a 'whole school' approach which includes group workshops, online resources and individual academic supervision. Drawing on research into supervisors' experiences (Cornelius and Nicol, 2016), this chapter outlines a range of strategies that support the development of master's students' writing skills.

Our experience is probably typical: in many areas of social and health sciences, master's students engage part-time in distance or blended studies alongside their professional activities. Programmes frequently include a 'capstone' project or other enquiry-based course that requires independent investigation and the writing of a lengthy report or dissertation under the guidance of a supervisor. Students produce a high-quality academic product larger than any other they may have produced up to this stage of their studies, and this can appear overwhelming. Students may become isolated and demotivated if not carefully supported.

In our case study, students often enter the 'Work Based Project/Dissertation' course, which is the final element of all master's programmes in our School of Education, anxious about the process, apprehensive about their ability to conduct a suitable investigation and daunted by the prospect of writing their first lengthy piece of academic work. Although expectations from level descriptors (such as those in the Scottish Credit and Qualifications Framework—http://scqf.org.uk) and theories of adult learning (e.g. Knowles,

Holton and Swanson, 2011) suggest that learners at this level should be resilient, self-directed, effective critical thinkers and accomplished writers, the reality is that development of these attributes may have some way to go. Confidence as well as writing skills may need boosting.

SUPERVISING MASTER'S RESEARCHERS IN PROFESSIONAL CONTEXTS

Master's students in professional contexts simultaneously enact multiple roles and identities: as professionals, researchers and students. Alongside study, they may have to accommodate their employer's expectations and demands, personal commitments and sometimes challenging financial circumstances. Their previous educational experiences are diverse, often some time ago, and from disciplines with different writing traditions and styles. Alongside this, supervisors may have preconceived ideas about supervision and anxieties of their own.

Master's students in professional settings negotiate connections between professional activity and academic study. This involves problematizing and critiquing the former and simultaneously taking a 'researcherly' perspective for the latter. Exploration of taken-for-granted assumptions about practice, and examination of difficulties arising from confrontations with literature which challenges habitual practices (Spratt and Florian, 2014), may require considerable supervisory guidance. For a critical researcher who is also a central actor in the study, exploring the insider-researcher role and associated ethical issues is a critical precursor to finding an appropriate academic writing style. Writing should provide clarity and objectivity when reporting research methods and findings, but also evidence of reflection and criticality.

To avoid unhelpfully optimistic assumptions about students' prior experiences, it is important to have information about students early on, preferably before supervision starts (Cornelius and Nicol, 2016). Detail about the student's cultural and educational background provides clues about the nature of the support they might require. There is a danger in assuming that an individual student is fully prepared for independent research and able to write appropriately (Grant and Graham, 1994). Early diagnosis of possible difficulties can surface through open discussion or evaluation of previous academic work and tutor feedback.

Social and emotional aspects are crucial, particularly as increasing numbers of students come from geographically and culturally disparate backgrounds. Practices such as group supervision are gaining favour as both a pragmatic solution where supervisor availability is limited and as an opportunity for peer support amongst students with similar interests and challenges (Maunder et al., 2012). A 'networked' approach develops a sustainable model of professional development which reflects current practices and helps to bridge academic study and professional practice. Within any community there will still be a significant one-to-one supervisor–supervisee relationship for most master's researchers. Supervisors find it important that these relationships are established and maintained reciprocally (Cornelius and Nicol, 2016). For effective communication, particularly when this takes place online with distance learners, clarity about supervisor expectation with writing is vital to avoiding misunderstandings about feedback.

A particularly significant area of supervisory tension exists between the supervisor's role as mentor and as the assessor who monitors academic standards (Anderson, Day and McLaughlin, 2006). While PhD assessment is normally undertaken by independent examiners, master's assessment is frequently done by the supervisor (in our School, with input from a second marker). This may create problems if a student thinks that they need to accommodate their supervisor's feedback uncritically in order to achieve a good grade. It can also be uncomfortable for a supervisor who has to provide feedback on draft materials prior to formal assessment. Issues related to power and control need to be managed carefully to avoid abuse or restrictions on student independence (Anderson, Day and McLaughlin, 2006). Documentation of discussions and feedback helps to bring any issues to the surface and is recommended (Anderson, Huggins and Winfield, 2015) in case of future disputes or appeals. Supervisors need to provide careful and realistic feedback on progress and writing at all stages to avoid misunderstandings or unexpected outcomes on assessment.

The majority of supervisors have a limited portfolio of experiences to draw on for strategies to support master's writers. In addition, as our research respondents noted, every master's student is different, so what worked for one will not necessarily work for another. An environment which considers the needs of both students and supervisors is essential when considering the development of master's researchers and their writing.

SUPPORTING MASTER'S WRITERS

Our model for support of master's students has developed along with the increase in interest and uptake in master's-level study in Education in Scotland. The late 20th century saw a significant growth in UK students undertaking master's-level study (Anderson, Day and McLaughlin, 2006) and it was recognized that Scottish Education needed to address issues such as technological change and globalization. In our School of Education, this resulted in a wider cohort of staff becoming involved in supervision and recognizing that new supervisors, as well as students, needed support. Team discussions, feedback from students, reflections on experiences of supporting and mentoring new supervisors and action research to support development of appropriate support informed the development of an approach that supports individual master's students within a generic framework.

Importantly, the development of academic skills for master's study takes a 'whole school' approach. Within a flexible study framework, a 'Critical Approaches to Academic Literature' course addresses the need for students to develop skills in critical thinking, reading and writing, along with sourcing and referencing literature. This course is recommended as a starting point for master's-level study, although some with appropriate prior experiences omit it. To accommodate this and allow course content to be re-visited if part-time studies take place over an extended period, self-study materials from the course are made available to all students. The 'whole school' approach requires that learning from the 'Critical Approaches' course is reinforced and applied across other courses.

Coherence of experience for all master's students in our School of Education is a second feature of our approach. Although drawn from diverse programmes, all students take a common 'Dissertation/Work Based Project' course. Supervisors can work effectively with students across different programmes since the process itself is generic and students communicate with peers with similar interests or in similar cultural or geographical areas despite being on different programmes. Students have opportunities to make their own connections across a network of peers, including staff.

Generic support reduces the pressure on individual supervisors and provides consistency to students. This also diffuses some of the issues of supervisor power by giving students access to alternative resources and perspectives. Generic support begins with an online course induction, outlining course expectations such as the need for high standards of presentation and writing, adherence to academic conventions such as referencing, and an independent and critical approach. The role of the supervisor is emphasized as one of 'guide' rather than 'instructor', and students are told that supervisors will not undertake close proof reading or correction of text. If students require support for academic writing, they are encouraged to be proactive early and seek other sources of help. Other generic resources include exemplars and links to external resources. Extracts and full projects are made available alongside book lists and other resources to support students. Writing challenges are a common issue on a blog hosted by the Course Leader and links are made there to a range of useful external resources, including the University of Manchester's *Academic Phrasebank* (www.phrasebank.manchester.ac.uk), books and online resources such as those by Wallace and Wray (2016).

The induction provides guidance on how to work with a supervisor. Drawing on work emphasizing the value of using structured approaches to initial supervisory meetings (e.g. Grant and Graham, 1994), a set of prompts is provided to help students manage their first interactions with their supervisor. These prompts highlight the need for thorough discussion of prior experiences and expectations, together with consideration of communication protocol.

Following induction, a regular programme of synchronous online workshops provides opportunities for students to articulate ideas and discuss issues with peers as well as independent tutors. Workshop topics range from critical reading to writing up, with recordings, associated resources and discussion forums available online. If supervisors reinforce the value of attending these workshops, students appear to become more independent as researchers and understand course expectations more clearly, which is beneficial to both partners.

Effective formative assessment, feedback and revision are key aspects of the generic support. Students are provided with feedback and feedforward on their writing throughout the course. They submit writing at several stages of the course, beginning with an 'initial thoughts' document which starts discussion of project ideas. In this short document, students outline emerging research ideas and provide evidence of engagement with literature, allowing supervisors to immediately assess the student's referencing skills.

A full proposal is submitted following 6 months' preparation and includes a draft literature review to allow evaluation of critical thinking, writing style and referencing skills. Formal feedback is provided using a structured pro forma. A second marker provides an independent perspective which gives weight and authority to the feedback. The proposal, including specific information regarding ethics, must be approved before the student can proceed, so this stage fulfils a gatekeeping role at which point potential problems, including writing issues, can be flagged before work proceeds too far.

Once research is underway, draft materials are submitted to individual supervisors. Supervisors will not proof read or edit, and take different approaches to review. One successful approach is to adopt a 'journal reviewer' stance, offering a few general comments, asking questions encompassing a range of issues and providing pointers to further resources. Questioning, as a technique for drawing out 'purpose' and 'reasons for actions', as advocated by Black et al. (2002), is recommended as a critical aspect of supervision and a useful approach to developing writing skills. Using questions allows issues to be explored without demotivating a student by returning a liberally annotated script. Supplementing questions with a few indicative annotations is usually sufficient to highlight a recurring writing issue, and this approach passes the responsibility for checking and editing back to the student. Following up feedback with discussion provides a further opportunity for students to process feedback and articulate next steps.

Supervisors formatively assess the full draft, focusing on the flow of ideas through the chapters, signposting for the reader and the importance of final sections, without providing any indication of the overall grade that the work might obtain. This important stage ensures that the student's final submission develops beyond a set of independently produced sections—literature review, methodology, findings and so on—to a coherent, professional product. At this stage, the supervisor is assisting with the effective communication needed to address the needs of assessors and professional colleagues. A specific end point to the formative feedback process is crucial since most supervisors will offer suggestions and criticisms every time they are given materials to review.

Common 'generic criteria' (Table 17.1) are supplemented by specific assessment criteria for each master's course, including the final project. The generic criteria become familiar to students and supervisors and encourage the development of necessary skills. Pro formas provide consistency and allow comment on both generic and specific criteria as well as feedforward—the clear articulation of 'next steps' which students must address in future

Table 17.1 Generic criteria for assessment at master's level*

Master's-level work should demonstrate advanced knowledge, understanding and enhanced capacity, and exhibit the following qualities of postgraduate performance:
• the ability to reflect on, and critically review, existing practice; • analysis that goes beyond description and demonstrates critical thinking; • exploration of underlying assumptions, theories, perspectives and policy foundations; • awareness of the need to provide evidence for statements and when drawing conclusions; • sharpness and appropriateness of judgement when dealing with complex issues and problems; • impartiality and balance in argument and inference; • high levels of inter-professional communication skills and use of academic writing conventions; • clarity and coherence through the effective and critical selection and presentation of information/data.

* Based on generic UK SCQF level 11 descriptors, designed to be supplemented by specific criteria for individual courses.

assignments. Feedforward for the master's project may include encouragement to continue with professional enquiry or to disseminate work in written or other formats within professional networks.

Finally, support for supervisors includes informal mentoring for new supervisors by experienced team members and engagement in second marking alongside colleagues to help develop an understanding of expectations. Supervisors have highlighted the lack of opportunity for focused discussion of supervision, and value this in workshop situations (Cornelius and Nicol, 2016). Sharing common problems and challenges enables the development of a supportive community of supervisors. This is important as no two supervision experiences are ever the same and assumptions about supervisor competence and confidence should be avoided. Close cooperation and communication between supervisors across different programmes of master's study have benefits for moderation and quality, ensuring that standards and experiences are common across programmes and between supervisors.

Our experience enables us to suggest the following recommendations for supervisors supporting master's writers in professional settings:

- Become part of a wider community of supervisors in order to share the experiences and challenges of supporting master's students.
- Take advantage of opportunities to work with other supervisors (for example, by second marking for experienced colleagues) to enhance your understanding of wider expectations and appropriate standards of writing.
- Ensure that initial meetings with students are used to explore prior writing experiences, begin to challenge assumptions, explore the insider-researcher role, identify support needs and consider expectations.

- Familiarize yourself with generic support available for students so that you can direct them appropriately. This may include local or external workshops, websites and books specific to master's-level projects.
- Encourage your students to become self-critical writers who establish their own support networks. Use reviewing and questioning approaches rather than proof reading or editing of writing, but indicate when this is necessary.
- Understand the tensions between supervision and assessment and negotiate these carefully.
- Develop consistent approaches to assessment and feedback, across courses and programmes where possible, to ensure common understandings and practices amongst assessors and students.

Many students report that one of the key master's outcomes for them is that they have enhanced their academic writing. Writing improves with practice, and writing a master's thesis, possibly for wider dissemination, is an important stage in the development of writing confidence. It is both a privilege and a responsibility to support students appropriately so that the skills they develop will have an impact in their professional settings as well as help them achieve their academic objectives.

* * *

Supporting honours and master's students—things to do

- Expect students will be novices and in need of overt explanation about writing; adopt a 'show and tell' approach.
- Balance the desire to complete on time with the need to develop researcher writing skills.
- Foster writing within a managed schedule.
- Give timely feedback.
- Ensure that the literature review, ethics application and methods are written early.
- Encourage students to read completed theses as examples of the genre.
- Where possible, work with other supervisors to provide scaffolded support.
- Encourage feedback from multiple sources.
- Acknowledge potential external pressures (employment, family commitments, etc.).
- Use exemplars to encourage student self-efficacy through emulation.

Part VI

Thesis by publication or performance-based writing

Cally Guerin; Sharon Sharmini; Barbara Bolt

Edited by Susan Carter

THESIS BY PUBLICATION

Supervisor: *[Getting doctoral students to write] has actually been harder with candidates who are pursuing thesis by publication. The tendency is to put off writing until [the] research is complete. This leads to an imbalance in input and reduces the influence I have as a supervisor in helping them develop a mature academic writing style . . . less time for trial, error and personal reflection before refinement.*

Student: *I believe in storytelling, even in academic writing, things should progress from A to D over B and C. While I can stick to that rather well on a smaller scale (say within one paragraph), my stories are not that entertaining or thrilling and over the whole text. My supervisor helped me a lot to see the flaws and make them a) better to understand and b) fit to common standards of publications.*

PERFORMANCE-BASED WRITING

Supervisor: *In Fine Arts, the trauma (word used advisedly) of having to write such a large document, that usually supports and opens up the practice, can be transformative . . . most candidates come in from a studio-dominant background . . . [s]o writing is ALMOST ALWAYS an issue.*

Student: *[S]aying things such as a piece is too emotive, your style too journalistic, your opinions are uninformed etc. are not helpful unless you assist a person in identifying what this means in terms of writing style and giving them ideas, examples or suggestions on how to better this.*

This part acknowledges that thesis-by-publication (Thomson and Kamler, 2013), practice-based or performance-led doctorates have particular issues requiring supervisory management, and commonly there is a lack of consensus as to what is expected (Butt, 2013; Starfield et al., 2012). Management of a publications-based thesis will differ from thesis-as-monograph management. Arguably, writing per se will dominate more than with a monograph: the thesis by publication has a prime focus on situating the researcher within their topic's discourse community. It is usual for monograph producers to begin with an extensive literature review and a full proposal that describes both research methods and thesis structure, with a projected timeline. A full proposal for the publication route needs to cover methods, discrete article segments and their coherency, with a detailed timeline. Publication along the way is arguably 'a visible response to policy-led pressures for research productivity' (Boud and Lee, 2009: 7). Although, as Guerin (2016: 33) notes, publication-based theses are 'generally considerably shorter in most cases', managing them also entails taking account of article submissions, intended journals, peer-review turnaround and response to review time. Guerin (2016) finds this to be an exercise in connectivism, where 'learning consists of the ability to construct and traverse . . . networks' (Downes, 2012: 9, cited in Guerin, 2016: 33). Likewise, when performance or practice is supported with an exegesis, the focus shifts and attention is thrown onto writing's interrelationship with the other expressions of original thought.

Students opting for publication need to proceed more like seasoned academics from the outset, with a focus on finding publishable moments whenever they:

- review literature to establish the dimensions of their initiating problem, the method they will use within a methodological frame, and the field;
- gather data;
- analyse data, and reflect on it.

Early supervisory discussion needs to cover what publication entails, and how students might identify article-sized aspects of their research project and choose target journals accordingly. It's often useful to begin by selecting likely journals and then to work with the student to choose topics for articles amongst the different stages. In this part, Cally Guerin (Chapter 18) considers the benefits and possible drawbacks of thesis by publication that initiates students into the realities of publication. In Chapter 19, Sharon Sharmini follows through with advice about protocols that can help smooth the examination process for publication-based theses.

Similarly, when writing is auxiliary to another doctoral component, such as performance, exhibition or practice, the production schedule and skills development must be planned and managed differently. As with disciplines that cross semiotic boundaries—e.g. Mathematics, Computer Science—it can be hard work getting doctoral students to write persuasively because the skills that brought them to doctoral level are not necessarily those used in producing formal academic English. Frequently those who are brilliant kinaesthetically or performatively are not strong writers. Their supervisors may also be aware that formal academic writing is not where their own strengths lie. Here Barbara Bolt (Chapter 20) anatomizes the 'double thesis', which combines performance, practice or creative work with writing, considering how supervisors might balance 'the doubled activity of making and writing' as a healthy partnership within the whole doctoral journey.

Chapter 18

Feedback from journal reviewers

Writing a thesis by publication

Cally Guerin

Research students receive writing feedback from multiple sources including supervisors, peers, and language and literacy experts (Aitchison, 2014; Aitchison and Mowbray, 2015). Assessing and responding to all these multiple voices and forms of feedback, many of which may contain similar advice but some of which may be quite contradictory, is a major challenge for those developing their confidence as research writers in their discipline. For those presenting their research in the form of a thesis by publication, even more voices are added to the cacophony of advice received; that is, further feedback is provided by peer reviewers through their evaluation of the student's journal articles and book chapters. While this has benefits for the students (and their supervisors), it can also have major drawbacks which should be considered when making decisions about the thesis-by-publication format (Guerin, 2016).

There are, of course, significant advantages for aspiring researchers who enter into the world of peer review through submission to journals and edited collections; indeed, this might be seen as a pedagogical element in doctoral education (Aitchison, Kamler and Lee, 2010). Until now, the system of peer review has been regarded as the gold standard for those seeking to have the credibility of their research verified. The process of single or double blind review is (in theory, at least) intended to allow unbiased evaluation of new research, an evaluation that is supposedly free from being influenced by the author's existing reputation, or indeed, the lack of reputation in the case of novice scholars. Peer review intends to elicit the opinions of experts who are well informed not only about the topic and research methods in question, but also about the readership of the particular journal and its likely concerns. Hence, it is expected that only high-quality research will be published as an outcome of the process.

However, there are flaws in such a system, especially in the contemporary academic research environment (Ware and Monkman, 2008). For example, reviewer feedback can be ill-considered and expressed unkindly—sometimes harshly or dismissively—by academics and researchers who rush through the process. Although supposedly experts, reviewers can turn out to have relatively limited knowledge of the field, being fairly new to it themselves, or they may be unsympathetic to the topic or approach. While journal editors generally do their very best to find appropriate reviewers, it can be difficult to get anyone at all to take on yet another voluntary, unpaid reviewing task in the 'accelerated academy' (Carrigan, 2015, 7 April). This is further exacerbated by the failure of many research institutions and universities to recognize reviewing work in academic workloads.

Then, the reviews produced by two or three reviewers may provide conflicting directives. Usually, more than one review is sought in the interests of avoiding the possibility of personal prejudice, but this can introduce the need to decide to whose opinions it is most important to attend—and, in the worst case, can lead to the situation where it is impossible to satisfy all reviewers.

From the perspective of a master's or PhD student attempting to prepare a thesis by publication, the peer-review process imposes extra challenges on top of those faced by other scholars engaging with this system. One important concern is that there can be significant delays between submitting articles and chapters and receiving feedback on that writing. As mentioned above, it is not always easy for editors to find suitable reviewers who have time to undertake the task; once reviewers have agreed to do the work, they do not always meet the agreed deadlines anyway. For students, such delays can result in disjointed progress on their research; after long periods, they may need to revise writing they had previously regarded as finished (the 'whack-a-mole' effect, referring to a computer game where moles keep popping out from underground and the player hits them on the head as they appear—see Guerin, 2016).

For novice scholars who are only just getting established, negative reviews may be utterly devastating and demotivating. Some academic journals and editors do have a specific policy of nurturing new writers, taking time to provide detailed feedback and explaining why the current document is not yet ready for publication. However, many prestigious journals with high impact factors (that is, the kind of journals where students will want to place their work in order to establish their credibility) do not have the time or resources to undertake such development activities for the deluge of submissions they receive. Negative reviews are difficult for any researcher to receive, no matter how experienced, but can be even more dangerous for research students. Reviewers sometimes hide behind the impersonal nature of blind review to express irritation with the article or chapter. From a student perspective, harsh criticism from a stranger can be even harder to accept than if it comes from supervisors or advisors with whom they have existing relationships (Can and Walker, 2011). Further, follow-up face-to-face discussions with supervisors, after receiving the written feedback, allow students to obtain further elucidation of comments and justify their writing choices

(East, Bitchener and Basturkmen, 2012). Without this reciprocal exchange, students can be thoroughly discouraged and seriously doubt the value of their research projects more generally.

A further problem in the feedback gained through peer review is that the advice might conflict with supervisors' opinions. In these situations, having worked closely with supervisors and acted conscientiously on their suggestions about the writing, students find that supervisors, so-called experts in the field, have very different opinions from language experts about what is correct or appropriate. It is easy to see how that is likely to undermine the student's confidence in their supervisors, particularly when the supervisor had believed that the piece was ready for publication.

But these are worst-case scenarios, and for many research students, the experience of seeking peer review through the process of writing a thesis by publication is a validating experience (Guerin, 2016). Many report that they greatly value the insights that new eyes bring to their project and the communication of their research (Netsinghe and Southcott, 2015; Presthus and Bygstad, 2014; Robins and Kanowski, 2008). The opportunity to make their work available to scrutiny by those already established in their discipline can result in that work being taken seriously by people outside the immediate research group or supervisory team. This in turn confirms the students' emerging researcher identities, assuring them that they are thinking and behaving like other researchers in their discipline.

The challenges and benefits outlined above make it clear that there is an important pedagogical role for supervisors and advisors in helping their research students interpret and respond to peer-review feedback. Ideally, supervisors as 'publication brokers' (Kamler, 2010) can guide research students in the appropriate forms and processes as they negotiate the feedback from this external source. They can help the student to assess which elements of critique are legitimate and helpful, how the suggestions work to strengthen the individual paper, and how such changes might inform the rest of the thesis as well. Supervisors can also work with the student to consider whether and how other review elements need to be refuted through careful argument. This then provides the opportunity to learn how those arguments can be presented diplomatically, and how to make a case for certain choices that have been made in the research design, analysis or communication.

Caution must be exercised when making decisions about the thesis-by-publication format, as the necessary engagement with the process of peer review has major implications in terms of the feedback it brings to the research student. Those who are potentially discouraged by harsh criticism from an unknown reader may find this a dangerous path to follow; but for those who are ready to put their work into the broader research community and accept the resultant judgements, receiving feedback from reviewers can be a wonderfully invigorating and affirming experience.

Chapter 19

Supervising a thesis that includes publications

Sharon Sharmini

Increasingly, doctoral candidates incorporate publications in their thesis. In some institutions (for example, in Malaysia and Taiwan), it is mandatory to publish at least two ISI (Institute for Scientific Information) ranked papers prior to submission of the thesis for examination. In this chapter, I present the implications of a study that investigated how examiners assess a Publications-Based Thesis (PBT). A case study approach with mixed methods was used with data gathered from examiners who had more than 10 years' experience in assessing PBTs. Data were procured through a survey (n=62), interviews (n=15) and examiner reports (n=12). The survey was analysed using a descriptive analysis, while free-form comments and interview data were analysed using a general inductive approach. A literature search on the types of PBTs and how examiners approached assessing theses (Bourke, Hattie and Anderson, 2004; Holbrook et al., 2004a; Johnston, 1997; Mullins and Kiley, 2002) indicated a paucity of research exploring how examiners assess a thesis with publications. The implications derived from the views of examiners from this study are thus useful for supervisors who supervise theses that include publications.

Publications-based theses include *PhD by publications*—the thesis consists entirely of published papers; *hybrid PhD*—publications such as articles or conference papers are inserted in lieu of some chapters; and finally, *PhD with publications appended*—aspects of the monograph thesis have been published and are appended in the thesis (Sharmini et al., 2015). Supervisors who intend to supervise doctoral candidates interested in doing a PBT could consider the following suggestions from experienced examiners who have assessed PBTs. Their advice is especially relevant as not all examiners are familiar with PBTs, and thus may face challenges in assessing work that has undergone rigorous peer review and has already been accepted.

INCLUDE A COMMENTARY

Supervisors should advise candidates to include a commentary regarding publications in the Introduction, explaining which parts of the thesis have been published, where the articles have been published and the status of the publications (e.g. under review, accepted, etc.). Examiners would rather be informed early in the thesis of the possible repeated information in the chapters than be agitated by repeats while assessing the thesis. To avoid this, the Introduction should say early on that the thesis consists of published materials and that there may be repetitions. Some institutions require the removal of duplicated material, and expect candidates to ensure formatting consistency.

DECLARE ROLE OF AUTHORS

It is a norm that supervisors mentor candidates into publishing—some supervisors are generous with their contribution and refrain from listing their own name as a contributor in the paper. However, with the increasing pressure to publish, many supervisors work with the candidates and earn co-authorship based on established protocols. When multiple authors are listed in a publication, 'it gets harder to distinguish the candidate's work' (participant). There is variance in habits too: some supervisors see fit to contribute more to students' work as part of their teaching role; others do very little work, but believe that supervision's oversight entitles them to authorship. This creates confusion and ethical ambivalence during the examination.

A step forward would be for the candidate to provide a statement declaring the contribution of multi-authored publications, itemizing how much each author has contributed, possibly as percentages. Information on what each author has contributed—for example, who designed the study, collected and analysed the data and/or wrote the draft—would also be useful. This may sit in the Appendices, and should be signed by all contributors. Copyright consent from publishers should also be located in the Appendices.

ENSURE THAT THE CANDIDATE IS THE FIRST AUTHOR

Besides raising concerns with the role of multiple authors in publications, PBT examiners have raised issues on the author order. The candidate must be first author on any writing included in the thesis. If the candidate is not the first author, it would be wise not to include that publication in the thesis, but to reference it, explaining what work the candidate contributed. It is possible to append such publications in the thesis.

Two existing guidelines to address authorship order are those by the American Psychological Association (APA) (2012) and the Computing Research and Education Association of Australasia (CORE, 1999). The APA guidelines clearly stipulate that the student is given credit for their work when publishing and they would normally be the first author. The CORE guidelines clarify that supervisors should share authorship with the candidate as 'it is often the case that the paper would not have existed without ongoing input from the supervisor' (CORE, 1999, Supervision section, para. 3 and 5). The Vancouver Protocol developed by the International Committee of Medical Journal Editors (2009) is another tool that can be used to ascertain author order. This protocol stipulates that authorship credit is based on substantial contribution to conception and design, acquisition of data, or analysis and interpretations of data; drafting the article or revising it critically for important intellectual content; and finally, approval of the version to be published. Importantly, the acquisition of funding, participating in data gathering or general supervision of the research does not constitute authorship. Quite commonly, supervisors should not be co-authors, but rather, should be gratefully acknowledged.

AIM FOR QUALITY-ASSURED PUBLICATIONS

Publications in top-ranked journals, high-impact-factor journals and international peer-reviewed journals positively influenced most examiners. Publications as book chapters, local peer-reviewed journals and refereed conference proceedings were much less highly valued. However, it should be noted that there are disciplinary differences in opinion as to what types of publications are highly valued. Computer science and information science academics view peer-reviewed top-ranked conference proceedings as equivalent to top-ranked journals. Conversely, examiners became suspicious about publications in unknown or low-quality conferences, especially when the work could not be found online. Such publication tended to influence examiners negatively.

Supervisors could guide doctoral candidates to assess the value of publication outlets prior to embarking on submission. The ranking of journals, impact factors and readership should be considered. Supervisors could advise students to be vigilant about some rapid online publications, which do not provide a rigorous review and thus are virtually worthless. The Directory of Open Access Journals (https://doaj.org/) provides information on reputable publishers. Quality assurance comes from rigorous review of the work.

ENSURE COHERENCE

Examiners raised concerns that the thesis could become less coherent when publications were inserted as chapters, particularly in hybrid theses, where some chapters are publications, while others are more conventional thesis chapters. Examiners criticized unconventional layout, which made it difficult for them to see the flow of logic as the text appeared disjointed, repetition disrupted the flow of ideas and the overall coherence of the thesis was lost. To the examiners, this layout did not present an overall picture. The issue of coherence in hybrid theses is potentially a problem, especially since coherence is an important criterion for judging a thesis (Holbrook, Bourke, Lovat and Fairbain, 2008).

In order to avoid these problematic assessment criteria, supervisors can advise doctoral candidates to have introductions or bridging sections that weave the publications together so that there is a storyline. A general discussion chapter that ties together and highlights the results of the chapters could be included. It would also be useful to inform examiners about the structure of the thesis (that it includes published work) in an introductory chapter. It is also advisable for candidates to rewrite chapters to reduce repetitions, so that the thesis is threaded together in terms of content.

FACILITATE PUBLISHING

In any PhD programme, supervisors play a pivotal role—they teach, mentor and guide the candidate by passing on their knowledge. This form of supervision is viewed as apprenticeship learning (Delamont, Atkinson and Parry, 2004; Holdaway, Deblois and Winchester, 1995) in an active learning environment (Pyhältö, Stubb and Lonka, 2009). Once supervisor and candidate have established whether or not a publication route would be beneficial for the candidate, and a PBT is chosen, supervisors will mentor candidates to write an article. At the initial stage, this could include selection of an appropriate journal, with the student then reading articles from the journal and identifying key patterns, linguistic bundles and the different sections of the article. Candidates should note how the target journal typically structures an argument, how much referencing and theorizing is usual, how much detail is given about methods. They will need to identify and meet journal formatting requirements. Later they must go through the psychological challenges of the revision process. Getting feedback and assisting with the revision process are also key mentoring roles for the supervisors. The supervisors' role is to facilitate learning, and over time, the candidate is scaffolded into publishing practices. Supervisors could encourage candidates to share and disseminate their research in conferences and department seminars. The feedback that is provided during these dissemination events develops confidence in presenting the research and the feedback can also be used to write for journals.

Publication-based theses are becoming more common for two reasons: for measuring research outputs (Aitchison, Kamler and Lee, 2010) and responding to increasing competition in the job market (Jackson, 2013). A PBT is ideal for those who want to venture into an academic career as the mentorship and guidance provided by the supervisors 'would offer possibilities for developing a range of research literacies, that is, skills required to read, understand and produce research in an academic context' (Badenhorst and Guerin, 2016: 37). These are essential skills beyond the PhD. The recent *Review of Australia's Research Training System* (McGagh et al., 2016) has called for a shift towards assessing the doctoral candidate and the skills gained rather than the thesis alone. This call and the advent of PBTs are relevant to the ever-changing landscape of doctoral education.

Chapter 20

Finding my voice(s) in the creative arts thesis

Barbara Bolt

Practitioner-researchers engaged in practice-led research are most often required to prepare what we may call a 'double thesis' for examination—a body of creative work which may be exhibited, written, presented, performed, uploaded or displayed *and* a written dissertation/exegesis/exposition, an academic treatise that provides the context of and argument for the research. Aware of multiple definitions in different countries and communities, I use the term 'exegesis' here for the written document and 'thesis' for the double thesis as a whole. This makes the task of producing (rather than writing) a thesis a much more complicated project for the practitioner-researcher than for a graduate researcher who 'writes a thesis'. Film-maker Jenni Thornley observes that:

> At times I felt something split or schizophrenic about the doubled doctorate . . . It's as if the doubled form creates a greater chance of risk, as one has to create and navigate a self-reflexive discourse within each work and between two works; one has to listen and intuit the conversation informing each of them. Yet the very crucible for praxis lies here.
>
> (Thornley, 2014: 149)

For Thornley, as for many other practitioner-researchers, the question of where the writing takes place in a doubled doctorate is a troubled one. She asks: 'Can a film write the doctoral thesis? Is the exegesis an after-thought laden with unfinished business? Or is the interstice between "artefact" and "document" a potentially creative space where "praxis"—volatility between theory and practice—is forged?' (Thornley, 2014: 136). As supervisors, we would hope that the 'interstice' between the making of the artwork and the making of the writing is a creative space. To that end, the task of feedback is to open up and hold open that space.

This chapter speaks to the challenges faced by supervisors and graduate researchers in this doubled activity of making and writing to address the question: how can we as supervisors provide the guidance and feedback to enable the practitioner-researcher to find confidence in writing and develop their writing voice? What strategies are useful in developing a dialogic voice between the creative work and the writing? In order to address these questions, I obtained ethics committee approval for the research project: 'How I found my voice: the experience of PhD candidates writing a dissertation as part of the creative arts thesis' (ID 1545755.1). This chapter draws on responses from six graduated practitioner-researchers to the following three questions:

1 What challenges did you face in the writing task of the PhD?
2 What was the single most significant factor in helping you find your own voice in writing the dissertation/exegesis/exposition?
3 How would you describe the relationship between your approach to your practice and your approach to writing?

The chapter is framed around principles of supervision, staging the research, locating yourself and writing into the research, and finally writing through and out of practice. Student participants are named as the authors of their comments throughout.

PRINCIPLES OF SUPERVISION

In an Australian Government Office for Learning and Teaching (OLT)-funded project, 'Building distributed leadership for effective supervision of creative practice higher research degrees' (LE12–2264), Jillian Hamilton and Sue Carson (2013) identified *12 Principles for the Effective Supervision of Creative Practice Higher Research Degrees*:

- Adopt a student-centred approach
- Embrace diverse projects, practices and working methods
- Ensure your students believe in the validity of creative practice research and its experimental nature
- The theory and practice need to speak to each other
- The theory and practice might not be done simultaneously, despite the need to work together in the completed work
- Balance the big picture and attention to the detail
- Provide frequent, constructive feedback
- A supervisor should also attend to the practice in the studio
- Provide support while managing interpersonal relationships
- Milestones are time consuming, but ultimately rewarding components of the journey
- Don't feel limited by boundaries as a supervisor, but be aware of regulations
- Reflect, discuss and share your practices with colleagues.

(Hamilton and Carson, 2013: 4–15)

These principles make apparent the need to keep the theory and practice in dialogue with each other and, for us as supervisors, to keep the practice at the forefront when giving feedback on the writing practice. However, the principles also point to the fact that supervision and feedback operate in an improvisatory space with each supervision, and each supervisory session has a unique character. While these guiding principles may assist initiation into supervision and help us navigate our supervisory practices, our own experience of supervision, first as graduate researchers and then as supervisors, *and* feedback from our practitioner-researchers offer a way forward. The route is always freshly negotiated each time.

DEFINING THE RESEARCH

Responding to the question, 'What challenges did you face in the writing task?', one of the participants, Lani Seligman, noted:

> In the early stages ... the parameters of defining the research can feel quite counter intuitive to practice based research which is often experienced as being more exploratory and open. However, without the definitional framework there are infinite points of connection that are difficult to frame within the writing process. Defining the research directs the process of writing towards something and this in itself leads to finding your 'voice'.
>
> (Seligman, 2016)

Estelle Barrett introduced the term 'staging the research' (2007: 185–205) as the process of setting out a provisional plan or research design defining the parameters for the research. Defining the research in creative practice research is, for many, one of the most difficult problems of the research process. Practice is by its very nature open and explorative, while research requires a question that can focus the scope of the project and direct the research (Biggs and Büchler, 2009: 8). The need to articulate a question that limits the study often seems antithetical to many practitioner-researchers, yet it is the question that enables the research to begin.

Even at this early stage of setting the parameters for the research, the inter-responsiveness between the practical and the theoretical concerns is paramount. Artist and academic Sean Lowry identifies how writing is integral to creating a dialogue that needs to proceed from the very beginning of the project: 'since practical and scholarly written components are typically inter-responsive, the dissertation needs to be considered right from the outset in order to avoid becoming an adjunct illustration formed in retrospect' (Lowry, 2014: 340). Developing a daily writing practice from the outset most assists the practitioner-researcher to find a voice. Respondent Lynn Mowson describes

> the practice of writing every day in the studio which I did for the final year. Setting a routine of writing 250–500 words a day or thereabouts. As the time

> went on it became easier and the writing more useful. I wish I'd started this from the beginning.
>
> (Mowson, 2016)

Writing can support the development of thought behind creative performance.

LOCATING YOURSELF AND WRITING INTO THE RESEARCH

Practitioner-researchers are well schooled and fluent in the language of their practice and their discipline. They are creative practitioners first and foremost and have come to academia to deepen their understanding of practice *through* research. However, when it comes to preparing their written dissertation/exegesis/exposition, practitioner-researchers often feel that they are strangers and second-language speakers in the practice of academic writing. Thus, the question of finding one's voice or voices is a difficult one for many practitioner-researchers.

Lowry identifies that there is a 'difference between describing one's own practice and the task of analyzing the ideas that underpin it against a carefully framed ground' (2014: 343). It is framing the interplay between the two that differentiates the research from its antecedents and precedents that situate the researcher in the field. As Lowry notes,

> unless some form of frame is constructed in order to place the creative work in relationship with a significant question or problem, the solipsism that potentially emanates from simply grandstanding one's own creative work can invite a situation in which distinctions between art and researcher are . . . confused.
>
> (Lowry, 2014: 346)

The conceptual and theoretical framework adopted by the practitioner-researcher provides a means through which *to locate the researcher and the enquiry* within the context of the historical, social, political and contemporary context.

Research requires that the researcher position themselves and their research in the field and this means finding an appropriate voice or voices with which to write. Mapping the field of theory and practice through others' literature logically calls for a third person or analytical narrative—Benjamin identifies . . . Nelson says . . . Beckett's plays . . . etc. However, how does one speak about one's own process, one's practice and the artwork that emerges from the research? In other words, how does one move between the third-person exegetical work in the conceptual framing of the research to the 'I' of the first-person experience as a practitioner-researcher in process? How does one talk about the artwork without becoming solipsistic (Bolt, 2014)?

In her confirmation paper, visual artist Vanessa Godden articulated the complexity of the 'voices' that enable her to position herself as a researcher and also to move between the third person, to situate the practice and the research in the field, and the first-person reflective and narrative voices that allow her to draw on personal experience to locate herself in the research.

> Throughout the chapters I will use a braided process to transition between three distinct voices: analytical, reflective, and narrative . . . The analytic voice is meant to aid in building pragmatic connections between the art works I produce and existing theory and fine art influences. The reflective voice uses autobiographical histories to demonstrate how other people's perceptions of me inform my perceptions of myself. Narrative extractions from personal journal entries serve as renderings of the experiential basis for this research project.
>
> (Godden, 2016: n.p.)

Godden's project works with autobiographical material as a 'medium' of the practice, and this braiding of voices enables her to move between positionalities in the writing. 'Braiding' different voices into the weave of the exegesis/dissertation/exposition is always a challenge. However, practice and the examples of other theses enable the practitioner-researcher to find their particular voice or multiple voices.

WRITING THROUGH AND OUT OF THE PRACTICE

> From the outset I wanted the research and writing to have more than a purely exegetic function. I saw writing as a generative and creative act in itself. The challenge was to maintain a productive interaction between research and writing, and making, throughout the project.
>
> (Ron Left, 2016)

Writing through and out of the practice is critical for forging the praxis in the thesis. In discussing how she overcame her preconceptions that she could not write, academic and visual artist Simone Slee noted the most significant factor in finding her own voice:

> Centering myself within the process of the art work's production was the most important factor in garnering my voice within the writing. Once I enabled this to occur the project began to drive its own agenda developing an autonomy that was also akin to an artwork itself. Commencing with the artwork this firstly generated the research questions that then enable these [initial propositions] to be tested, sometimes contradicted, adjusted and clarified and provoked new questions as they applied to the work. In this approach I placed myself as another material in the artwork's production, literally 'inside' the artwork itself and spoke objectively from this perspective. The use of the first person voice facilitated making concrete these concepts associated with the process . . . myself as a material. This approach was consistent with the conceptual premise of the artwork itself and is in contrast to observing and describing the work and the practice from the 'outside' as if it were an object considered from a distant perspective.
>
> (Slee, 2016)

Writing through practice, rather than on or about the practice, positions the practitioner-researcher in the work and in the process. Yet this is not a solipsistic exercise of 'I' as originator that infects some exegetical work. Rather, it is a questioning that operates both materially and conceptually. What has happened through the research process? What questions does the work ask of current theory and practice in the field? What has been put in doubt? What has opened up? Here the artist as interlocutor is no longer on the outside objectifying the artwork or offering themselves up as the genius creator of the artwork. The practitioner-researcher is forced to question the work of art rather than describing, explaining or interpreting the artwork. Thus, the writing becomes a generative and creative act in itself. The aim is not to collapse into the artwork, but rather, questioning becomes the tool mapping the movement that happens through the research process and through the artwork. Constant and restless questioning from within the practice isn't concerned with the artwork in itself, but is more concerned with an open field in which the artwork emerges as but one 'effect' of the research. The interplay between what the artwork is, and what the process and the artwork reveal or do, is the work of art. Questioning becomes the vehicle through which the writing may proceed and it is the supervisor who can facilitate this task of questioning.

SEEING DOUBLE

> In an ideal world I think I'd love to approach my writing more like my making, and my making more like my writing! My practice is full of half-baked explorations, flights of fancy and 'trying things out', whereas my writing tends to be highly methodical and planned. As it is, the relationship between them is one where I use my practice to think through the ideas that come out in my writing . . . I would like to start exploring how I can respond through creative writing to my practice and blur the line between the 'academic' and the 'creative' of the writing discipline.
>
> (Travis Cox, 2016)

Practitioner-research is a unique mode of research that places the author's process and artwork at the heart and centre of the research. An inter-related creative and academic 'double' thesis requires fluency in both the language of art as well as the language of academic writing, and this doubling requires the supervisor to be engaged with both the studio practice and with the writing. Doubling also occurs in the writing itself, where the practitioner-researcher takes on and moves between different and multiple voices required to make sense of the engagement, whether it be addressing the field or addressing personal experience. What this says is that there is no such thing as 'objectivity' in research, only different and situated positioning. Finally, the writing emerges out of and in relation to practice via a constant questioning through the research. This enables the practitioner-researcher to shift from a preoccupation with the artwork to a concern with the work of art. This ultimately is what research is about.

ACKNOWLEDGEMENTS

I would like to thank Travis Cox, Vanessa Godden, Ron Left, Lynn Mowson, Lani Seligman and Simone Slee for their generous and insightful contributions in helping me to understand the challenges and opportunities offered by writing in the research process.

* * *

Thesis by publication—things to do

- Overtly explain the publication process (journal requirements, peer-review process, responding to comments).
- Discuss pros and cons of journal selection.
- Scaffold student publications through conference and seminar presentations.
- Award the student 'first author' position as early as possible, respecting authorship conventions.
- Help students respond to reviewer comments; share your own peer-review experience; highlight the importance of audience awareness.
- Encourage the student to clarify the 'sum of many parts' nature of thesis by publication (relationship between articles, potential duplication of information, formatting variations, etc.) before final submission.
- Show how reviewers' comments provide guidance for improving the entire thesis.

Thesis with performance—things to do

- Discuss the 'double-thesis' relationship between text and performance throughout.
- Overtly discuss voice and the authorial performer/critical analyst shifts of voice.
- Stress the importance of writing early and routinely as a thinking activity.
- Show how theory enables the candidate to situate themselves in relation to performance.
- Suggest that issues/tensions/challenges associated with the multiple voices of researcher-performer be foregrounded and critically analysed within the thesis.

Part VII

Maintaining and gathering momentum

Paul J. Silvia; Rowena Murray; Susan Carter

Edited by Susan Carter

> ***Supervisor:*** *There comes a time when the writing matters more than anything but the student has entered the period in which deep personal and thought mechanisms change. At this time it's hard for the student to articulate her understanding and her confidence about writing takes a blow. It's challenging to build confidence, encourage the transition to her new way of thinking, and keep her writing.*
>
> ***Student:*** *My biggest issue is procrastination (I am doing this survey instead of the writing I intended to do), and I don't need to read more about writing, I need to actually DO the writing and get feedback on it. That is what helps me most.*

Somewhere in the research project many research students become demotivated towards the writing they need to do—our data from both supervisors and students confirmed loss of momentum with writing to be fairly common. Awareness of time pressure activates some, but also enervates others. Quite commonly, students slump in the second half of a doctorate, some into stultifying depression (Mewburn, 2012, 8 May). It's exasperating for supervisors when deadlines slide past unmet, and students' fear of failure and risk aversion harden into task aversion (Onwuegbuzie and Collins, 2001) so that generating written work becomes abhorrent. Students in such stages can be greatly helped by peer support from fellow writers and participation in generic writing workshops.

Nonetheless, supervisors play a major part (Golde, 2005) in sustaining doctoral students through the challenges of intellectual and writing blocks that feature as a significant difficulty in one extensive longitudinal study (McAlpine, Jazvac-Martek and Hopwood, 2009). Two things are at stake here. One is timely completion of a passable thesis. Maybe more important is the student's personal growth into a researcher who can both handle the pressure of generating writing when the process is tedious, and appreciate the intense pleasure when the process is going well (Lamott, 1995).

Writer's block is a blanket term that Silvia (2010: 45–46) has debunked entirely: 'Saying you can't write because you have writer's block is merely saying you can't write because you aren't writing. It's trivial. The cure for writer's block—if you can cure a specious affliction—is writing.' Conversely, neurologist Alice Weaver Flaherty (2004) considers writer's block to be linked to inactivity of the limbic system, and notes that exercise can help to stimulate this part of the brain effectively (and legally, a benefit over other stimulant options). Whatever the cause of students' loss of writing momentum, it is something that supervisors encounter frequently and need to prepare for. Part VII offers assistance.

In Chapter 21, Paul J. Silvia turns the spotlight onto the supervisors, by questioning how they model productivity with writing and good citizenship when it comes to deadlines. Rowena Murray (Chapter 22) describes her practice of writing in the same space as students, with breaks for feedback, as a means of keeping them writing and motivated. She also provides suggestions for short writing tasks that students can cover in an hour's writing. Susan Carter wraps up (Chapter 23) with a variety of exercises that supervisors might use to nudge stalled students over the obstacles of writer's block.

Chapter 21

Writing methodically

Teaching students by our words and deeds

Paul J. Silvia

Most of English's tackiest clichés turned out to have a kernel of truth. In this chapter, we'll look at a few of the clichés that guide how I teach graduate students to write methodically. Like most supervisors, I have no grand theory of writing mentorship informed by cutting-edge pedagogical theory or research. Instead, I have a gallimaufry of ideas gleaned from talking with and watching successful graduate mentors and some lessons learned from my many mentoring mistakes.

We want our students to write productively: they need to get their big curricular projects (e.g., theses and dissertations) done on time, and in most fields, they need to publish smaller projects along the way. For me, productive writing is methodical writing: writing consistently during the normal work week (Silvia, 2007), and choosing writing projects reflectively (Silvia, 2015). If people write methodically, they will usually end up writing an appropriately freakish amount. But how do we teach our students to be methodical writers?

'TALK IS CHEAP'

We teach through our actions, which allegedly speak louder than words. In all things, we lead and teach by our example. Our students learn by watching our actions, and they are always watching—and occasionally doing respectable impressions when we're not around. To teach methodical writing, then, we must model methodical writing. As Bandura (1997) has pointed out, people learn how to do challenging tasks by observing others. Obviously, by watching experts we learn the nuts and bolts of how to do the task, along with useful strategies and shortcuts. More subtly, however, we learn confidence. When we see someone similar to us do a task well, our sense of self-efficacy increases. The goal seems realistic and within our capacities.

What do we supervisors model for our students? What do they see when they see how we write? Let's ponder some common writing scenarios a graduate student might observe.

- How do we handle deadlines? The weekend before a grant is due, do we drag some cases of bottled water and protein bars into the attic and pound out a proposal in an eyebrow-singeing burst of typing? When the deadline for an invited book chapter looms, do we quip to our students, 'Being late is no big deal—no one ever gets those in on time'?
- How do we handle negative feedback? Do we howl and seethe in front of our students when we get bad reviews on a manuscript? The grad students might hear us extoll the wisdom of peer review, but do they see a bubbling cauldron of wounded pride and grievance?
- How do we plan our writing? Do we wait for huge chunks of time that aren't there? Do we stuff our writing into evenings, weekends, and holidays? Have our students ever heard us say, 'Things are just too busy—that paper will have to wait until the semester is over', or, 'This time of the year is too crazy to get any writing done'?
- How do we give feedback? Complaining about slow reviewers is perhaps our birthright, but are we the slow reviewers other writers complain about? If we promise our students to get comments back to them within a week, do we?

Talk is cheap. If we aren't modeling methodical writing in our deeds, we can't expect our students to learn it from our words.

'SLOW AND STEADY WINS THE RACE'

The question of how to teach methodical writing, then, is also the question of how to write methodically ourselves. I see methodical writing as having two branches. The first is writing consistently—writing week in, week out, regardless of whether that week is a busy week or a slow week or any week when students are on campus, smoking and staring at their smartphones. Big projects get done by working on them one day at a time. Slow and steady might not win the race, but it will get your book finished.

Writing consistently, like exercising consistently, takes commitment and planning to pull off. Scholarly writing is discouraging for most of us. We're working on long-term projects that will face an over-educated and critical audience. What appears on the page always sounded better in the brain. The academic week is stuffed with urgent-but-trivial tasks, ceaseless interruptions, and more drama than an Icelandic film festival.

Writing schedules are a bulwark against the chaos. Research shows that professional writers typically write at the same times and same places (Boice, 1990; Goodson, 2012; Perry, 1999). Academic writers should probably write daily, like professional writers do, but any times will work so long as they are consistent. I think 4 hours a week is a good target—most people find it easy to claim and defend 4 hours, and it's a lot of time when used well—but you can pick a suitable number. For many years, I wrote from 8 am to 10 am Monday through Friday. Once I had babies, I shifted to 5 am to 7 am. Now I'm in the middle: 7:50 am to 9 am. I know many productive writers who write twice a week (e.g., two blocks of 2 hours) or even once a week (e.g., one monstrous 4-hour block). So long as the time and place are the same, the act of writing will become habitual, another part of the daily routine, instead of something that you force yourself to do.

The second branch is writing reflectively—choosing your writing projects based on meaningful priorities. Of all the things we could write, what should we write first? What projects are our most important ones? What projects probably don't merit the time? Essentially, everything can get published somewhere (Silvia, 2015), but the opportunity cost of writing is enormous: hours spent on one project are hours not spent on other possible projects. Deciding which ideas should be written up and which should be written off takes some discernment.

Once we have whittled down projects to those worth writing up, we need to decide which one to write first. People use all kinds of rules for setting writing priorities. Some people start with the oldest project first, a sort of 'first in, first out' rule; others start with the newest project, a sort of 'last in, first out' rule. Some people focus on the project that is closest to completion; others start with the project that needs the most work; still others start with their most cherished idea. And some people are buffeted by deadlines, focusing on whatever task is most overdue or has the angriest co-authors.

I first work on projects with upcoming deadlines (e.g., a deadline for a chapter, or a deadline for comments from a co-author), and then I tackle (1) manuscripts with an invitation to resubmit, (2) whatever project is closest to completion, and (3) new manuscripts written from scratch. Projects involving grad students get a nudge upward. I haven't found a good way to juggle long-term and short-term projects, such as how to write a book while writing articles with grad students. And I suspect that I occasionally avoid writing complicated papers by working on simpler ones first. No one approach works for everyone, however, and we needn't overthink writing priorities. So long as we write consistently and reflect on which project is the best use of our limited writing time, we'll write enough.

'YOU LEARN IT BY DOING IT'

Being a good role model is the hardest but most effective part of writing mentorship. But beyond that, we need to get students writing. 'You learn it by doing it,' as the saying goes, so obviously we should teach students writing by working on writing projects together. They will learn it by doing it, and they'll see how we think about and handle writing's many decisions.

Naturally, we should start by encouraging the students to set writing schedules. Graduate students' weeks are just as chaotic as ours, between taking classes, collecting data, and needling each other on social media, so teaching them how to set up and defend a successful schedule lays the groundwork for writing productively. As mentors, we should respect their scheduled time by not interrupting, scheduling meetings, or e-mailing them kombucha recipes during that time.

Other chapters in this book describe ways for faculty to involve students in writing and explain how to get students going early. Writing early is crucial and can't be overstated. Many faculty delay getting students writing out of a well-intentioned desire to let students get their feet on the ground, focus on their early years' coursework, and gain some background knowledge. But if we learn writing by doing it, we need to do it, no matter how gnarled and alarming the early pages might be. As for gaining background knowledge, writing is a way of teaching others and ourselves (Zinsser, 1988). Having a writing project forces us to do the reading, thinking, and vexed muttering to oneself that are the hallmarks of scholarship.

People learn faster when they get feedback faster. When grad students are working on writing projects, mentors should meet with them to discuss it at least every few weeks, if not weekly. The alternative is a go-it-alone model, in which students struggle through the project themselves, face a tricky decision, choose the wrong direction, wander deep into the thickets, and then get airlifted out by their mentor a few months and dozens of useless pages later. Beginners do learn from their mistakes, but they learn more efficiently when experts take the time to teach them.

Often students work exclusively on a single sole-authored project, such as a big thesis or dissertation that will end up as a book or monograph. Students need ongoing guidance and good role models to learn how to pull off big writing projects. Even when not writing with students, mentors can teach and model a consistent approach to long-range scholarly works. In such cases, mentors help students to set short-term goals: tracking down sources, reading, taking notes, making structural decisions, and developing an original argument for the work.

Although one size doesn't fit all, I meet weekly with my small but valiant group of graduate students. Everyone commits to a weekly writing goal. We start by checking in on the last week's goals, then set new goals for the coming week. I take part, too: I set goals and 'fess up when I don't meet them. Our weekly goals and our backlog list—the unwritten projects waiting in the wings—go up on the lab whiteboards, which keep us on track, give witness to our writing ambitions, and provoke occasional twinges of abject panic. And, week by week, it gets done.

As promised, I don't have a grand vision of writing mentorship. My approach boils down to a few simple ideas.

- If I don't model good habits, students won't listen to what I tell them about methodical writing.

- Weak writers improve by writing and then talking about what they wrote, so students should get involved in writing as soon as possible.
- If I encourage consistent writing and talk about writing constantly—even in the rambling and repetitive way that I suspect one of my students does an excellent impression of—the graduate students will somehow become better and wiser writers.

Chapter 22

Writing prolifically

Rowena Murray

There are times when doctoral students feel demotivated towards their writing. However, in the final phase of their studies—when time is running out—they need to write more than ever, and perhaps more productively than ever. This may involve students changing how they write and supervisors changing how they give feedback. Some students welcome the vision of the final straight and strive to cross the finishing line, but others find change in writing patterns and supervisor feedback disconcerting.

For the purposes of this chapter, 'writing prolifically' means writing and revising more regularly, and often adopting more productive writing habits. The chapter provides examples of activities and suggestions for feedback that supervisors can use to help students establish productive writing patterns. I build on Aitchison and Lee's (2006) doctoral student writing group pedagogy, particularly 'making writing "normal business" in the doing of research' (2006: 265), Lee and Murray's (2015) framework for supervising doctoral writing, and my research on productive academic writing habits (Murray 2015a, 2016).

SPEEDING UP THE DRAFTING–FEEDBACK–REVISING CYCLE

Supervisors can help students to write more productively by providing structure for writing and revising. They can define not only the structure of academic texts, but also the structure of academic writing practices. The Structured Writing Retreat approach (SWR) is one way of doing this (Kempenaar and Murray, 2016; Murray, 2015b; Murray and Newton, 2009). The SWR principle sees supervisors and students working on writing at the same time and in the same place, with a structure that allows a pattern of immediate feedback to intersect the bursts of writing. It offers multiple opportunities to help students establish good writing patterns.

Specifically, the SWR experience suggests that the following practices stimulate student writing:

- writing with peers in the same room (the 'typing pool' model);
- goal-setting for writing, i.e. setting and monitoring specific writing objectives;
- writing in fixed time slots to establish discipline and resilience;
- talking briefly at the start and end of writing slots or days, to take stock of progress and reset goals or set new writing goals;
- taking regular breaks, good nutrition and hydration and physical activity.

This combination of practices increases writing productivity. It also shows students how to minimize the risks of extended periods of sitting (Thow, 2015). In dedicated writing time within a group writing dynamic, students find it easier to 'unplug' from internet, email, Facebook and phones, and start writing quickly. They find it easier to write whether they feel like it or not. They find it easier to keep writing. For this to work, it helps if supervisors not only explain these practices but also create structured writing time for students, at least at first. If this approach is new to students, supervisors have to guide them on specific writing goals for each time slot. Then they can tailor their feedback to those goals: to what extent did the students achieve what they set out to do?

Setting up a period of dedicated writing/revising time provides multiple opportunities for writing feedback. This can mean anything from a 2-day residential retreat to 90 minutes' writing. In planned breaks within structured writing sessions, supervisors provide feedback on students' texts, but also on their writing intentions, interpretations of feedback and emerging thesis arguments. Students can immediately act on feedback, and supervisors can quickly comment on serial revisions. This cycle improves students' understanding of the criteria to be applied to their writing—and helps them to plan writing and revising tasks. It speeds up the drafting–feedback–revision cycle. Supervisors give feedback on students' texts and additionally focus on ways to improve productivity. In addition, when supervisors themselves write during structured writing sessions, it improves their own productivity.

Key tasks for supervisors are, therefore, helping students to set specific goals for each writing slot and checking the extent to which they achieve them. Revision tasks can also be defined as specific goals; that is, defining the scale and word count for each revision. Supervisors need to think about writing and revision in terms of specific tasks. This involves breaking down complex writing/revising tasks into sub-tasks, or sub-sub-tasks, and explaining to students how they can do this, so that they learn to set realistic goals. The next section provides examples, with suggestions for supervisors' feedback to increase productivity. These activities are especially helpful when students need to work productively through difficult thesis-writing stages.

ACTIVITIES FOR WRITING PROLIFICALLY

Supervisors can design writing tasks for students to work on in 60- and 90-minute slots, several of which can make up a writing day. Supervisors' feedback will then focus on both the agreed writing goal and the next writing goals. Here are three examples of writing tasks that supervisors can use, and feedback they can give to increase productivity. Each task combines components that are associated with productive academic writing.

Working on the macro and micro levels of thesis writing

- **The task is to write a 750-word thesis summary** (Murray, 2016).

A thesis summary has a paragraph on each chapter. It can be included in the thesis at the end of the Introduction, but its first purpose is prompting decisions on chapter contents. It prompts students to construct the macro thesis argument as a set of micro chapter arguments. A thesis summary helps to maintain students' focus in their writing and revising.

Supervisors can prompt students to set sub-goals for writing a thesis summary. Break the 750 words down into paragraphs. Allocate a number of words per paragraph. Align research aims with conclusions; align first and last paragraphs. Students can rehearse, review and adjust these decisions in discussion. It takes only minutes to read a draft 750-word thesis summary (perhaps several times), another few minutes to construct feedback, a further few minutes to discuss it with the student, and a few more minutes to plan the next revision for the next writing slot.

When productivity is the goal, supervisors and students should define tasks in specific terms. Making writing goals specific means using numbers: the number of minutes in the writing slot, the number of words of text to draft or revise, the number of verbs to define the writing tasks (e.g. 'Chapter 1 provides a rationale for . . . Chapter 2 reviews . . . Chapter 3 defines . . .') and/or the number and scale of revision tasks (e.g. add, unpack, clarify, explain, cut). Supervisors and students can then review this approach, discuss the pros and cons of making writing goals specific, and the impact on their thinking of focusing on specific writing tasks.

Sample of Supervisor's feedback:

- Some of these paragraphs are longer than others—why is that?
- You use generic terms here, e.g. 'the literature is reviewed'. Specify which literature and why. What did you leave out?
- Possible to have an equal number of words for all chapters, or not, for a reason?
- Match your aims, at the start of the thesis summary, and claims, at the end.
- To what extent did you achieve your goal in the time allocated?

Producing precision in academic writing

- **The writing task is multiple revisions.**

The process of producing multiple revisions speeds up when supervisors work with students on their writing-in-progress, in dedicated writing time, with both student and supervisor writing in the same place, at the same time. In this way, they perform the process of academic writing *as* multiple revisions—thus normalizing it for students. Supervisors can prompt discussion of writing-in-progress—the process of gradually working towards precision and clarity in writing and talking about what 'precision' means. This brings assumptions and misconceptions into the open, so that supervisors can address them and define specific revision tasks.

Just as supervisors can help students set specific writing goals, they can also help them to set specific revision goals:

- Insert definitions of terms.
- Insert link words at the start of paragraphs and sentences.
- Make connections clearer; e.g. 'However', 'Moreover', 'Nevertheless', etc.
- Qualify assertions of contribution to knowledge.
- Insert modifiers, such as 'perhaps' or 'suggests' or 'can be of benefit'.
- Signpost what each chapter/section does and does not do explicitly.
- Allocate a specific period of dedicated revision time to each writing task.
- Tighten prose.

Students can monitor their revision goal achievement—thus working towards developing self-efficacy in relation to their writing (Bandura, 1997) and learning to set realistic goals themselves. Supervisors can point to parallels between applying this criterion to publications and thesis writing in order to provide a rationale for multiple revisions, and to explain the steps in the process not just in the abstract, but as they happen (Murray, 2015b).

Sample of Supervisor's feedback:

- Define 'precision' in writing.
- Review examples of relative levels of precision in the student's writing.
- Some of your assertions to contribution go beyond the evidence provided.
- Introductions to chapters and sections do not say exactly what they will do.
- To what extent did you achieve your goal in the time allocated?
- Let's list ways to make your writing more precise in the next revision.

Constructing coherence

- **The writing task is to 'match' thesis abstract, summary and chapter introductions.**

This task gives students opportunities to work on the coherence of their thesis arguments. When they draft chapters, even after multiple revisions, the thesis argument may still not be clear. Revising the thesis abstract, 750-word thesis summary and chapter introductions so that they match shows the mechanics of argument construction.

Constructing coherence usually takes many feedback–revision iterations, and supervisors can help students to sustain writing through these iterations by suggesting different writing strategies for drafting and revising their Conclusion chapter. For example, if the study had three aims or research questions, these can be used to write three headings for three sections in the Conclusion chapter. Supervisors can prompt students to think in terms of specific numbers of words per section; for example, 1000 words on each aim, explaining how the study achieved each aim.

Paradoxically, it may be productive—in terms of producing lots of text, but also for creating coherence—to use strategies for simply generating text. While a writing goal of 'generating text'—freewriting for 5 minutes, for example—seems pointless to some supervisors and students, it can help students clarify what they want to say. Supervisors can encourage students to use other text-generation strategies, and use them for their own writing (Murray, 2016). They can help students to understand and adopt these strategies.

Sample of Supervisor's feedback:

- Use the same words in your abstract, summary and chapter introductions.
- Link your study's achievements explicitly to your study's aims.
- How productive do you feel your writing is at this stage?
- Your goals for your next revision should be to . . .

FEEDBACK FOR PRODUCTIVITY

This chapter draws on my experience of working with doctoral students in many Structured Writing Retreats. I wrote and revised this chapter at two of these retreats. Writing support is communal. For example, I discussed grounded theory—in which I am no expert—with another student who, although I am not her supervisor, asked me to read a section of her analysis chapter, and I suggested she discuss it with a student who had recently completed her doctorate using a grounded theory method. During a break, I asked one of my PhD students how she was getting on with her literature review and made suggestions. I helped another with coding transcripts. I had several short discussions about the PhD examination, which focused the thinking of those writing thesis Conclusions.

These discussions give me insights into how these students were thinking, writing and revising. As a facilitator at writing retreats, I ask everyone about progress and make suggestions as appropriate, but with my doctoral students, I provide individualized support, specific to the writing they are doing in that moment. As their supervisor, I can focus on what they can do to solve problems with, in and through writing. In the breaks from writing, I can check whether my support helped and how their writing has progressed. Thus I can learn how to help them manage their writing so that they can be productive. I can also see signs that they are writing more productively, and our completion rates are improving.

Supervisors who have no experience of writing retreats can adopt a 'try it and see' mindset. They can be assured that there is evidence for this approach, and can take an inquiry-based approach in their own writing feedback processes. This structured approach answers the call for 'more deliberate structures in subject disciplines to scaffold doctoral publication' (Kamler, 2008: 283). This chapter has described how such a structure could support the range of writings that doctoral students have to produce, and it has shown how supervisors can create these structures.

Speeding up the drafting–feedback–revising cycle helps students to 'write prolifically'. They develop productive writing practices that they can apply alone and in other student groupings (Aitchison and Guerin, 2014). The key benefit may be in connecting writing, thinking and knowledge construction in writing discussions. Yes, each of these potentially discrete activities has its own components and actions, but immediate-feedback discussions can pull them all together. Rather than talking about and performing research and writing as if they were separate activities, talking about writing-in-progress makes it possible to see, construct and manage the links between them.

Chapter 23

Strategies for helping students through writer's block

Susan Carter

Writer's block has long been an issue haunting writers of fiction (King, 2001; Lamott, 1995; see also Winokur, 1987) and academic texts alike (Elbow, 1998a). Unsurprisingly, the research project that underpins this book picked up on a common frustration for supervisors: *'Some students seem reluctant to produce written work, which makes it very difficult'* (supervisor respondent). The supervisor's challenge is to re-inspire, and re-energize—but this is hard when you are busy yourself. Neurologist Alice Weaver Flaherty (2004) devotes attention to the role of the brain in affecting writer's block or its opposite. Sitting just behind the ears, the limbic system activates creative motivation and engenders meaningfulness (Flaherty, 2004). Flaherty argues that writing procrastination is 'usually better treated by putting the writer in limbic or motivational state than by cognitive strategies such as making a To Do list' (2004: 16). Somehow students have to be given back their mojo. Supervisors can stockpile a smorgasbord of approaches to get doctoral students writing again when they stall. Small exercises intended to nudge students past the block can help trigger renewed creative energy for the task of writing.

Supervisors in our research endorsed Paul J. Silvia's sentiments in Chapter 21, that academics have to model a good relationship with writing and give speedy feedback: *'I try my best to stay on top of it by setting deadlines for myself as well as for the student'* (supervisor respondent). Survey participants found that, when students did experience writer's block, they also became elusive and uncommunicative: *'The times when communication has a tendency to drop off without careful monitoring is when a student is having trouble writing'* (supervisor respondent). Hard though it is to be patient when students avoid contact, we need to appreciate that academic writing is daunting to newcomers. Peter Elbow (1998b) has convincingly argued that challenges around writing are exacerbated by academia's penchant for rigorous critique. It can feel as though producing writing is inviting attack. Elbow speculated that there's 'something deeply wrong with an educational system that made people who were smart think they were stupid' (1998b: xiv) and found through teaching practice that peer writing groups are powerful for prompting writing flow because they seem supportive rather than critical. One of our study's participants confirmed that '*Usually they [doctoral students] stop writing out of fear, so it is primarily a matter of working through that and finding strategies to unlock their writing again*' (supervisor respondent). Flaherty (2004) speculates that perhaps the emotional turmoil of writing—she reports 'ricochet[ing] daily between euphoria and terror' as a writer (2004: 11–12)—may be essential for creativity. The trick to breaking down writer's block could be in selling this thought to students: pain is part of the creative process; get used to it.

Some students need support from either generic learning advisors or counsellors on managing their emotions. As professional educators, supervisors should take some responsibility for initiating potentially hard discussions that address the ongoing issues crucial to successful thesis completion. Paul J. Silvia (2010) suggests the practical solution of using Excel to keep track of small daily tasks. In this model, the author sets one writing task for each day of their working week, preferably one that is doable within a timeframe that can be as small as 30 minutes if there are other pressures (Silvia, 2010). The task is best when specific, not just 'work on Chapter 5', but 'two paragraphs on definition of writer's block', say, or 'cut 300 words from pages 2–27'. Each day the author must state whether they have achieved the goal or not—failure-averse doctoral students (and academics) often find it preferable to just do the work rather than type 'not done' in the achievement column. Then at the end of each week, those small chores add up to progress.

Following advice elsewhere throughout this book will also help to avoid student blockages. However, a supervisor should also have a raft of exercises at hand. You might suggest any of the following to the writing-blocked student:

BREAK IT DOWN TO DOABLE

Find the easiest chunk of writing work that will take 30–50 minutes. Tell me what it is and get it to me by tomorrow. We'll repeat this daily over the next 2 working weeks.

FREEWRITE

Write without regard for grammar, punctuation, structure or logic: just write without stopping for 10 minutes. Elbow's (1998a) 'freewriting' method is established as a sound pedagogy that frees up your subconscious mind to bring its thinking into what you write. Later, return and revise freewritten prose into something more academic.

SELF-AUDIT ON WRITING HABITS

- Acknowledge the successful working practices that you have: list what you do reasonably well. What might peers find useful? Do you help your colleagues enough by talking about writing?
- Consider what is working well so far in the writing you have produced: what do you like about it? How is it new/exciting/significant? Write that down in a note to yourself.
- List the areas of work that are not so successful for you. What bad habits do you currently have that might be rectified? Number the negative points in order of most important to least important. Are the most important things on your list of unsuccessful factors also the hardest to rectify, or not? Pick the three things you would most like to improve. Identify short, middle-range and long-term goals for writing habit rehab.
- Can any of the improvements be made more easily with someone else's help: mine as supervisor, your partner's, the learning advisor's, the IT help desk, a counsellor, the librarian specialist in your field . . .? Might asking for help carefully and clearly give some leverage? Put a symbol by any items where help from another would make a difference. Can you designate a time when you will solicit help? Add this to your diary now (or at least today).

DEVELOP YOUR INNER SLAVE AND MASTER

Just for 2 weeks, try splitting into two people, the master writing-manager and the slave writer-worker who must do as she is told, no more and no less. Imagine you are doing this to learn how to be an effective manager of employees—you might need this skill after graduation.

The writing-manager needs to take care of the writer-worker, who is a valuable resource, while at the same time getting maximum productivity from them. Construct a timeline with specific and manageable goals for each day of the following week that your writer-worker can cross off once completed. It is important that these are achievable tasks. Don't ask for more than 1 hour's work daily for the next week. Designate a small section of a chapter, maybe just providing topic sentences for each paragraph. Or maybe ask her to finish a significant piece of reading and write her thoughts on it. The writer-worker must set aside the allotted 1 hour (or 1.5 hours if you think you might be slow) for the chores that have been given and complete them each day, taking the manager's deadlines seriously.

The overall task is big, yet commitment to manager and worker roles can make it achievable. Value each other and work in a tandem of mutual respect. (Yes, this is one person splitting into two, but it works only with conscious commitment to playing two separate roles convincingly.)

ORIENT YOURSELF IN YOUR THESIS

1 Revisit your research proposal and early outline of thesis structure—emend if you think it needs it.
2 Remind yourself of your initial ideas (and enthusiasm) for the research project. Have you captured that enthusiasm somewhere in your introduction?
3 Have research questions or goals changed? Why? Write that short story: originally, the plan was . . . However, because of x, y and z . . .
4 Picture the thesis as a whole so that you have a better sense of how each of its parts functions in the overall context.
5 Re-examine your existing written work/chapters written so far. Make notes of the key elements of chapters you have already been working on. Is there something missing that would be easy enough to write?
6 Tally words in each section. Make a table or chart and review the word count in 1 month's time.
7 How is the next stage in your thesis going to draw on or link to prior sections? It can really help you to get back in if you pick up the existing threads with a mind to reworking them into forward movement.

DO THE MATHS

Establish the ideal final length, probably around 80,000 words for most theses that rely primarily on prose. Calculate approximate word lengths for each chapter, and, where possible, each section within chapters. This gives a guide as to the level of detail you have word space for. Once you can see how small and manageable a section is, write that section.

SOCIALIZE AS A RESEARCHER

Being exposed to the research of others in your field has many benefits and is always stimulating—or even inspirational. Plan towards giving a seminar or conference paper. Having a specific time-bound target motivates you, and writing a discrete entity like a conference paper is a good reminder that you can in fact produce polished and finished work.

Find or make a writing group or writing buddy. Receiving feedback from your peers is stimulating, and laughing at pedantry together defuses the challenge (Thesen, 2014); it may also help you to identify particularly strong (or less strong) elements of your work for development. Having to articulate your ideas can assist you in their clarification. You could also participate in (or set up) a reading group with other doctoral candidates in your discipline in which you discuss particular articles, readings, theories or methodologies.

MAKE IT LUXURIOUS

Try taking your laptop somewhere special and working there. Many of us find cafés ideal—there is background noise, but once the laptop is open, you need to perform being a writer in a café. Some dress up and go upmarket with their laptop. Others stay home in their dressing gowns with the cat on their knees.

ESCAPE DISTRACTION

If your office makes for distraction, swap offices. Find a part of the university with a good view and a desk and work there. Go somewhere without Wifi and leave your phone behind, preferably for a long wet weekend.

ESTABLISH A ROUTINE AND RHYTHM

Many writers find it helpful to work at a particular place and for a regular (and reasonably consistent) time. Some have theme writing music. Having specific times in which you work (at specific places) will also help you to maintain a balance with the rest of your life.

STAY FIT AND HEALTHY

Neurologist Alice Weaver Flaherty (2004) found that the limbic system in the brain is what affects motivation and meaning-making. She also found 'grudgingly' that exercise stimulates the limbic system—and is legal and non-harmful, unlike other possible stimulants. Try taking reasonably vigorous exercise, thinking about the writing you need to do while you are doing it, and then writing for an hour afterwards.

TREAT TIME OUT AS TIME FOR ARTICULATION WORK: AND CONSCIOUSLY DO IT TOWARDS WRITING

Flaherty (2004: 7) argues that 'The fallow periods that some writers call block are, for others, a fermentation process in the creative process'. Inger Mewburn (2012, 6 July) notes that before you can write, you need to do a great deal of thinking and reading and note-taking. She notes that:

> It takes time to find, read and sort through information and even more time to organize it in such a way that it is useful . . . I find myself resenting the amount of time I spend on these kinds of activities because all this articulation work [citing Starr, 1999], although laborious, doesn't really feel like legitimate work. I find myself feeling anxious and fretting as I do it. I have to resist the urge to skip it and just get to the writing. I like writing because it feels and looks more like 'proper work' to me . . . But I have to constantly remind myself that writing, like cooking, is just the place where all that articulation work becomes visible.
>
> (Mewburn, 2012, 6 July)

You could keep a tab on the work you are doing that supports writing but is not writing. Then look to see if small bits of writing could be threaded more cohesively into the reading and thinking work.

SEEK INSPIRATION FROM AUTHORS WHO WRITE ABOUT WRITING

Joan Bolker's chapters 'Getting to the Midpoint' and 'Interruptions from Inside and Outside' may be helpful in practical terms if you are in a bit of a slump, or struggling with the middle stages of the doctoral degree (Bolker, 1998: 63–79; 80–98). Flaherty (2004) writes beautifully, addresses her own emotions with writing in relation to personal tragedy, and interestingly applies neurological methods to understanding writer's block. Stephen King (2001), describing his relationship with his own prolific writing, may exemplify an author seeking to manage his limbic system—he makes vivid his tussle with both addiction and writing. Lamott (1995) and Silvia (2010) are valuable for the humour and humanity that they bring to writing. They differ in that Lamott fully explores emotion, whereas Silvia discounts it and focuses on practical methods for staying on top of writing. Rowena Murray (2011) does not underplay the challenges and complexities of doctoral writing, but persists with small-step approaches to working through these.

DOCTORATE AS DEVELOPMENT OF INNER SELF

I'm finishing on my favourite idea, one that I believe is true, about what is most valuable and hardest to learn. Accept difficulty as an incentive: if it is tough, it means you are learning those characteristics of heroes: perseverance in the face of adversity; self-reliance; persistence to the end—and how to keep a sense of humour and proportion. Learning how to manage both self and project through difficulty is one of the greatest benefits a graduate can take away: these are skills of use to family and social relationships, career, sport, hobbies . . . almost every aspect of life (Leonard, Becker and Coate, 2005). Difficulty is what makes a PhD worth having. More importantly, handling difficulty is one of the most empowering types of learning that doctoral students can do.

* * *

Maintaining and gathering momentum—things to do

- Model good practice; share tips and techniques that work for you.
- Encourage regular 'writing as a habit' (time, place, word count).
- Set tangible, bite-sized tasks; respond with prompt feedback.
- Encourage talking about writing (especially about why the student is *not* writing).
- Tackle problems early; offer practical solutions.
- Encourage a healthy work–life balance.
- Stress the value of down-time (relaxation/reflection) to help clarify and refine thoughts.
- Suggest new approaches to (re-)stimulate productivity.
- Focus on the whole journey: personal growth, transferable skills.
- Acknowledge—and celebrate—milestones along the way.

Part VIII

Keeping the examiner happy

Gina Wisker and Margaret Kiley; Susan Carter; Sue Starfield

Edited by Deborah Laurs

> ***Supervisor:*** *[O]ne of the single most frustrating things in my profession is telling a student that X is needed right through the process, being ignored, then having the examiners say that it was required—at which point the student takes note.*
>
> ***Student:*** *The best feedback predicts the 'what about . . .?'-type statements an examiner might raise.*

Examiners need to sign off that a thesis meets quite specific doctoral criteria. Doctoral writing must display evidence that the student has chosen methods knowingly, fully aware of limitations and alternatives. It must demonstrate analytical competence with literature, which requires discrimination about what is included, and accurate emphasis on what literature is important, and for what reasons. Research questions, hypotheses, definitions and arguments all need to be expressed accurately at macro and micro levels to an outside audience: most importantly, the examiners. It is sensible for students to be aware of examiners' requirements from the time they begin revision (Trafford and Leshem, 2002). Revising writing with a reader-needs perspective is always sound. Turning the imagined reader into the examiner, and drawing on research from examiners' reports brings this lens into precision. On the basis that research students must develop deep-level writing awareness, this part draws attention to the need for audience awareness that enables clarity of expression throughout the doctoral process, with a particular focus on how the meta-level requirements might be developed through writing feedback.

Gina Wisker and Margaret Kiley (Chapter 24) unpack the implicit Threshold Concepts associated with doctoral study and suggest ways in which supervisors can 'nudge' students towards their mastery and its demonstration in writing. In Chapter 25, Susan Carter emphasizes supervisors' responsibility in helping students to anticipate examiners' questions, and then addressing them in writing before submission in order to preempt them arising in the first place. She begins with the typical criteria that examiners sign off on and suggests how to strengthen writing accordingly. Sue Starfield (Chapter 26) focuses on the end game by identifying what does indeed make experienced examiners happy (or vice versa) when reading doctoral theses. Arming students with this awareness empowers them before submission.

Chapter 24

Helping students demonstrate mastery of doctoral Threshold Concepts

Gina Wisker and Margaret Kiley

Research into the characteristics of successful PhD theses (see, for example, Bourke, Hattie and Anderson, 2004; Holbrook and Bourke, 2004; Kiley and Mullins, 2004; Lovitts, 2007; Mullins and Kiley, 2002) suggests that examiners expect to see evidence of a variety of relatively abstract, rather daunting achievements and skills. We propose that this might be because satisfactory completion of a PhD indicates a contribution to knowledge as well as providing evidence of conceptual, critical and creative research and articulation. This evidence demonstrates a range of related disciplinary or inter-disciplinary understandings and skills at the doctoral level. Terms such as 'conceptual framework', 'critical perspective', 'contribution to knowledge' and their abstract indicators are examples of those rather elusive aims in doctoral research. For candidates to be able to bring such achievements into their writing, focused, accessible and timely feedback from supervisors is essential.

Supervisory feedback, both oral and written, offers specific advice, based in the broader understanding and recognition of what those rather abstract terms indicate in practice. In the light of the importance of the written contribution, which is what examiners see, we suggest that research into Threshold Concepts at the doctoral level provides a particularly helpful framework for feedback on students' written expression and articulation of their research practice and achievement.

Threshold Concepts (Meyer and Land, 2005, 2006a, 2006b) are those concepts that are critical to a learners' understanding of a discipline. The Threshold Concepts understanding of learning has been applied to 'learning to be a researcher', with theory and argument identified as concepts that often challenge learners (Kiley, 2009). Understanding these concepts is seen as being critical to successfully crossing the various conceptual thresholds at stages in the research journey, and to becoming an effective researcher (Kiley and Wisker, 2009; Wisker, Kiley and Aiston, 2006). Therefore, one of our roles as supervisors is to find and develop the feedback language to bring these essential Threshold Concepts and conceptual threshold crossings into doctoral students' view, so they can recognize and embark on the journey to demonstrate them in the written thesis.

Every doctoral student is different, every project is different, and each has its own nuances in relation to questions, problems, processes, research, modes of articulation of the question and the achievement of research outcomes and processes. Ensuring clear and appropriate feedback on conceptual levels of work is the most sensitive area, and as supervisors, we have to find ways to express the abstract, the complexly conceptual, and help to make it accessible through our feedback so that candidates can own and translate what it means into their own work and expression.

THRESHOLD CONCEPTS AND CONCEPTUAL THRESHOLDS IN DOCTORAL LEARNING AND EXPRESSION

There are a number of characteristics of a Threshold Concept (Meyer and Land, 2006b)—for example, boundedness, irreversibility and transformation—which have been applied to a number of concepts that supervisors, when interviewed, consider are the most challenging for their own students. Threshold Concepts related to learning to be a researcher include: argument/thesis, theory, framework, knowledge creation, analysis, research paradigm, creativity, scholarly writing and 'doctorateness' (Humphrey and Simpson, 2012; Kiley, 2009, 2010; Trafford and Leshem, 2009). Each of these concepts requires the learner to engage deeply and conceptually. Once the concept is fully understood and the conceptual threshold crossed, the learner is then able to demonstrate this understanding through the range of behaviours, skills and abilities expected from an effective researcher in relation to their research work, and their articulation of it.

Additionally, it is helpful to be aware of some of the behaviours that candidates exhibit while coming to terms with these concepts. One common behaviour is using mimicry (Bhabha, 1994; Wisker and Savin-Baden, 2009), where learners use terms and phrases that they understand to be critical in their discipline, but of which they have little or no understanding. Many successful researchers report engaging in mimicry as PhD candidates themselves, until one day they actually understood what they had previously been pretending to understand and talk about.

Meyer and Land (2006b) also suggest that another feature of grappling with understanding a Threshold Concept is 'stuckness'. Research at the doctoral level (Kiley, 2014) suggests that many candidates feel as if they are 'going round in circles', or 'knocking their head against a brick wall' when they are in a stuck place. This is often when candidates consider withdrawing from their programme and where the idea of 'nudging' them across Threshold

Concepts can be very helpful when giving feedback. Such nudging might include offering advice about overcoming writing blocks and fostering discussions leading to fuller, clearer understanding (Wisker and Savin-Baden, 2009; Wisker, 2014) and breakthroughs in writing.

MANIFESTATION IN THESIS WRITING

According to researchers across a range of different countries, examiners generally agree on similar qualities in describing what delineates a 'good' thesis (Denicolo, 2003; Holbrook et al., 2004a, 2004b; Lovitts, 2007; Mullins and Kiley, 2002). Likewise, as Mullins and Kiley (2002: 378–379) found from interviews with supervisors, there are also commonly shared views about the characteristics of a poor thesis:

- lack of coherence;
- lack of understanding of the theory;
- lack of confidence;
- researching the wrong problem;
- mixed or confused theoretical and methodological perspectives;
- work that is not original;
- not being able to explain at the end . . . what had actually been argued in the thesis.

These characteristics relate closely to the Threshold Concepts outlined above. For example, from their written and oral reports, examiners frequently talk about the need for a coherent argument; that is, telling a story that is supported by evidence/data. This, we argue, is reflected in the Threshold Concept of *argument/thesis*. A lack of understanding of theory relates closely to the Threshold Concept of *theory*. Holbrook, Bourke and Fairbairn (2015) note that examiners' reports stressed the following as important in relation to theory: '"accuracy and completeness", "grasp", "alignment", "coherence and consistency", "treatment of findings and discussion", and "dimensions of contribution"' (2015: 75). However, they argue that examiners' comments on theory vary by discipline, with a far higher percentage in disciplines such as Education and Humanities and Social Sciences, more generally followed by Science and specifically by Health (2015: 79). Examiners don't always comment on theory, but candidates who 'achieve distillation in communication, thinking, and maturity of insight about theory are recognized by examiners as particularly high achievers in that area' (Holbrook, Bourke and Fairbairn, 2015: 84).

Another comment made frequently in reports concerns the (lack of) evidence of critical analysis, reflecting the Threshold Concept of *analysis*. Unsurprisingly, most reports highlight contributions to knowledge. For candidates, understanding that their research should make an original contribution to knowledge reflects the Threshold Concept of *knowledge creation* in learning to be a researcher. Methodology/research design is another criterion commonly noted in examiners' reports and discussions, and links with the two Threshold Concepts of *framework* and *paradigm*.

A number of examiners make mention of the candidate who has taken a creative approach to their work. This use of the word 'creative' is not specific to the creative arts, but refers more to the candidate who tried for something outside the norm or tackled a risky project, but didn't quite manage to meet the requirement. In this case, the Threshold Concept of *creativity* comes into play. Finally, the scholarly nature of the writing in a thesis is generally one of the main criteria expected by institutions when sending theses to examiners. Trafford and Leshem (2009) suggest that when a research candidate can bring together all these various components of a doctorate, then the student has achieved 'Doctorateness'.

FEEDBACK AND NUDGING

In relation to the achievement of Threshold Concepts and conceptual threshold crossings in doctoral work, Wisker, Cheng and Morris (2010) developed the notion of 'nudging': a set of focused, individually nuanced but persistent strategies to urge or prompt students into working at an increasingly more conceptual, critical and creative level—and expressing this in their work. Some of these practices are quite generic, some discipline-specific, and others target the specific stage of writing a student is at. They include:

- offering models and explaining what they initiate in terms of thinking;
- engaging with questions of articulation;
- suggesting that students find models themselves;
- prompting and exemplifying ways in which students can engage with theories and concepts and take on any of these to underpin their questioning, research processes, research journeys and scrutiny and interpretation of data.

This feedback and nudging should also influence articulation of the doctorate as a whole in writing. Whereas a supervisory comment such as 'you need to theorize' will convey little and is likely to waste time in terms of agonizing about its meaning, students can be guided, not by tracked changes, but by examples and suggestions and questions, linking words, rephrasing and integration of critical text with their own arguments and findings, as models to take through the rest of the piece of writing.

Some of the nudges are local and specific, some are open questions. For example, when urging theorization, a comment such as, 'How does the idea of Baudrillard concerning space offer insights here?' nudges critical thinking in a specific form, and also sets up a pattern for ensuring students' integration of critical works with their own. Offering a perspective, even to the extent of sharing a quotation or an example of someone else's work where a theorist's perspective offers clarification, will enable greater insight and clearer expression. The point of good feedback is to engage thinking and dialogue, to enable and empower rather than to humiliate, confuse, give answers (except when correcting factual errors) or substitute the work of the supervisor for that of the student. Feedback engages student and supervisor in a creative critical dialogue on the work, with the product being evidence of learning that will satisfy examiners' expectations.

Feedback, like any teaching and learning, is a dialogue between the supervisor, the student's understanding as expressed in their writing, and finally the examiners (and, if the thesis is published, future readers). The supervisor offers a view of the specific actions needed in the written work to ensure clear expression, and enable readers to understand the student's achievements. Supervisors need to learn the language with which to give useful feedback to enhance students' precise articulation of their understanding. Feedback that is confusing, abrupt or generic is probably caused by supervisors just not having the words to engage. Our aim in giving feedback is specific guidance, engagement with specific needs at different stages, in terms of both the discipline and the writing. Good feedback is empowering when it nudges conceptualization, then articulation. With good feedback, we are inducting students into the gradual use and ownership of appropriate expression, as they move through stages of mimicry to increasing confidence in their own 'voice', and articulate complex ideas and understandings. Their writing should showcase their achievements to best effect.

Chapter 25

Building bulwarks

Defence in thesis writing

Susan Carter

The thesis stands amongst the most defensive of textual genres. Like many creatures, its survival rests on a convincing display of defence: the primary reader is a rigorous examiner. That person, working beyond their day job, often in snatches, is charged with checking that the institutional criteria of the master's or doctoral degree are met. As a fairly standard example, the Statute for the Degree of Doctor of Philosophy at the University of Auckland (2012) requires that the doctoral thesis:

- is an *original contribution* to knowledge or understanding in its field
- meets *internationally recognized standards* for such work
- demonstrates *knowledge of the literature* relevant to the subject and the field or fields to which the subject belongs, and the ability to exercise *critical and analytical judgement* of it
- is satisfactory in its *methodology*, in the *quality and coherence* of its expression, and in its *scholarly presentation* and format.

(University of Auckland, 2012, n.p.; italics added)

Students need to *demonstrate* in writing that they have met these criteria, attesting that they possess research skills for future independent work (as defined by the UK Research Councils, n.d., for example). This need to demonstrate makes the thesis a highly prescribed genre (Carter, 2011). Supervisors can shore up their students' defences, because the criteria that guide examiners can also inform research students (Boulter and Denicolo, 2002; Trafford and Leshem, 2002; 2008). Although examination is not an early concern, it can direct both early-stage thesis writing and final revision before submission.

ENSURING SATISFACTORY CHOICES

As methodological decisions are made in the first few months of the doctorate, students should be encouraged to write down the rationale behind choices in clear formal language (for example, why they rejected some methods or theories, how they delineated sample size, etc.), in order to pre-empt examiner questions. Some choices will emerge from early supervision meetings; directly thereafter, students can be encouraged to write up their reasoning. Whatever they produce in these early stages is likely to find a place within the thesis as a means of *demonstrating* methodological soundness. Writing at the time of choosing ensures that the reasoning won't be forgotten later, forfeiting the opportunity for patently clear defence. A confidence-booster for students is that this activity generates relatively easily written words, with the by-product of generating early pieces of writing so that supervisors know what they are in for and can begin the feedback process.

Examiners warm to introductions that convey the student's motivations for the project (Carter, 2008)—fostering writing in the early phase makes it more likely that this first glow of enthusiasm will infuse the prose. Once students recognize the need to formally defend their research, they can begin to develop skills in packaging their thoughts for the convenience and pleasure of readers (Sword, 2009). Later, in the revision stages, supervisors can remind students to check whether they have documented the decision-making process clearly enough in the thesis. Such attention to detail can help ensure, when the thesis is submitted, that at least some of Glatthorn's (1998) commonly-asked examiner questions won't arise:

> - Why did you choose that particular method? Why did you not instead use this other method?
> - Can you clarify for me how the particular method you chose relates directly to the problem you have chosen to study?
>
> (Glatthorn 1998: 186–188)

Examiners expect the rationale for the study to be clearly explicated—the early stages of writing are a good time to describe the thinking processes underpinning hypotheses or questions. Examiners will want to see the following (adapted from Denicolo, 2004, 114–116):

- a rationale of general approach closely argued giving a reasoned case for rejecting other possible approaches;
- justification of research design presented, taking account of potential advantages and limitations; research techniques argued as theoretically and practically relevant to the research problem;
- reasons given for rejection of possible alternatives, rationale provided for amendments to standard tests and procedures or for detailed design of innovative techniques.

Questions such as these can be used to guide feedback at all stages of students' writing.

CRITICAL AND ANALYTICAL SKILLS WITH THE LITERATURE REVIEW

In the early stages, the tsunami of literature to be covered seems overwhelming, and the scope, argument, methods and questions of the project are likely to be still under negotiation. Nonetheless, students must learn to make sense of the literature as it relates to their own study, a task where writing, thinking and reflecting are closely intertwined. They must make meaningful notes to save themselves from having to circle back round. Ideally, these notes should construct a meta-narrative of the relevant research discourse: what were the monumental shifts; what points are contested; who sides with and against whom (Hart, 1998). Encouraging such questioning can feed into further writing that helps establish the student's own position within the discourse. Students need good supervisory support to cope with such mentally challenging work (Carter, 2015, 27 November). As they begin to find their 'voice', students also need to be encouraged to trust themselves as writers with full entitlement (Guerin, 2013, 1 September).

Writing up one's choices from the outset can help to fit literature into the research project rather than being overwhelmed. A couple of Glatthorn's questions ask about research niche interest: 'When you reviewed the literature, why did you decide to review that particular area of study?' and 'You have reviewed the important literature, but I fail to see what use you make of your review. Can you clarify for me what you learned from the review of literature?'(Glatthorn, 1998: 187). Writing should pre-empt such questions.

Supervisors could set students the task of drafting questions relating to their research to ask of each piece of literature that they review. Such questions will come from the field of study—in literature studies, for example, my question was simply, 'Why do I like or dislike this?' Often, though, questioning may consider sample size, methods, theory, funders, etc.; when doctoral students begin to feel comfortable about routinely interrogating what they are reading, they become increasingly enculturated to critical analysis and review. In this way, supervisors can subtly ensure that feedback on exploratory literature review drafts scaffolds students' learning on several levels. Textually pre-empting examiners' questions will also satisfy graduate committees during the provisional year review.

WHAT IS THE 'ORIGINAL CONTRIBUTION'?

Assessing the significance of their original contribution can trouble students. The term 'originality' is vague, and often undefined and unquantified (Tinkler and Jackson, 2004: 117–118). Supervisors might like to share with students Tinkler and Jackson's range of what can be considered 'original' within their field, such as:

- Research on new areas of study, data sets, questions, hypotheses, problems, links between topics/data sets and so on.
- Research processes
  - New applications of established research tools—for instance, methods, instruments, conceptual tools, modes of analysis, procedures, theories, 'practice'—to different or new research topics.
  - Significant refinement of established research tools or development of new research tools applied to established or new research topics.
  - The application of new perspectives to research topics.
- Research outcomes (intentional or unintentional)
  - New or substantially revised solutions, products, theories, knowledge, interpretations, approaches, ways of doing research (methods, instruments, conceptual tools, modes of analysis, procedures, applications of theory, 'practice').
  - New syntheses of theory, knowledge or ways of doing research.
  - The opening up of new or neglected areas for fundamental and significant further research.

(Tinkler and Jackson, 2004: 117–118)

Such a list may assist students to identify their original contributions, and it's also useful to remind them to *overtly state* what is significant about their research in

- the introduction (areas of study, processes and outcomes);
- the methodology (processes);
- discussion and conclusion (outcomes and their significance).

In many disciplines, when students adapt or modify theory or method, the explicit inclusion of words such as 'novel' or 'original' adds weight to persuade the examiner of the thesis's original contribution.

MEETING 'INTERNATIONALLY RECOGNIZED STANDARDS'

It is probably typical of New Zealand academics to spell out the need to be 'recognized internationally': we are a small isolated country wanting to be taken seriously. However, all institutional criteria will expect the standard of doctoral research and writing to look professionally expert.

Increasingly, doctoral students opt for thesis by publication or publishing along the way. Even when writing a stand-alone thesis, students should aim for a voice that is authoritative and confident, and clearly expressed. Thesis prose should look publishable within an international peer-reviewed journal. In a survey investigating peer reviewers' adjudication of 441 abstracts submitted for an international conference, Berkenkotter and Huckin (1998: 111) identified the following factors in accepted abstracts:

1 clear definition of a problem or need;
2 novelty; and
3 ethos, in that 'high-rated abstracts also typically project more of an insider persona', i.e. competently use terminology and literature of the discipline.

Their first criterion is the project's evident significance (Ferris and Hedgcock, 2014). Glatthorn (1998: 186–188) identifies typical oral examination questions, such as 'Why did you choose that particular problem? Why did you not study this other problem instead? What exactly were you trying to find out? I'm unclear about the meaning of your problem statement', questions that students should pre-empt in the written thesis. To encourage students to understand how to show an insider persona in writing, supervisors can ask them to find three articles by experts and highlight text (words, phrases and clauses) that convince them that these authors are discipline experts. Students can then emulate similar lexical, tonal and rhetorical strategies in their own work once their attention is drawn into the implicit workings of disciplinary discourses.

MAKING THE 'QUALITY AND COHERENCE OF WRITTEN EXPRESSION' EVIDENTLY 'SATISFACTORY'

This book suggests many approaches that supervisors can adopt to help research students reach their full potential as coherent and stylish writers. Doctoral students, in particular, need to learn to masochistically welcome the review process and become inured to the reiterative nature of good academic writing, the slog involved. The more people who give feedback at every stage of production, the more sets of collegial eyes looking for ambiguity, linguistic tangles and inaccuracies of any kind—helping with defence—the better. The ultimate question is whether 'the text of [the] thesis [is] sufficiently transparent with a perfectly clear intended meaning' (Boulter and Denicolo, 2002: 43). Family and friends can helpfully signal to students when they lose track; writing that is reasonably clear to non-experts will usually satisfy examiners. Explaining a complex passage verbally to someone else often shows students the need for sharper expression, or a few extra words, to strengthen the written document. As far as final quality is concerned, some students can afford professional proofreading, and some institutions provide assistance. Nevertheless, it's important to remind students that the final responsibility is theirs alone.

FINISHING TOUCHES

This chapter began with the idea of examination as the end-goal and closes in the same way. Awareness of examination practices and expectations that colours early writing should also guide final revisions. Before submission, encourage students to make a complete sweep of the entire document, checking that the joinery of their defensive bulwarks is sturdily and visibly in place. Trafford and Leshem (2002) usefully provide a set of critical questions you might adapt to help your student critically review their own work:

- How did you relate the various stages of your research one to another?
- What is your contribution to knowledge?
- How important are your findings and to whom?
- How do your main conclusions link to the work of [other famous scholars]?

(Trafford and Leshem, 2002: 8–9)

Allowing students to respond to this self-critique aided by a set of critical questions equips students with a practical workerly framework for self-reflection. Pre-submission pressure can add tension to the supervisory relationship; by emphasizing the examination criteria, you can distance yourself, highlighting that it is the academy itself demanding high standards.

Chapter 26

What examiners value in a PhD

Sue Starfield

Students and supervisors are often surprised when I talk to them about the research into what examiners look for in a PhD thesis. Almost apologetically, I'll explain that it's an area of growing interest. John Swales, the well-known applied linguist, coined the phrase 'occluded genres' (Swales, 1996) to describe genres that are not publicly or easily available. The PhD examination process and the examiners' reports that make our hearts sink or soar are typical examples of hidden or occluded genres. Fortunately, we now have some research that shines a light into examiners' preferences. This information is particularly important for students and their supervisors in countries like Australia where there is typically no oral defence or viva, and examination is based solely on the written thesis. There is, however, much that supervisors, everywhere, can take from the research into examiners' expectations, to inform the guidance they provide to their students from the earliest stages of the thesis journey until submission.

As one of the experienced PhD examiners interviewed in Mullins and Kiley's well-known study (2002) explained:

> A PhD is a stepping stone into a research career. All you need to do is to demonstrate your capacity for independent, critical thinking. That's all you need to do. A PhD is three years of solid work, not a Nobel Prize.
>
> (Mullins and Kiley, 2002: 386)

A quick Google search of Nobel Prize winners suggests there is some truth in this—many are quite elderly by the time they earn the coveted award and it seems unlikely that they would have received it for their doctoral project—although that may well have started them on the path to future glory. So the key message here is, 'get it done'—do it well, but see the PhD as a time-limited stage in your career development.

One of the key messages that can be distilled from the research is that first impressions count. Experienced examiners decide very early on whether the assessment of a thesis is likely to be 'hard work' or 'an enjoyable read' and their initial impression of the quality of the thesis is usually formed by the end of the second or third chapter—often by the end of the literature review. 'It is unusual that if someone does a poor job of the literature review that they will suddenly improve' said one experienced examiner (Mullins and Kiley, 2002: 377). Supervisors do need to make it clear to their students that chapters like the literature review that are often drafted early in the thesis process need to be kept updated and revised, often substantially, prior to submission.

We would all like our students' theses to be in the 'enjoyable read' category. What can we do to get them there? Here are some of the things that a study of examiners' reports (Johnston, 1997) tells us:

> - Examiners approach reading a thesis with an air of expectation and even enthusiasm, but this disappears if the thesis is not *reader-friendly* [emphasis added].
> - General impressions and overall presentation of the thesis are particularly important.
> - The reader needs to be assisted through the use of summaries, logical sequencing, signposts and removal of excessive repetition.
> - *All* readers require assistance to understand the work.
> - They feel distracted and irritated by poorly presented work.
> - They appreciate well-written, interesting and logically presented arguments.
>
> (Johnston, 1997: 340–341)

Mullins and Kiley (2002: 378) note that 'sloppiness' is one of the words most commonly used in negative responses to theses. Sloppy presentation suggests to the examiner that the research might well be sloppy, and they read the thesis with a more critical eye. One of the examiners interviewed by Mullins and Kiley noted just how significant a role the student's perceived 'lack of care' can play in the examination:

> I give my students strong advice on how not to 'flip' an examiner from 'reasonable' to 'unreasonable' by having irritating things in the thesis such as typos and other careless textual mistakes that indicate lack of attention to detail. Once flipped (and I am aware of this happening), I am irritated and I have to work very hard at overcoming this irritation and not letting it influence my view of this thesis, although this is not easy.
>
> (Mullins and Kiley, 2002: 378)

Just the other day, I was chatting to a PhD student who was about to submit his PhD thesis for examination and just waiting for the supervisor's final sign-off. I ran through a couple of the key things that need to be done before final submission. Semi-jokingly, I said, 'Have you checked your Table of

Contents?' The student visibly paled: 'Table of Contents? No one's mentioned that.' As I had fairly recently examined a thesis without a Table of Contents, I knew just how that oversight 'flipped' me from a well-disposed to a slightly more suspicious examiner. A fellow experienced examiner's account of how he approaches examining a thesis illustrates the importance of the Table of Contents in the assessment process:

> First of all I look at the structure to see if there is a logical progression. I look at the table of contents just to see whether it makes sense from that point of view. How much space is devoted to a certain section. You know roughly what should be there. I guess I try and find what is the contribution of research and hopefully there is a section there which outlines the contributions of the research and then once you know what they claim what they have done other than the results that they have achieved then you can verify it is their actual work.
>
> (Kiley and Mullins, 2004: 130)

Is it part of the supervisor's role to remind a student of the necessity for a Table of Contents? I certainly believe we should encourage our students to look at recently submitted theses in our Schools and Departments that have been well received by the examiners. These theses can provide students with a sense of what is expected of them. In addition, there are a number of online repositories which host completed PhD theses, and we should encourage our students to consult sites such as *Trove* (http://trove.nla.gov.au/) or *Proquest Theses and Dissertations* (www.proquest.com/products-services/pqdtglobal.html), to which many universities subscribe.

As Johnston's (1997: 345) study argued, examiners do not approach a thesis as 'experts in the field who will judge accordingly', but 'just like readers of any new piece of writing'. A reader-friendly thesis is the outcome of multiple drafts; it is vitally important that supervisors communicate this message clearly to students from early on. Feedback from readers including, but not limited to, the supervisors is essential. Supervisors should encourage their students to join writing groups and other writing support initiatives where possible. In the final stages, I like to recommend that a proof-reader or at least a reasonably literate friend read through the entire thesis prior to submission. It has to be someone other than the author who, towards the end, will not see typos, grammatical errors, repetitions and illogicalities. Some may need an editor for more help with grammar and language. Whichever the route chosen, redrafting takes time. Count back from the submission date and build in the time needed for the final polishing—it always takes longer than anticipated. But as the research shows, the effort put in to craft a reader-friendly text will be worth it. The research points to numerous negative comments focusing on the need for proof-reading that seem to have an impact on the overall assessment, such as:

> I lost count of the number of times that singular nouns were referred to in the plural—an irritant that should not have survived proofreading. This added to

> the overall impression that the work was rushed and not subjected to adequate preliminary review.
>
> (Johnston, 1997: 339)

Chapter 11, 'Before You Submit', in *How to Write a Better Thesis* (Evans, Gruba and Zobel, 2011) has a great checklist of all the many things that need to be done to polish the final draft of the thesis. I encourage all the students I talk to at workshops and seminars to print it out and use it.

Kiley and Mullins (2004) also asked examiners how they went about reading the thesis. Rather than sitting down and reading from cover to cover as one might a novel, the majority of the examiners surveyed begin with the abstract, introduction and conclusion and, of course, the references. At a later stage, when they have a good chunk of time, they will read the thesis through in a more linear way. Again, first impressions are important: a clear abstract with no typos; a well-written introduction that has not been written in haste a week or two before submission; and a thought-through conclusion that clearly shows how the questions raised in the introduction have been addressed go some way to shaping that positive first impression. And, of course, as I mentioned above, an up-to-date reference list including all articles, chapters and books referred to in the thesis helps too. Contrary to the advice on many thesis-writing websites and blogs, I advise my students and the supervisors I talk to of the importance of drafting the introduction early in the writing process. While there may be some truth in the view that the introduction can only be written once the thesis is complete, my view is that having a working draft which can be regularly updated helps student and supervisor keep track of the thesis's evolution.

From another negative comment, we learn that a high-quality literature review should do more than 'review' a body of literature. It should be structured as an argument for why this research needs to be done:

> [C]learly the author can examine and review a complex body of literature. However, a literature review must carry a major part of the argument in the thesis, the argument that convinces the reader of the need to investigate the to-be-specified research questions.
>
> (Holbrook et al., 2008: 351)

This is a perspective that many students fail to grasp and that supervisors can guide them in developing. As another examiner wrote: 'literature reviews whilst exploring every facet of the related research should pivot around the central argument of the thesis and flow the reader through the justification for the research' (Holbrook et al., 2008: 351).

Examiners' reports also provide insight into other aspects of what constitutes a 'good' thesis. For example, Holbrook et al. (2008: 350) point to expectations that the literature review will be linked with the findings of the thesis, a point that might otherwise remain implicit. A negative comment thus stated: 'I was a bit amazed that relatively few references were given in the discussion and conclusion sections, which are typically the parts of the work in which the results are compared to the earlier work', whereas a more positive one commended the candidate for 'a very good effort . . . made at tying the results back into the existing literature'.

I have found that this dimension of the discussion section—where the student begins to show their contribution to the field through reference to previous literature—is often not apparent to students. Here again, the supervisor can make sure the student is aware of this function of the discussion chapters.

The number of students who actually fail the PhD examination is extremely small. Many will, however, be required to do revisions, with Holbrook et al. (2014) revealing that formative comments constitute a large proportion of the examiners' reports they analysed. In the words of one of the examiners interviewed by Mullins and Kiley (2002: 383), doctoral assessment provides 'an opportunity for the students to be able to incorporate comments so that it [the thesis] sits on the library shelf and glows more brightly'. In conclusion, it is worth emphasizing the reciprocal relationship that exists between examining and supervising: becoming an examiner of doctoral theses can help us become better supervisors as we, too, are pushed to articulate what we expect in a 'good enough' thesis.

* * *

Keeping the examiner happy—things to do

- Draw students' attention to examiners' expectations from the outset:
  - encourage self-audit (*What skills/concepts/behaviours are required to achieve 'doctorateness' within my field? Which do I need to work on? How will I do this?)*
- Acknowledge writing process and production, as well as content-related issues.
- Anticipate—and pre-empt—potential examiners' questions:
  - encourage the keeping of a running record of all process-related decisions (why this setting, why this method [and not others], how data was analysed, etc.)
- Encourage students to take every opportunity to explain research to different audiences:
  - informal peer-group discussions
  - publications in related journals
  - seminar and conference presentations
- Empower students to present themselves to best advantage:
  - ask questions (*Do you like/dislike this article? Why? How is it relevant?*) so students justify decisions and thinking processes within their writing
  - encourage looking at published theses for exemplars of what to include (and where)
  - stress the importance of tying the whole thesis together (cohesion between 'introduction and conclusion'; research questions clearly answered; signposts and linkages between sections; consistent formatting; literature linked to research study, etc.)
- Provide feedback in good time, allowing months (not weeks) for final polishing and proofreading.
- Foreshadow likelihood of further revisions in light of examiners' comments.

Part IX

Writing feedback as nudging through identity transition

Claire Aitchison; Alet P. Olivier; Deborah Laurs, Lisa Chant, Susan Carter and 'Ema Wolfgramm-Foliaki; Eva M. Brodin and B. Liezel Frick; Tai Peseta and Sarah Barradell; Anthony Paré

Edited by Susan Carter

> ***Supervisor:*** *I think that the relationship with the supervisor is the most important area where authorial voice develops, because you are in dialogue with your supervisor and you receive the supervisor's feedback on your work. So, I think that that relationship between supervisor and student is the space where authorial voice happens.*
>
> ***Student:*** *I was nervous as I wasn't sure about the standard of work required at this level. I wasn't sure what to expect: it has been difficult to develop a 'voice' and writing style. I got so used to getting negative feedback that I took on the identity of 'bad student'. Except then . . . I got really good feedback and I was so shocked I had a little meltdown and anxiety attack.*

Consider for a moment your own lived experience of being an academic. You probably spend most of your week chewing through chores, making hectic cycles round your teaching, research and service requirements. There's a need to factor in time for reporting, too. Amongst this, there is little time for most of us to angst over whether we are imposters (Archer, 2008; Turman,

2001) as research writers. Yet most doctoral students operate in a self-conscious limbo of becoming rather than being: researcher identity is bothersome. This part focuses on the fact that writing feedback is not just about producing text, but about producing a confident research writer.

Part IX considers how supervisors can support their students' transitioning identities, development of writing voice, and competence within the academic community. We argue that research students need 'more than conversations about their substantive research. They also want focused "insider" discussion about "the rules of the game", what it means to be a scholar' (Walker and Thomson, 2010: 3); writing feedback is strongest when it conveys in concrete terms how writing demonstrates discipline epistemology and scholarliness. In some disciplines such as Social Sciences, word choice and emphasis carry theoretical weight, so that novice authors need considerable linguistic control as they construct their own position within their prose.

In the delicate zone between encouragement and discipline training, supporting the development of doctoral students' identity as it appears in their writing can be fraught. As always, there are considerations when working across cultures: 'Many international students are not making decisions about their research question, research approach, and intended outcomes . . . on a solely individual basis, but have to take into account their audience and sponsors back home' (Robinson-Pant, 2010: 148). With all students, there is scope for them and their supervisors to talk past each other, and for considerable emotional pressures to ensue. Nonetheless, growth into full researcher identity emerges from the struggle.

In Chapter 27, Claire Aitchison maps the centrality of the individual and follows this up with suggestions for supervisory practice that enable students to find themselves as academics and researchers. Alet P. Olivier (Chapter 28) draws on linguistic theory to offer concrete approaches that might help students to establish their own voice in writing. Deborah Laurs, Lisa Chant, Susan Carter and 'Ema Wolfgramm-Foliaki (Chapter 29) demonstrate the influences of indigeneity and culture on multiple positionings of self, factors significant for many research students. Chapter 30, by Eva M. Brodin and B. Liezel Frick, offers a model for supporting students' creativity and strengthening their confidence as researchers. In Chapter 31, Tai Peseta and Sarah Barradell (supervisor and supervisee respectively) consider the myriad 'voices' with which a student author speaks herself into being. Finally, in Chapter 32, Anthony Paré brings identity back into textual ethos, giving the last word to the word.

Chapter 27

Writing an identity into being

Claire Aitchison

There is no better way for a doctoral scholar to come to know who they wish to be in the academy than through writing and through sharing writing experiences with others. 'Who am I now?' and 'Who do I want to become?' are the central *questions of becoming* that face all doctoral scholars. Doing doctoral research is not simply an intellectual activity. Learning is transformative—and most especially at doctoral level, when scholars must grapple with high-stakes projects and big ideas that speak to the core of who they are, and wish to be.

As doctoral students struggle to make sense of complex ideas and to place themselves into a new dynamic intellectual environment, they are engaged in a process of identity formation; a continual process of becoming. For student writers, this venture into the unknown can be both exhilarating and confusing. Over 3–5 years of candidature, students will test out different understandings of knowledge and of themselves as they make sense of their research, the field and their own place within it. Ontological and epistemological questions interrelate over the entire course of candidature—and beyond—providing students with previously unavailable possible new selfhoods.

There is now a considerable literature recognizing the mutually constitutive relationship of identity formation and doctoral study (Barnacle and Dall'Alba, 2013; Green, 2005; McAlpine and Amundsen, 2007; Petersen 2012, 2014). Kamler and Thomson (2014) refer extensively to the mutual writing tasks of 'textwork' and 'identitywork' that constitute the ongoing process of becoming. The difficult search for identity progresses over the course of candidature as an engaged scholar is continuously reassessing what they believe in relationship to what they read, discover and write. Doctoral learning is 'as much about identity formation as it is about knowledge production' (Green, 2005: 153) and thus is an acutely affecting endeavour.

At the early stages of candidature, students are strongly defined (by others and themselves) by what they don't know. Ultimately, the successful doctoral scholar needs to project a sense of themselves as an expert, a discipline insider, able to communicate appropriately and with authority as a member of an international group of colleagues. The shift from novice to expert necessitates shifting uncertainty self-narratives towards confident and competent personal identities.

This move from novice to expert is unnerving—at times excruciating. Small wonder, then, that some students find it so difficult as to be traumatizing (Lee and Williams, 1999; Starfield, 2010). As research programmes continue to expand worldwide and bring in a greater diversity of students, many will feel an intense sense of alienation and disorientation as they move from one educational context, language of communication and culture of learning to another. The challenge to write with authority 'may be felt more acutely by students who are writing in a language other than their first' (Cotterall, 2013: 3). So-called 'non-traditional students' such as multilingual, multiliterate and international students may feel particularly disconnected if the strengths of their former identities, strengths that got them into a doctorate, seem inadequate and mismatched.

Doctoral scholarship draws students into contested networks of aspiration, desire and imagination. Rizvi (2010) says that globalization enables international students to imagine far broader professional futures, requiring expanded 'transnational identity work'. Increasingly, this plays out for scholars operating in a global job marketplace where an academic identity needs to be maintained online through publications and international profile building. In the competitive global market for researcher graduates, doctoral scholars are known via their publications, which represent high-value cultural capital (Aitchison, 2017). Their writings are the vehicles for doctoral students to develop and market their new self-hoods as scholars with established credibility.

Identity formation occurs both during the writing process and in the written output. The construction of knowledge through writing is an embodied state, not just a cognitive activity (Barnacle and Dall'Alba, 2013); a student who is writing is 'more than just a brain' (Cotterall, 2013). Words on the page are distinctly different from personal cogitations. Words on paper publicly reveal a person's inner thoughts, not only displaying ideas, but also exposing their author to their own critique and public scrutiny. The process of constructing a text requires the author to be not only a producer, but also a reader and consumer of their own words—and a critic of their own thinking.

Meaning is made in the act of writing and at the same time this act inscribes a certain identity on the writer that is both separate, and yet also integrally part of the evolving self-hood of the author. Struggles over academic identity and meaning-making are realized in, and through, writing.

SO HOW CAN WE HELP DOCTORAL STUDENT IDENTITY FORMATION THROUGH WRITING?

The increasingly more audited and output-focused context of doctoral education favours a 'mastery approach' (Barnacle and Dall'Alba, 2013) that threatens opportunities for play, creativity and experimentation in writing. This narrow framing is at odds with the benefits to be accrued from a writing-rich doctoral candidature, which maximizes learning through the provision of numerous writing opportunities. It is more important than ever before for institutions, supervisors and students themselves to resist the pressure to produce always-publication-ready, perfect doctoral writing. Reserving and promoting spaces for experimentation and learning through writing, where identity and meaning-making are valued, supported and scaffolded, is a central challenge in contemporary scholarship. This isn't a job for supervisors alone; however, there are many opportunities for supervisors to make a difference.

I have written elsewhere about how writing groups can be key sites for the development of identity construction (Aitchison, 2009, 2010; Aitchison and Lee, 2010). In these safe spaces, individuals can play with different personal and professional identities, assume different voices, experiment and practise, play to an audience and get feedback to alter, adjust and recalibrate identities within supportive and authentic communities. Writing groups also provide opportunities for novice writers to see how others wear different identities—the person you laugh and joke with in discussions of writing may adopt a serious tone as an author: that of the incisive, objective, even aloof scientist or the reflective practitioner, the social scientist.

In the close-up-and-personal space of student–supervisor relations, there are frequent writing-related pedagogical opportunities. For example, in one study (Aitchison, 2015), a supervisor described how he asked his students to respond explicitly to the provocation, 'Who are you?', when working on early-to-middle stages writing. Supervisors also revealed how timing and process can be critical influences on the development of an authentic student voice: 'It gets a little bit weird, knowing how far to edit somebody's work—when do you do it for them, and so on' (Aitchison, 2015: 9–10). This quotation reveals how identities change over exchanges on writing—supervisors may sometimes act as a critical friend or collaborator making few interferences in the text, but they may also adopt a gatekeeper role, strongly directing and correcting student writing. A healthy learning environment will foster a capacity to accommodate all of these roles and for them to be adapted for different kinds of student writing and purposes, and for difference stages of developing expertise.

There are many strategies that supervisors can initiate to bring rewarding and transformative writing experiences into doctoral scholarship. Kamler and Thomson (2014) provide many useful and detailed examples, as do Aitchison, Kamler and Lee (2010) and Carter and Laurs (2014), for example. Nevertheless, for this volume, I offer the following four principles and practices I believe especially useful for supporting Kamler and Thomson's (2006) 'textwork and identitywork'.

Build secure environments for risk-taking in writing

When students are given permission to write 'messy drafts,' they use writing for thinking and meaning-making. Requesting both messy and polished work, depending on the task, and actively discouraging student use of external editors, can be powerful practices for fostering identity formation. Supervisors can usefully model constructive supportive reviewing and feedback practices with their own students as well as facilitate such practices amongst their students; for example, in supportive collaborations between scholars of different strengths and stages of candidature.

Encourage exposure to other writers and writing

Students benefit from joining writing-related networks and communities beyond the supervisory space. Encourage students to participate in a wide variety of writing 'events' and networks, from locally delivered workshops to online global communities and activities. For example, AcWriMo, which stands for Academic Writing Month, is a wonderful global network of research writers who come together as an online, networked community each November. It is easy to recommend this to doctoral students who can simply join in at the PhD2Published website (www.phd2published.com/acwri-2/acbowrimo/about/). In these larger forums, students can practise their evolving identities with a degree of anonymity and independence while being connected to wider 'families' of doctoral scholars experiencing the same fears and successes.

Clarify expectations of writing early and throughout

Clarify supervisor expectations and ways of working with writing early on. For example:

- discuss students' writing-related strengths and needs;
- clarify submission and feedback arrangements—outline expectations regarding frequency, types of writing activities, size of submissions and turnaround times;
- work together to construct an annual and whole-of-candidature writing and publication schedule;
- explain expectations and approaches to writing for the public domain, covering issues such as authorship and ownership, quality of writing, integrity and editing.

Reject secrecy and competitiveness

Make writing processes open and transparent. Demystifying writing processes by engaging *with* students in the joy and pain of writing can help them. In addition, there is much to be gained by encouraging students to join or form writing groups where they can read and critique each other's work. Practices such as these demonstrate a valuing of the process of writing—not just the output. They also reassure students that they are not alone in their discomforts of self-doubt.

Chapter 28

Negotiating agency through authorial voice in thesis writing

Alet P. Olivier

SO, WHAT IS VOICE?

Authorial voice is often regarded as a mystical, fuzzy, elusive, slippery notion. Literature provides a cacophony of disparate definitions, conceptualizations, approaches and applications (Matsuda, 2001; Sperling et al., 2011; Yancey, 1994). To ensure a common understanding of voice, the following definition is offered: 'Voice is the amalgamative effect of the use of discursive and non-discursive features that language users choose, deliberately or otherwise, from socially available, yet ever changing repertoires' (Matsuda, 2001: 40). Voice is often still steeped in the emergence of Western individualism in the United States, and concomitantly, is associated with self-discovery and emphasis on self-expression in writing. Voice implies individualistic expressivist writing (Yeh, 2012), but is also dependent on the social context of writing. During the 21st century, a few major contributions have initiated the exponential growth of voice, advocating the importance of voice in academic discourse and investigating its role there (Hyland, 2004; Ivani , 1998; Prior, 2001).

One of the paradoxes of voice is that although it is widely used in discourse writing, there are few guidelines for applying voice in practice, perhaps because of the theoretical maze around it. A new awareness of a 'pedagogy' for voice is emerging, both theoretically and empirically: 'Research into voice in academic writing, while not extensive, is growing and is varied in a healthy way' (Tardy, 2012: 41). Empirical research valuing voice pedagogy validates this need: when their teachers 'empowered' them, students were able to develop a strong voice and 'transform this power' within their writing (Yeh, 2015: 205).

The 21st century needs a reconsideration of voice, addressing its complex and layered disposition in academic discourse. A continuum of approaches towards a voice pedagogy varies in terms of degrees of voice instruction.

One study advises that voice 'should be treated as a relatively minor concern' (Helms-Park and Stapleton, 2003: 256). Others, however, offer a cautiously optimistic approach (Ivani and Camps, 2001: 31), suggesting that 'critical awareness' could promote voice as a mechanism to 'help learners maintain control'. This could be realized through awakening, encouraging, sensitizing and prompting students to voice possibilities. On the next level is advice to actively facilitate, assist, help and guide writers in developing their authorial voice (Canagarajah, 2015; Guerin and Pickard, 2012). Further along the continuum, and providing a yet more forceful approach, supervisors/advisors can encourage agency and empower students to become critically voiced writers in negotiating levels of meaning making (Canagarajah, 2015; Yeh, 2012). Furthest along the continuum lies a very recent approach, suggesting that voice can actually be *taught* and *learned* like other text qualities (Burke, 2010; Canagarajah, 2015; Matsuda, 2015; Zhao and Llosa, 2008). Supervisors and advisors could choose any of these points on the continuum to match students' level of voice development. This chapter provides material that will allow supervisors and advisors to support their students' conscious development of voice.

IS VOICE JUST AN IMPORTANT PART OF OR A PREREQUISITE IN RESEARCH WRITING?

The reality that voice is a vital part of academic writing and is critical for membership of the academic discourse communities has been confirmed by research: '[A]ll writing has "voice" . . . [as] an integral aspect of self-representation in academic discourse' (Hyland, 2008b: 20). Developing an appropriate academic voice is a process that takes time, since the '[assertions] of authority in texts are not always obvious or transparent to novice writers' (Guerin and Picard, 2012: 37). Thus, voice should be addressed as a prerequisite of research writing.

DOES ACADEMIC WRITING AND FINDING VOICE COME NATURALLY?

While examples of individual 'diligence and brilliance' that can get writers a long way (Hyland, 2013: 69) do exist, the literature on academic writing is replete with the reality of writing as a site of struggle (e.g. Ivani , 1998; Wellington, 2010). Even at postgraduate level, research writing is often 'a formidable task' in which 'many doctoral students are left to struggle on their own rather than being carefully scaffolded to craft professional research writing' (Chang and Tsai, 2014: 525, 540). A scaffolding approach to writing instruction at doctoral level is recommended (Kamler and Thomson, 2006). Unfortunately, even at universities with dedicated writing centres, graduate students seem to receive little assistance in writing (Garbus, 2005: 172). Since an increasing number of students worldwide are undertaking postgraduate research (Wisker et al., 2003), institutions have started to realize the need to provide effective writing assistance. Recent publications have confirmed the importance of advanced writing development that addresses the need for postgraduate and doctoral writing assistance (e.g. Basturkmen, East and Bitchener, 2014; Cotterall, 2011; Guerin and Picard, 2012; Paltridge, 2003).

WHAT IS THE SUPERVISORY ROLE IN PROMOTING AGENCY IN DEVELOPING STUDENT VOICE?

Pedagogy is the science and art of teaching. The supervisory relationship is a pedagogical relationship (Basturkmen et al., 2014), and this also applies to developing voice. Embedded in any research supervisory relationship is the reciprocity of agency. The notion of 'agency' in a pedagogy for voice construction points to voice as having agentive features; supervisors and advisors can encourage agency and explore how students negotiate this agency (Canagarajah, 2015) to develop an '"agentive" voice' (Matsuda, 2015: 154).

The nature of promoting agency in voice, like the supervisory relationship and pedagogy overall, entails organic and exponential growth along a continuum, as discussed above. Supervisors aim to incrementally develop skills without restricting the development of voice through 'rigid rules' (Zhao and Llosa, 2008: 164), a fixed formula or attaining a predetermined level. They should aim to 'empower students to be critical and voiced writers in constructing their own meaning' (Burke, 2010: 313). In their instruction, supervisors/advisors need to raise students' awareness and sensitize them to recognize voice in prose, assist them to find good models, and promote and establish agency, thus empowering students to find their own voice.

DISCURSIVE (TEXTUAL) FEATURES OF VOICE BECOME TOOLS FOR WRITING WITH VOICE

I propose that voice can be viewed through two lenses: as individualized and as socialized. The individualized voice shows authorial stance, and is how writers present themselves and their opinions in the text. The socialized voice acknowledges the social context of writing in which academic writing is essentially an interaction between writers and readers. Further, the socialized voice has the intra-textual task of guiding readers through the text and organizing propositional content, and the inter-textual task of engaging with the voices of others from sources outside the text as well as engaging with the reader.

Find below two useful charts (Tables 28.1 and 28.2) describing these multiple functions of voice and linguistic features with examples to achieve them.

Although voice is a prerequisite in research writing, it is not acquired instantly, but develops along a continuum. A 21st-century approach to voice should go beyond expressivist writing to include writing as a social endeavour so that students are sensitized to the available choices and options

Table 28.1 Expanded table for individualized academic voice in research writing

Linguistic devices for individualized voice		
Individualized voice or stance: ways in which writers present them in the text to convey their judgements, opinions and commitments; a writer's unique and recognizable imprint associated with authorial presence in the text.		
Hedges	Writers stand back, allow an amount of vagueness about their personal attitude towards propositional content; withhold commitment and open dialogue; give a plausible interpretation rather than certainty	*Adverbs (and related adjectives)*: apparently, generally, essentially, perhaps, possibly, unlikely *Adjectives*: an apparent, a likely explanation . . . *Conjunctions*: but, however *Adverbial phrases*: to a certain extent, in general, in my view *Verbs*: appear, assume, suppose *Modal verbs*: can, could, may, might, must, ought, should, would (not)
Boosters/ emphatics	Writers intrude into their writing to stamp their personal authority/ voice onto their arguments; emphasize certainty or underline writers' conviction about their arguments; present their work with assurance	*Adverbs (and related adjectives)*: clearly, obviously, certainly, definitely, evidently, obviously *Interjections*: of course, indeed *Adverbial phrases*: without doubt, in fact, of course *Emphatic verb to be*: the truth of the matter is that *Verbs used in combination with personal pronoun I/we*: believe, find, know, prove, realize, think
Attitude markers	Writers take an affective attitude to propositions, conveying surprise, frustration, agreement, rather than commitment	*Adverbs and adjectives*: admittedly, appropriately, disappointingly, expectedly, fortunately, remarkably *Verbs*: agree, astonish, disagree, prefer, am/was . . . disappointed
Self-mentions	Writers project their explicit stance in relation to their arguments, discipline and readers	*Personal pronouns*: I, we *Possessive pronouns*: my, mine, our, ours

for voice development. While voice cannot be prescribed by predetermined formulas, it can and should be negotiated. Along a continuum of sensitization, facilitation, guidance and instruction, students' agency in advanced academic discourse can be enhanced by applying features of voice as tools and strategies. Examples of these tools, functioning as discursive features of both individualized and socialized voice, have been provided to assist supervisors and advisors. Their use may empower students to become critical and voiced writers who achieve the amalgamative effect of the multiple nuances of voice.

Table 28.2 Expanded table for socialized academic voice in research writing

Linguistic devices for socialized voice			
Socialized voice: associated with the disciplinary groups to which the writing and the writer are linked. As a result of the writers' choices from certain discourses, they align their work with particular texts and authors and engage with the reader.			
Linguistic devices for intra-textual voice			
These help to organize propositional content and guide the reader through the text.			
Logical/ discourse connectors	Express additive, causative and contrastive relations, rhetorically conveying the argument		*Conjunctions and adverbial phrases*: but, so, after all, therefore, furthermore, although, because, in other words, in comparison with, except for, due to, accordingly, on the other hand, consequently, similarly
Sequence/ frame markers	Refer to discourse goals; sequence, labels, predict stages and shift arguments		*Prepositions*: *sequencing*: in (chapter x), finally, first, first of all, firstly, last, lastly; listing (a,b,c) numbering (1,2,3), next, secondly, subsequently, following, finally *Label stages*: at this point/stage, in brief, in conclusion, in sum(mary), so/thus far *Topic shifts*: now, well, let us return, right, then . . .
Explanatory markers/ code glosses	Elaborate propositional meaning		Namely, as, like, for example, e.g., *viz*, such as, in other words, that is
Endophoric markers	Expressions referring to other parts of text		See (fig 1), in section/chapter, part 1, example X, Fig X, page X, Table X, below, later
Linguistic devices for inter-textual dialogic voice: communicating with sources outside the text			
Dialogistic alternatives: research writers cite other voices and acknowledge dialogistic alternatives. Research writing consists of multiple voices outside the text that create a dialogistic backdrop for the text. Supervisors and advisors should be vigilant for writing that falls short of an argument and voice. *Verbs pertain to 3rd person* (singular or plural).			
Disclaim: disclaim formulations reject, overrule and offer counter-arguments	Denial/negation: firm position of denial towards propositional content		*Used in combination with verbs*: no, never, do . . . not, does . . . not, cannot, will . . . not
	Counter: often used with denials to state counter position Concession: concede to a counter expectation		*Conjunctions used in combination with verbs*: sure, yet, but, still, however
Proclaim: formulations are contractive as	Concur	Affirm Concede	*Verbs*: X affirms, agrees, acknowledges

continued . . .

Table 28.2 Continued

they limit the scope of the dialogistic alternatives in different ways	Pronounce	*Verbs*: X concedes, admits *Verbs*: X contends, must agree that
	Endorse	*Verbs*: X shows, proves, admits, demonstrates
Probabilize: refers to alternative positions	Evidence	It seems that, it is possible
Entertain: recognizes proposition as part of the communicative context	Likelihood/ probability	*Modals*: will, must, may *Verbs*: X thinks, supposes
	Hearsay	*Verbs*: it is said that, understood that
Attribute: the writer's authorial voice engages with external voices, emphasizing dialogistic communication	Acknowledge	*Verbs*: X states, argues, believes, says, acknowledges, presents, according to
	Distance	*Verbs*: X claims, contends, alleges, attests

Linguistic devices for inter-textual dialogic voice: engagement with reader

Engagement: communicating and rhetorically positioning; interaction between the writer and the reader; co-construction of voice.

Reader pronouns	Explicitly communicating with reader; pertaining to 2nd-person pronouns to claim solidarity	Personal pronouns: you, your
Personal asides	Address readers directly, by commenting on an idea	Parentheses ——; brackets (often, it is true . . .); (this, by the way is . . .)
Directives/ relational markers	Instruct the reader to perform an action	Imperatives: consider, note, imagine, you can see that plus modals of obligation: must, should, ought
Questions	Rhetorical questions	Am I the only voice in the desert crying for the dire need of writing assistance to students?

Chapter 29

Cultural identity/researcher identity

Managing multiple positionings

Deborah Laurs, Lisa Chant, Susan Carter and 'Ema Wolfgramm-Foliaki

Cultural identity impacts on academic identity. When research students come from historically marginalized groups, supervisors have an additional task in ensuring they are supported through often difficult identity transitions. This can be hard, yet success fulfils some of the responsibilities of any tertiary institution: public benefit. And there are considerable rewards when cultural knowledges are applied to supervision, enabling supervisors to learn and develop their own understandings in the process of engaging with those of others.

Our case studies come from New Zealand Māori and Pasifika doctorates, but points demonstrated here are relevant for many cultures. Around the world there are many historically underrepresented groups who find it hard negotiating a western system and producing formal academic writing that demonstrates both an authentic voice and mastery of a set of generic expectations that seem alien. Scaffolding the development of new skills, while acknowledging prior knowledge, can be challenging. As doctoral supervisors and researchers from Anglo-European, Māori and Tongan backgrounds, we draw upon a funded research project (Carter et al., 2016) to suggest practical approaches that may help; in addition, we make the argument that there is interesting potential to make use of different worldviews when it comes to supporting the development of a research identity.

PROBLEM

There is little need to rehearse the social inadequacy of education when outcomes fail to fully represent all those within the community: unequal access to success calls for action (see a strong response in Smith, 1999).

Nor is there need to reiterate the difficulty of identity transition that the doctorate entails, given its requirement for perseverance in the face of the unknown (Lovitts, 2008) when constructing a new persona through research writing (Kamler and Thomson, 2006). These challenges are further nuanced by gender (Carter, Blumenstein and Cook, 2013), globalized experience (Ali and Kohun, 2007) and indigeneity (McKenzie, 2005). Thus, without arguing points we take as given, our case study exemplifies the fairly typical historic colonial inequity that plays out as an ongoing shortfall in Māori and Pasifika educational success in New Zealand.

New Zealand government statistics reveal the shortfall in doctoral success between Māori or Pasifika candidates and everyone else in the country. Our national foundation document, the Treaty of Waitangi, protects Māori sovereignty rights; that is, right to agency. Agency, however, is difficult to achieve without equal opportunities for success, and the New Zealand government has backed its rhetoric about achieving equity with targeted funding: 'Māori (and Pacific) doctoral completions have received an "equity weighting" which funds them at double the rate of non-Māori (or non-Pacific) completions' (McKinley et al., 2009: 2). Academics need to take the problem seriously.

The success gap has narrowed over the last decade (Carter et al., 2016), but there are still insufficient Māori PhD graduates and supervisors experienced in Māori research methods to cope with the increasing numbers of these students making it through to higher-degree study. Researchers into Māori and Pasifika experience highlight academia's nature as a political space (Grant, 2003; Jones, 1999; Middleton and McKinley, 2010; Smith, 1997, 2007) that comprises 'unresolved and competing demands between . . . disciplinary knowledge bases and indigenous knowledge' (Kidman et al., 2015: 14). Indigenous students can find themselves as outsiders on all fronts—regarded by their own people as outsiders because they are now academics, yet nonetheless not feeling as though they fully belong within the academic domain (Wolfgramm-Foliaki, 2016a). Supervisors sometimes need to support indigenous students in negotiating these tricky boundaries.

METHODS

As a team, we held two fora for doctoral students and supervisors (University of Auckland, 20 November, 2015; Victoria University of Wellington, 11 March, 2016). As part of the full-day programme (which also included workshops on building relationships and working with international students), a targeted *hui* (colloquium gathering) enabled participants to share their experiences around writing feedback for Māori and Pasifika candidates. Approximately 40 people took part, and two research assistants took notes. Here, we present the anecdotal advice from these sessions, further supported by the literature, the authors' personal experience and guidance from other cultural experts.

LITERATURE

Literature tends to emphasize the challenges for Māori and Pasifika research students, who typically have family commitments (McKinley et al., 2009, 2011) and financial difficulties (Theodore et al., 2016: 606). Theodore et al.'s (2016) study (n=626) shows that the majority of Māori graduates 'studied full-time . . . and were employed while studying. One third were parents (32.9%) and nearly half were first generation students (48.4%)'. Of these, 'females were more likely to be parents, to study extramurally, to work part time, and to have a long-term medical condition, impairment or disability' (2016: 609). Such factors are likely to mean that Māori and Pasifika doctorates take longer and require supervisory patience in acknowledging perseverance.

It is always wise to establish whether students are the first in their family to attend university. Such students may be unfamiliar with points that academics take for granted: ensuring these students are comfortable asking questions helps them fit in more readily (Wolfgramm-Foliaki, 2016b). Spell things out clearly: for example, which deadlines are negotiable and which will affect survival. Check that you both share the same understanding of what is required to complete the project and what needs to be done next at each stage. Then, as always, we suggest that it is good practice to encourage students to partake of other support provided by counselling and scholarship services, librarians, student learning advisors and peers: first-in-the-family students may need this support even more than most.

Supervisors can find it discomfiting to discover that Māori and Pasifika students inhabit a worldview different from their own (Engles-Schwarzpaul, 2015: 1250). When the research involves students' own communities, supervisors may suddenly find themselves in the role of learner, a learner with very little experience. In such cases, Engles-Schwarzpaul reminds us that:

- a supervisor is not, in the first instance, a purveyor of knowledge;
- postgraduate students already have substantial and refined pockets of knowledge to draw on; and
- [students] are able to activate networks of distributed knowledge, often outside of the University.

(Engles-Schwarzpaul, 2015: 1252)

It can be important for supervisors to set aside the need always to be expert when working across cultures, and to be willing to engage in learning alongside, or guided by, their students.

Such advice is borne out by the practical suggestions on supporting indigenous students from our research. We premise these findings on two cultural concepts. The first is the Māori notion of *whanaungatanga* (the complex, almost untranslatable, network of holistic 'family-like' connections that exist between oneself and others). The second is the Pasifika concept of *va*, which views the space between people—and between people and things—as a uniting, rather than a separating entity: alive and in need of maintenance.

When considering good practice for our priority groups, Māori and Pasifika, we felt that these indigenous concepts, with their emphasis on building and nurturing interpersonal connections, are probably of use in most supervisory relationships. We suggest that doctoral writing feedback works best when there is *whanaungatanga*—that is, respect and loyalty, on both sides—and when the differing roles and responsibilities within the supervisory relational space (*va*) are mutually acknowledged and maintained. Transparency around the best ways of working together—with supervisors and students spelling out their respective expectations, including what each knows and doesn't know—has merit for all supervisory relationships.

Regarding thesis production, students from indigenous cultures may often be more attuned to oral communication than to formal writing. Marking up manuscripts with feedback is helpful, but supervisors should also make time to discuss their comments with the student; such conversations are probably where the most progress with ideas will occur. It's often easier to simply tell students what to do, rather than lead them towards understanding by asking questions. Nonetheless, adopting a question-posing approach ensures that it is the students themselves doing the thinking and writing. Questions provide opportunities for students to draw upon their cultural knowledges and find an authentic voice. That autonomy is further advanced when supervisors consciously work around the power differential to promote a mutual, dialogic, learning relationship. The process becomes one of learning together.

Due respect for the student's wider network of family and elders is also important. Within Māori and Pasifika cultures, knowledge is held in common. Hence, even without direct community involvement, a Māori or Pasifika student is always operating in relation to a body of knowledge and experience that transcends their individuality. In fact, one PhD student argued that the elders who raised her speak through the words of her auto-ethnography (Baker, 2014). Supervisors need to be aware of, and acknowledge, the communal knowledge that colours their students' work, particularly if the research directly involves the community, and to assist students to accommodate these elements within the academic setting.

Indigenous students are often leaders within their communities and warrant respect for the roles they play outside academia. Showing students that you value them holistically, always beginning by asking about the non-academic aspects of their lives before moving to more formal supervisory matters, is another way of signalling respect. Likewise, sharing meals and encouraging students to be part of departmental seminars or celebrations can help indigenous students recognize that the university is also a community. Academia then can be seen as simply another form of *whanaungatanga* ('extended family'), with relational spaces (*va*) that need to be nurtured, just as within their cultural communities.

LIVED EXPERIENCE

If indigenous students choose to use culturally-based research frameworks, it may be necessary for supervisors to learn alongside them. Indigenous theories and methods (Denzin and Lincoln, 2008) have a growing place within the academy, adding to the existing body of western approaches. Often they invoke metaphors of creation that highlight co-construction of knowledge. Here, as an example, one of our research team, Lisa Chant, shares her experience as a Māori researcher:

> *Tukutuku* is a form of story-telling and knowledge transmission through the weaving of dried plant-based materials. I watched as my grandmother wove *tukutuku* wall panels, bringing the histories and knowledge of her people, Ngati Whatua and Ngati Wai, together with her knowledge and experiences as the wife and mother of Māori Anglican ministers. She wanted to create *tukutuku* for her son to use in delivering his Māori sermons to his community, and to give strength and support to Māori and non-Māori staff working with Māori patients and clients in a local community health and social services provider. When it comes time for my grandmother to join my grandfather, these panels will be part of the voice she leaves behind for us to cherish, and to use when teaching her great-grandchildren how to weave their own contributions into their community's spirit.
>
> Using the same *kaupapa* (principles) used by my grandmother—and my parents—I wove Māori research theories and methods throughout my PhD (Chant, 2013), in order to contribute, not only to global academic discourses, but also to indigenous epistemology, within the health sector. I sat with my PhD supervisors and advisors, Māori and non-Māori, all of whom had their own preferred research frameworks. I listened to and watched them engage with the *matauranga Māori* (knowledge) research frameworks that had evolved during my studies and involvement with the Māori community over the years. I witnessed their increasing engagement with Māori contributions to research frameworks, and saw how they wove that knowledge into their relationships, frameworks and knowledge-sharing within the academy. This has built my confidence to engage with and learn from other indigenous and non-indigenous peoples about how to weave their preferred research frameworks and cultural knowledge into research work we might do collaboratively in the future.

The incorporation of culturally-based knowledge systems for theoretical and methodological debate remains a contested space within western academic systems, mainly due to their limited exposure in peer-reviewed publications. However, awareness is growing. For instance, Linda Tuhiwai Smith's (1999) work on decolonizing research methodologies foregrounds Māori epistemologies within the academy, as does the use of Pasifika theoretical frameworks such as *tivaevae* (quilt-making) from the Cook Islands (Maua-Hodges, 2001, cited in Thaman, 2009: 5) and *kalakala* (garland-weaving) (Thaman 1993, 2003) from Tonga, as well as the Tongan data-gathering *talanoa* approach (Vaioleti, 2006). We have written in more detail about the evocative metaphors underpinning Pasifika pedagogical models (Carter et al., 2016). Elsewhere, Maggie Kovach (2010) situates indigenous methodologies within the academy from her perspective as part of the Plains Cree and Saulteaux peoples, and authors from multiple cultures contribute to Denzin and Lincoln's edited (2008) *Handbook of Critical and Indigenous Methodologies*, a work which students can cite to establish the credibility of their use of cultural frameworks.

Supervisors who are open to other ways of knowing by acknowledging their own lack of understanding both empower students and make it easier for them to express what they do not know about academia. The process can be seen as the trading of cultural expectations. It can also be useful for supervisors to develop their own support networks, developing a general pool of skills and knowledge about working with indigenous students. Doctoral supervision *always* requires a meeting of worlds, and a student and supervisor from different cultures need to negotiate each other's world-views with care and respect. This means being open to learning about other ways of knowing and researching; this means fostering *whanaungatanga*; this means acknowledging the student as learner *and* teacher, and as a member of their wider community (child/parent/sibling/partner); this means being aware of, and caring for, the complex interpersonal connections (*va*) that make up supervisory relational spaces. As western and indigenous supervisors, together we make the argument that getting to know the whole student—drawing on pedagogies, metaphors and mythologies from indigenous cultures—can enrich the supervisory repertoire for research writing support.

ACKNOWLEDGEMENTS

Funding from Ako Aotearoa (National Centre for Tertiary Teaching Excellence) Northern Hub for this project enabled the excellent support of John Wei as research assistant. University of Auckland summer research scholar (2015/2016) Daniel Badenhorst reviewed the literature on Māori and Pasifika pedagogies. We are indebted and grateful to Te Kawehau Hoskins, Georgina Stewart, Mera Penehira, Alison Jones, Tanya Samu, Matiu Ratima and Melanite Taumoefolau (Auckland) who gave advice and read drafts to help keep us on track, and to Teresia Teaiwa and Rawinia Higgins, who led the Wellington-based writing forum discussions. With sadness, we pay particular tribute to Teresia (1968-2017): inspirational poet, scholar and leader.

Chapter 30

The SISA matrix for feedback fostering doctoral students' creativity

Eva M. Brodin and B. Liezel Frick

Originality is a key expectation of doctoral work across the world (Association of American Universities, 1998; Australasian Qualifications Framework Advisory Board, 2007; Lovitts, 2005; New Zealand Qualifications Authority, 2001; United Kingdom Quality Assurance Agency for Higher Education, 2008); it underlies the notion of 'doctorateness' (as defined by Trafford and Leshem, 2009: 305). However, it is still too often described by supervisors as an 'I'll know it when I see it' phenomenon—which is not helpful for students trying to see what is expected of them at this level of study. This creates room for different interpretations of what constitutes original doctoral work between students, supervisors and examiners (Gelling and Rodríguez-Borrego, 2014). Due to implicit and varying understanding of originality, it is not self-evident how supervisors can provide feedback to support doctoral students' creative development.

Feedback is often used as a motivational strategy and behaviour modification tool in organizations (Ilgen, Fisher and Taylor, 1979), but little is known of its effect on creativity (Zhou, 1998), especially regarding doctoral education. Hence, this chapter introduces the SISA matrix that enables more than just text-based feedback. Our point of departure is that feedback is involved in all kinds of pedagogical interaction, whether it is oral or written, focused on ideas or actual manuscripts, and that it includes conscious or unconscious forms of feedback to students. *Every* pedagogical interaction is a kind of feedback to the doctoral student, sometimes beyond the supervisor's intention.

The SISA matrix is founded in research on creativity and feedback in general, as well as in our previous work on developing doctoral creativity. The matrix consists of four interrelated fields of reflective practice that aim at supporting doctoral students' creative development:

1 *Self-examination of the supervisor's own expectations* (connected to self-critical reflection);
2 *Identifying creativity together* (connected to conceptual reflection);
3 *Strengthening the students' authority* (connected to contextual reflection); and
4 *Alternating between steering and freedom* (connected to developmental reflection).

Although reflective supervisory practice is introduced in the SISA acronym order, the matrix is not sequential. Rather, the fields are actualized in an interactive way throughout the doctoral students' creative development. It should be noted that supervisory reflective practice not only supports students' learning, but has the potential to develop supervisory capacity.

SELF-EXAMINATION OF THE SUPERVISOR'S OWN EXPECTATIONS

One of the fundamental aspects of providing constructive writing feedback actually precedes the feedback process itself: supervisors' expectations of their students' ability. The supervisor's expectations should neither be too high nor too low, but appropriate to the student's capacity to make progress. Even though this might sound self-evident from an educational point of view, many studies have revealed problems in this regard (e.g. Babad, Inbar and Rosenthal, 1982; Reynolds, 2007; Turner, 2015).

When supervisor expectations are too high in relation to the student's capacity, this can lead to a doctoral journey of continual failures rather than incremental success. The potential for creative performance will decrease if the student starts to have serious doubts about his or her own capability, and hence loses motivation and self-efficacy (Bandura, 1997). According to Turner (2015), this scenario is not unusual with inexperienced supervisors. Because their own doctoral studies were a fairly smooth learning process, these novice supervisors initially expect the same level of competence from their doctoral students. However, when doctoral students cannot live up to supervisory expectation, both supervisor and student soon experience crisis in the doctoral thesis work. Turner's (2015) study points to the importance of having high, but *realistic*, expectations of the student's ability.

It is even worse when the supervisor has too low expectations of his or her doctoral student. According to a classic study by Rosenthal and Jacobson (1968), younger school children (irrespective of talent) perform better if their teachers expect them to attain good results, as in the *Pygmalion effect*. Babad, Inbar and Rosenthal (1982) verified that high-school students (irrespective of talent) perform worse if their teachers expect them to attain poor results, which is called the *Golem effect*. These effects arise because teachers approach their students differently, both implicitly and explicitly, depending on their expectations of students' capability (Brophy, 1983; Harris and Rosenthal, 1986). Similar results have also been found in higher education

(Feldman and Theiss, 1982; Reynolds, 2007) and in work organizations outside academia (Kierein and Gold, 2000). We suggest that doctoral education is no exception.

Thus, supervisors need to pay attention to their own expectations of their doctoral students' capability of creativity, for example, and critically ask themselves *why* they have these beliefs. This is especially important in cases where the doctoral student does not match the demographic norms in academia. For instance, the ideal of the autonomous scholar appears to disadvantage women (Johnson, Lee and Green, 2000) and international students (Manathunga, 2014). Furthermore, when international students (independently) seek contact for learning the social rules in the new culture, they run the risk of being discursively misconstrued as dependent (Goode, 2007). Supervisors need to avoid stereotyping students: if the supervisor expects a doctoral student to be less critical, creative or independent for some reason, these expectations will tinge the feedback provided, and hence the student will almost certainly not get the chance to actualize the full width of his or her creative potential. Accordingly, constructive feedback for enhancing doctoral students' creativity or any other ability relies upon a genuine and realistic belief in the student's capability.

IDENTIFYING CREATIVITY TOGETHER

Providing feedback on aspects with clear conventions of writing—such as referencing and formatting prescriptions—is far easier than commenting on aspects such as argumentation and the scientific merit of the work. Even more challenging are the more opaque elements of scholarly writing, particularly the notion of creativity. A first step in this direction is to grasp the concept of creativity at a theoretical level.

Researchers generally agree that creativity is associated with something considered original and valuable. Plucker, Beghetto and Dow (2004) define creativity as 'the interaction among *aptitude, process, and environment* by which an individual or group produces a *perceptible product* that is both *novel and useful* as defined within a *social context*' (2004: 90; emphasis in original). The creative doctoral thesis thus is assessed to be both novel and useful among the community of peers. Moreover, creative scholarly contributions are generally recognized for being genuinely *original* and *relevant* to the field, beyond cumulative knowledge production and replications (Bennich-Björkman, 1997). As such, originality is espoused within the contribution to knowledge a doctorate is expected to make (Baptista et al., 2015) and may manifest itself in the study design, the knowledge synthesis, the implications and/or the way in which the research is presented (Wellington, 2013). Although originality is expected across disciplines at the doctoral level, its manifestation may differ between disciplines (Lovitts, 2007). Therefore, a second step towards providing feedback for nurturing doctoral students' creative development is to discuss how the student's doctoral work involves original and contextually relevant elements.

Phillips and Pugh (2005: 62) have helpfully identified nine different ways in which doctoral originality may be demonstrated. These comprise:

1 empirical work not approached before;
2 novel syntheses;
3 conducting new interpretations of existing material;
4 conducting research in contexts where it has not been done before;
5 applying an existing technique in a new area;
6 providing new evidence to an existing issue;
7 doing cross-disciplinary research and using new methodologies;
8 looking at yet unexplored areas within a discipline; and
9 adding to knowledge in novel ways.

These possible areas of originality may be linked to students' ontological (how they position themselves as scholars), epistemological (negotiate their understanding of and contribution to a discipline), methodological (deal with methodological challenges), and axiological (integrate themselves into a disciplinary community) transformation from novice researchers to becoming scholarly experts (Frick, 2009, 2010). The most important point for fostering the student's creativity here is that these insights stem from *the student* in dialogue with the supervisor. Thus, the feedback should not take the form of directions, but rather the posing of questions such as, 'In what way do you think your work is original at the moment? Who might be interested in your work now? What else can you do to emphasize the creative components of your doctoral work?'

Since these questions might be difficult for doctoral students to answer, especially at the beginning of their studies, it might help students to study Murray's (2006) list of possible original contributions together and take the feedback discussion further from there:

- Do you say something that no one has said before?
- Are you writing down a new piece of information for the first time?
- Do you add to knowledge in a way that has not been done before?
- Do you synthesize things that have not been put together before?
- Are you making a new interpretation of someone else's material or ideas?
- Do you give a good exposition of someone else's idea?
- Are you testing existing knowledge in an original way?
- Are you doing something in this country that has only been done elsewhere?
- Are you doing empirical work that has not been done before?
- Are you taking an existing technique and applying it to a new area?
- Do you work across disciplines, using different methodologies?
- Do you look at topics that people in your discipline have not looked at?
- Are you building on an original piece of work?

(Adapted from Murray, 2006: 59)

Such questioning may establish a learning environment that nurtures doctoral student creativity through joint goal setting that could underpin feedback mechanisms. Shalley (1991) found that setting goals in terms of both creativity and productivity enhanced individual performance in both domains, even when different types of goals were set simultaneously. Thus, if supervisors provide feedback that enables doctoral students to set their own goals for creative engagement and productive progress, incremental transformation towards the development of creative expertise may be fostered.

STRENGTHENING THE STUDENTS' AUTHORITY

Doctoral creativity depends upon an authorial argument within a wider body of knowledge. Kamler and Thomson (2008) point out that the lack of an authorial voice is typical in weak thesis writing. For instance, novice doctoral writers tend to make summaries of everything they have read and done, rather than highlighting the most relevant aspects (Deng, 2012; Maher et al., 2014). Paré (2014: 24) explains that this is because 'students are suddenly expected to enter their disciplinary conversations; not only must they speak *like* us . . . but now they must speak *to* and *with* us'. The bulk of creativity research confirms that the relational aspect is essential in all creative knowledge production as it is finally the community of peers who assess whether the contribution is perceived as new and relevant to the field.

The thesis reveals how far the student has made the transition into his or her scholarly field, since each discipline has its own playground for how the scholarly text should move forward. It is not only a matter of what words are chosen, but also how the object is described (concretely or metaphorically), in what ways references are included in the text, who the potential reader is, as well as how the author is positioned within the text (Bazerman, 1981; Parry, 2007). For instance, in an analysis of doctoral theses, Parry (2007) found that the text in natural science aimed at *reporting knowledge* in a condensed form, whereas the text in the humanities rather aimed at *illuminating a certain knowledge perspective*. In the natural sciences, the author *provides evidence*, while the author in the humanities needs to *convince* the readers why his or her perspective contributes to knowledge. Parry's (2007) detailed analysis gives more on how the author voice differs between disciplines. Nevertheless, the doctoral student also needs to know about what should be included in and excluded from the thesis (Kamler and Thomson, 2008, 2014). Thus they must grasp and use appropriately the contextually conditioned expressive codes to find their creative voice.

We suggest, then, that text-based feedback to the doctoral student involves overt discussions about the disciplinary features of the thesis text, pointing out how and why. Doctoral students appreciate explicit discipline-specific advice on writing style (Parry, 2007).

ALTERNATING BETWEEN STEERING AND FREEDOM

At the heart of the SISA feedback matrix, the balance between steering and freedom is the most critical aspect of nurturing doctoral students' creativity.

Creativity thrives when individuals are allowed to break boundaries and choose their own path. However, too much freedom can also hamper doctoral students' creativity (Brodin and Avery, 2014) since they need to know the scholarly territory before they can creatively play within it. Thus, the supervisor has a pivotal role in alternating between steering and freedom through the feedback provided, keeping the student on the playground to play freely without being disqualified. There is no universal recipe for this balance: it depends on the individual student and usually changes over time. Some students need clear directions right from the start, while others prefer to be directed or guided later on in their learning process. In all cases, however, the goal is to make doctoral students become more independent over time, which is a prerequisite for their creative development (Lovitts, 2008).

According to Hattie and Timperley (2007: 86–87), effective feedback decreases the gap between current understanding/performance and a desirable goal. This appears when the following goal-directed questions are addressed: (1) Where am I going? (2) How am I doing? (3) Where to next? Furthermore, each of these feedback questions can work at four levels: *task level* (whether the task has been executed correctly or wrongly); *process level*, including the necessary cognitive processes for understanding/performing the task (e.g. critical and creative thinking); *self-regulation level* (developing the student's inner voice control); and *person level* (developing the student as a person). However, simple applause has turned out to be the least effective feedback for students' development as it 'contains little task-related information and is rarely converted into more engagement, commitment to the learning goals, enhanced self-efficacy, or understanding about the task' (Hattie and Timperley, 2007: 96).

Supervisor feedback forms a core formative component of all pedagogical interactions and operates at multiple levels. It plays a formative role in developing doctoral students' creativity. Zhou's (1998: 262–263) work on feedback valence and feedback style provides some clues as to how supervisors may alternate between steering and freedom through different feedback mechanisms that could be adapted:

- *Feedback valence* is the positive or negative outcome of the comparison between the individual's creative performance and situational criteria (in this case, the expectation of an original contribution to knowledge). Positive feedback valence notes that the student's performance was indeed creative; negative feedback valence that it was less creative than expected.
- *Competence feedback* is the information regarding the extent to which a student's ideas or solutions are considered to be creative relative to set normative criteria. Competence feedback may enhance creative performance by boosting students' intrinsic motivation.
- *Feedback style* refers to the manner in which competence feedback (both positive and negative) is provided, which can either be informational or controlling. Informational feedback is constructive, supportive and

informative, putting students in control of their own actions and behaviour. Such feedback is aimed at maintaining high levels of creative performance, or shifting the student towards becoming creative if they are not, by prompting self-determining actions in the creative process. Controlling feedback, on the other hand, emphasizes external criteria for creativity that the student is expected to meet—shifting the locus of control to an external reality rather than a self-determining one. Such feedback may inhibit when it lessens intrinsic motivation; steering feedback of this kind needs to be coupled with explaining the possible responses from the community of peers.

The combination of feedback valence and style provides students with information on where they are going, how they are doing, and where to proceed, and thus addresses task, process, and self-regulation levels of feedback, enabling their authority to develop.

The adaptation of Zhou's (1998) and Hattie and Timperley's (2007) frameworks presented here (Table 30.1) is useful as it does not rule out the possibility of alternative forms of feedback—not all feedback can necessarily be positive, and sometimes a more directive (or controlling) stance is required. It shows that feedback operates simultaneously at a variety of levels. It helps us to understand why certain forms of feedback would elicit more or less creative responses from students, and endorses our earlier point that feedback is entrenched in all pedagogical interactions. The supervisor would therefore need to change the feedback valence and feedback style based on the interplay between

- the individual student's abilities and existing level of competence (based on realistic expectations after a supervisor's self-examination of their own expectations);
- the requirements and complexity of the particular study (as jointly determined by the supervisor and student through conceptual reflection in identifying creativity);
- the student's level of authority as a researcher; and
- the stage of the study (where in later stages, students would be expected to require less steering, have more freedom, and provide more creative proof of their authority than in the earlier stages).

Zhou (1998) found that the ideal conditions for nurturing creativity are when positive, informational feedback is combined with high task autonomy. Such task autonomy is not always easy to achieve, especially at the onset of the doctoral study. The supervisory relationship is often an unequal one (Manathunga, 2007) where supervisors have significantly more epistemic, methodological and discipline-based power than the doctoral student, which makes it difficult for the student to claim autonomy and creative space agency. Though we have argued that both doctoral supervisors and students take part in negotiating their relationship, we also noted that supervisors often take the

Table 30.1 Feedback strategies and their effects on fostering creativity

Style \ *Valence*	*Negative*	*Positive*
Controlling	LOW CREATIVITY Feedback indicates that the student is not competent and does not meet imposed criteria (*task* level feedback). Student may leave feeling incompetent and controlled, with little intrinsic motivation to complete the task (*self-regulation* level feedback). This form of feedback elicits the least subsequent creativity from the recipient (*process* level feedback) from all different forms of feedback, and subsequently does not promote the development of student authority.	MODERATE CREATIVITY As creative performance is imposed by external forces in this form of feedback, the student may be deemed competent, but only on what was required. Thus, even though the student might feel affirmed initially at the *person* and *task* levels of feedback, there is little substantive evidence at the *process* and *self-regulation* levels of feedback, and subsequent creativity may be hampered, especially when the student is required to work independently.
Informational	MODERATE CREATIVITY Feedback points out that the *task* was not completed creatively as a result of the student's own lack of authority —thus a lack of *self-regulation*. The student may feel incompetent (*person* level feedback) and therefore not react creatively in subsequent tasks (*process* level feedback).	HIGH CREATIVITY Feedback declares the student competent (*task* level feedback) —thus capable of being creative —without external pressure aimed at a particular outcome. Student feels competent and self-determining (*person* level feedback), which leads to intrinsic motivation to be creative (*self-regulation* level feedback) in subsequent tasks (*process* level feedback).

Source: Adapted from Zhou (1998: 264) and Hattie and Timperley (2007).

lead in establishing this relationship that underpins the learning space (Frick, Brodin and Albertyn, 2014). Supervisors, however, have the responsibility to provide feedback that nurtures the development of expertise over time:

> If students' competence and personal growth are enhanced, their enculturation into the scholarly community through the recognition of their doctoral work may be facilitated. . . . If students are both competent and creative, it may facilitate their transformation into independent scholars.
>
> (Frick, Brodin and Albertyn, 2014: 261)

We argue that making a creative contribution is central to providing evidence of expertise, and that student creativity needs to be fostered to achieve this end. Pedagogies aimed at fostering doctoral student creativity need to take account of learning as a social process (Dawson, Tan and McWilliam, 2011), contrary to the traditional view of the doctoral candidate as an isolated individual immersed in a singular scholarly endeavour. In this chapter we agree with Hakkarainen (2013) that the human mind is capable of integrating collective activity and external influences in working towards making an original contribution. The SISA matrix introduced here highlights the importance of reflective feedback as part of pedagogical interaction, positioning both students and supervisors as active role players in knowledge construction. Active participation requires self-examination of their own expectations by supervisors, joint identification of creativity, the strengthening of students' authority, and alternating between steering and freedom as students progress towards becoming independent scholars with 'networked expertise' (Hakkarainen, 2013: 18). Supervisors who want to encourage creativity have to become boundary brokers, whose feedback helps students engage in relevant and diverse networks that enhance their awareness of what is distinct about their own work.

Chapter 31

Managing those haunting voices

A student and supervisor in dialogue

Tai Peseta and Sarah Barradell

FEEDBACK AS OPENING

While the individual student fittingly claims credit for authoring a thesis, the product itself might also be seen to represent the *effects* of the range of voices that a student is called on to assess, negotiate, and whip into shape. There are at least three discernible voices in play. First, there is the student's voice with its emerging authority fashioned through a process of intense anxiety, 'forged in fire' as Williams and Lee (1999) put it. Second, there is the supervisor's voice and its careful developmental view on the interactions between the research student, the thesis, the research community, and the bureaucratic requirements of the institution. And third, there are the demands of the disciplinary field(s) with particular mode(s) of constituting objects for inquiry, knowledge production, representation, and truth making.

For us (Sarah-student and Tai-supervisor), there have been at least two additional and significant socio-material contexts that insinuate themselves as voices on, and through, the thesis. One belongs to the pull of the profession—in this case, Physiotherapy—and its orientation to the clinical practice life-world of evidence-based patient care. The other is the intense pressure on doctoral students who are also academic staff to produce research outputs in line with the intensification of the accelerated academy (Vostal, 2016). These contexts offer up a strange and contradictory amalgam of voices that haunt and circulate throughout the journey for us both. Collectively, they manifest in very practical ways. For Sarah, there is a constant movement between her health science background in Physiotherapy and her desire to learn more about higher education as a social science; it manifests in her newfound attachment to experimenting with the textual representation of her research as a writerly and readerly endeavour (Brett, 1991); it reveals itself in the wrestling to be both faithful to, and analytical about, the lives of the participants who feature in her research. For Tai, the process of supervising a person, their research journey, and the production of a thesis must be attentive to constant—and sometimes—unpredictable transitions. It is never just the written thesis that is the object of feedback.

These voices contain a legacy and exert a presence that foreground the moving relation between identity, writing, and feedback. For Sarah, it has been important to identify and acknowledge those voices, to figure out how and when they matter to the PhD journey, the research, and the thesis, and to learn how and why to put them in their proper place. For Tai, there is a job of managing the dominance of any one voice, and offering pedagogies of challenge, fellowship, and feedback that do not seek to hurry Sarah out of those 'stuck places', but rather to encourage her in that liminal place of uncertainty and troublesomeness to be curious about writing's emergence and effects. Influenced in part by the growing literature on threshold concepts (Meyer and Land, 2006a, 2006b) and ways of thinking and practising (Entwistle, 2005), and because we both inhabit strong identities as teachers focused on student learning in different ways and for different reasons, the way we work together is mindful of how learning and identity formation are completely entangled in often unpredictable ways. It's not entirely a trouble-free space (Grant, 2008). Frustration, misunderstanding, and disappointment are in many ways inevitable effects of learning with, and from others, especially when the task involves the co-production of new knowledge bound by disciplinary and institutional conventions. And yet we have managed to negotiate together ways of attending to the delicate dance between identity formation and feedback, through a common focus on writing.

In the remainder of this chapter, we provide a glimpse into Sarah's portrayal of the voices that haunt her learning, how they linger and seep into folds and cracks of her evolving researcher identity. Tai then offers a response intended to describe the practices we have adopted that other students and supervisors might wish to try out together.

THE ASSORTMENT OF VOICES—SARAH

Voice 1: science and social science

I was a member of a reading study group before I started my doctorate. The group members were all interested in learning about higher education beyond the 'how to' of teaching. I was the most recent to join academia, coming from a clinical Physiotherapy background. One day we were asked to read three different papers and discuss which we liked best and were most effective. All these years later, I can still recall my observations of one paper in particular. It jarred with me strongly. I didn't understand the paper and this went beyond its content. The writing seemed flowery. There was a lot of theory. The author *sketched*, *explored*, *interpreted*, and *described*. The paper was written in the first person and the author laid bare both her struggles and hopes. It took me a long time to recognize what irked me that day. Where was the clearly stated research question that the paper would answer? Why was the author not *confirming*, *demonstrating*, or *concluding*? Where was the distance afforded by writing in the third person? These ideas about writing had been ingrained in me so much that a different writing style seemed less legitimate. When I started to write for my doctorate (on a topic sitting at the nexus of professional and educational practice), my own writing suffered from a set of assumptions that I had yet to acknowledge. My writing was clumsy and staid. I often presented arguments as absolutes. There was no sense of me in what I was producing. My writing was clinical, a testament to my scientifically-oriented past.

Voice 2: the reflexive researcher and the participants

My thesis is a heuristic phenomenologically-oriented inquiry. This has presented me with many challenges both as a researcher and a writer. The first is that the work is informed by an interpretative, not positivist, paradigm. The second is that writing is a form of analysis rather than 'writing up'. Third, it involves distinction between methodology and method where my own experiences are a crucial part of the discovery. It has taken considerable effort for me to find my own voice—what I want to say, what I have to offer the field—and have the confidence to learn different modes of expression. And this is before thinking about the voices of those who have participated in my study! When you write an ethics application, you explain how you will ensure that your participants' voices will be an accurate and trustworthy characterization. In my own methods draft, I note that I have written: 'Member verification processes also help to ensure that I am not misrepresenting statements or abusing the openings provided to me'. Sounds simple enough. But it is not necessarily straightforward when it comes to representing those voices in the eventual writing. I have recently finished writing small case accounts of all the participants from the first phase of my research. While they are written in the first person, I wrestled with that format for some time. Did it clash with any subsequent writing where I might use the first person from my own perspective? I spent a good 12-month period immersed in transcripts, and the accounts represent my analysis and interpretation of each person's experience. Each one has now been sent back to the participant for comment and this act brings with it more decisions. What if people disagree with what I have written? What sort of changes would I be willing to make? Whose research is it: mine, theirs, ours?

Voice 3: being readerly and being writerly

At high school and throughout my tertiary Physiotherapy studies, I was often praised for being a good writer. When I started my doctorate, I quickly learnt that I did not have the writing chops that I needed and wanted. One of my personal goals became to write better and to enjoy doing so. I wanted to write in both an imaginative and interesting manner, yet with substance and meaning. I sought to expand my vocabulary. I aimed for craftily constructed sentences. I started to read my work out loud to listen for repetition and awkwardness. In doing so, I hoped that journal editors would be more likely to send my work out for review, and reviewers would recommend my work for publication, and the audience would appreciate my work for what it said. I was hopeful that readers wouldn't be bored, but to be honest, when I thought about the response to my work, it was more from the perspective of the readership than the reader. It meant that my work was sometimes self-indulgent (i.e. too much of my story), overly fanciful at times (i.e. not clear and simple) and was often trying to do too many things that I thought important (i.e. meandering and not compelling), rather than paying attention to how my writing connected with, and aimed to affect, the reader.

ATTENDING TO THE STUDENT'S ASSORTMENT OF VOICES—TAI

The three tensions Sarah describes in her portrait of voices are likely to be recognized by other doctoral students. Sarah's focus on writing is writ large here in all sorts of intriguing ways: in her desire to be writerly and to be read by others as a capable and elegant writer; in writing about herself appropriately and in balance; in reacting to the writings of others; and in writing ethically and with care about the participants in her research. Sarah's writerly predicaments are also ones that I recognize as part of my research career.

Below, I share how we have negotiated our way through these writerly and identity provocations. This might provide possible strategies for supervisors and students in dialogue together, for supervisors learning from each other, and for students working in peer groups. In marking supervision as teaching as Connell did (1985), we make less of a distinction between 'this' or 'that' aspect of supervision being 'feedback'; rather, we see the supervision process itself as being caught up in a dynamic of feedback. Our practices together do not shirk the risks involved in learning, but they also take seriously the pleasures of education, and the identity transitions we encounter in managing the polyphony of voices around us. I flesh out four strategies below that are characteristic of our supervision:

1 Discuss the literature on research writing together

One thing we have come to appreciate together is the wealth of literature related to writing as part of doing a PhD, and as part of the labour of being an academic. These conversations enter our supervision exchanges regularly —on formal meeting agendas, in email when one of us locates a helpful resource, and over coffee when we catch up about other projects we are involved in together. In embedding this body of literature in my approach to supervision, my intention is twofold: it is to indicate to Sarah that she is not alone in her concerns about writing, but rather, in long historical company; and to learn how others have resolved (often temporarily) research writing challenges.

2 Read research as if you are engaging in dialogue with the writer

One telling difference between reading as a PhD student and reading as a supervisor is that I will probably know and have met many of the writers Sarah is encountering in her text for the first or second time. That knowledge about a writer (and their larger scholarly preoccupations) brings a raft of benefits that help a reader to contextualize the shape of an argument, and to see the research as an ongoing project of working through a set of complex ideas. Imagining the author in such a way can help students to see a person tussling with a set of ideas that are alive in the text, and that warrant inquiry and conversation.

3 Write to authors whose work you admire

There is a steady stream of researchers (in and out of our direct fields) whose writing we both admire. We understand that reaction to be educative. Examples of fine work deserve discussion, not only for content, but for how they work as pieces of persuasive writing. I often encourage Sarah to write to authors, to let them know their writing is being read, and to signal how it has offered a fresh insight into her own research. Part of receiving feedback, we think, is also being a generous and responsible giver of feedback too. It is one way for writers to get a 'feel' for the impact of their ideas beyond the communities they are travelling in.

4 Invite the student to identify what they are seeking feedback about in their own work

When Sarah produces writing intended for detailed discussion and feedback, what interests me first are her reflections on its qualities. I usually want to know what might be different from the last version; I want to know the aspects she feels most proud about; I want to know what still worries her about the piece; I want some insight into the questions she would like me to address specifically in my reading of it. This strategy means that I am able to access the piece of new writing, and Sarah's assessment of it, before we engage in discussion together. It provides me with knowledge of her thinking.

One variation we are experimenting with this year is the practice of group supervision. In our context, this involves three supervisors and six research students—with higher education research in common—coming together once a month for challenge, mutual feedback, and companionship. These communal meetings do not replace the dynamic of our one-to-one supervision, in part because the focus on writing and identity formation is particular to our entanglement. I suspect there are many supervisors also engaged in similar practices with variations here and there, working to develop students' sense of self as research writers.

Chapter 32

Thinking rhetorically

A pragmatic approach to texts

Anthony Paré

> . . . a work of rhetoric is pragmatic; it comes into existence for the sake of something beyond itself; it functions ultimately to produce action or change in the world; it performs some task.
>
> (Bitzer, 1968, 3–4)

As supervisors know, doctoral students often feel intimidated by the immensity of the dissertation. The relevant literature seems impossible to summarize and review; their data appear insufficient or uninteresting; and the need to speak with authority makes them feel like imposters. The dissertation, whether a monograph or a series of shorter manuscripts, represents the largest writing challenge students have faced, and they frequently have no systematic or deliberate method of approaching the task. Unfortunately, most of us have received little or no training as writing coaches, so we struggle to help our students, and our institutions rarely offer much support (Paré, 2011).

This chapter considers some of the ways in which a rhetorical perspective on writing can help doctoral students gain control of their dissertation project. For many, the word *rhetoric* has come to mean inflated or empty language—the stuff of political promises or advertising spiels—but it has an older meaning that lives on as a concern with certain key features of writing: the writer, the situation or context, the purpose of the text, the effect on readers, and of course the nature of the text itself. This older meaning continues to influence writing research and pedagogy through what is often referred to as the *new rhetoric*.

A new rhetorical perspective begins with the basic assumption that texts should *do* something, not just *say* something. They should have a strong intention to produce social action: to influence people's practices, attitudes, behaviours, and thinking. By encouraging students to adopt this pragmatic attitude and to identify the changes they wish to effect through their writing, supervisors can help students focus and direct their work. This chapter draws on rhetorical theory to raise critical questions about the dissertation, and offers concrete suggestions on how to help doctoral students answer those questions and join their disciplinary debates.

First, though, some clarification of what I mean by a rhetorical approach. Classical rhetoric was concerned with spoken language, and new rhetoric expands that focus. By using *discourse* here and elsewhere, I signal that broad inclusion, but my focus in the chapter is on the written dissertation. In its contemporary usage among writing researchers and teachers, *rhetoric* refers to any discourse used to influence the ideas or actions of others. This definition points to rhetoric's ubiquity. The fact is, we are *all* engaged in rhetoric, *all* the time.

As successful scholarly authors, supervisors are expert practitioners at the situation-specific rhetorical actions that constitute academia—that is, all the ways in which scholars use language to do their work. However, although we successfully perform these rhetorical practices, the challenge is to teach our students: we know how to do the writing, but we can't always talk about it. This chapter offers some theory and language to help in that task.

SITUATION AND EXIGENCE

The first key notions to consider are the *rhetorical situation* and the *exigence*. A situation is rhetorical when there is some problem or exigence that can be resolved by discourse. As a simple example, the situation becomes rhetorical when you have forgotten your watch and ask a friend what time it is. The problem is your need to know the time, and your question solicits a solution. Things become more complicated and formal, of course, when the activity grows in size and complexity and the audience grows in number and expectations, as it does with thesis writing.

Supervisors engage in many regulated rhetorical actions: proposals, reviews, grant applications, conference papers, articles, chapters, and so on. Doctoral students often produce term papers, comprehensive exams, research proposals, public defenses, and of course the dissertation itself. Each of these texts functions in a rhetorical situation by responding to some need or exigence, and each text has consequences, effects, outcomes; each text gets something done. Both supervisors and students need a clear sense of the situation, the exigence to which the dissertation responds, and the solutions it is meant to produce.

The bedrock exigence of all scholarly work, of course, is the need for new knowledge. We conduct and report research in order to add to a store of information, to change ways of acting or thinking, to introduce new perspectives—in short, to influence what and how we know about some phenomenon. In official documentation, the dissertation is often referred to as a 'significant', 'unique', or 'substantial' contribution to knowledge, and that alone can be a daunting expectation.

I have found that it helps students to think about their rhetorical situation as including an audience of their scholarly community, or some sub-set of that community, and an exigence or need within that community to which their dissertation will respond. Is it a gap in knowledge (the conventional motivation for research)? A limited perspective on some practice or belief within the community? A failure to consider theory or research from another tradition? To wrestle with this is to answer two key questions about one's research: So what? And, who cares? Students will gain a sense of direction if they can define and articulate the problem that their work will address, and they will have a more complete sense of the rhetorical situation if they know who shares their interest in the problem. In the end, their solution will only be as good as their understanding of the problem and the community that's interested in that problem.

To assist students in this analysis, I ask the following questions: what is the need or problem to which your work will respond? What are its consequences? For whom is it a problem? How will your research solve or lessen the problem? And because the gradual road to expertise often makes them forget the specialization of their topic, I ask students to explain the context and nature of their topic: in what area of human activity is this a problem? How could you help non-specialists see the importance of the topic? As an exercise, I frequently ask students to write as if they were addressing friends or family members or an audience of teenagers to explain their dissertation project. The non-specialist audience forces students to step back from the details of their work and to offer a broader picture.

A strong image of a readership helps students determine what should and should not be said, what arguments to anticipate, what is common knowledge, and how readers will likely respond. For some, attending conferences is a way to develop a sense of community, and I encourage students to go to smaller conferences and to join special interest groups, where identifying common concerns is easier.

But I also ask questions to make students think more carefully about their audience: will your readers be surprised, offended, challenged, or confirmed by your analysis of the problem you have identified? Will they find your analysis familiar or new? Will they agree with it and, if not, where are they likely to disagree? And I encourage them to become familiar with the journals that report on their areas of interest, because these will be the forums for their community. What topics are current? Whose work is cited? What methodologies seem preferred? Do the articles represent a conversation you would like to join?

In fact, joining students in their analysis of journal articles is one of the best ways for supervisors to lay bare the conventions of their disciplinary communities. All of the rhetorical elements introduced in this chapter, and far more, are at play in any given article, and a close reading with students will help them see these in action. An author's identification and definition of the problem is usually visible on the first page of articles, for example, as is a statement of purpose, as discussed below. Generally speaking, supervisors are members of the scholarly community which students wish to join, and can offer great help as cultural brokers by making explicit the values, beliefs, attitudes, histories, and controversies that shape our disciplines.

RHETORICAL PURPOSE: CONSIDERING THE EFFECT ON READERS

In academic writing, the author must either identify an exigence that members of the community recognize—a widely agreed-upon gap in disciplinary knowledge, for example—or provide a compelling argument for why their topic represents a pressing need. For scholarly texts to have credibility, they must speak to matters that others agree have importance and urgency. But once an exigence is identified or established, the author must also decide on the purpose or goal of their contribution. In my experience, doctoral students are often stuck with a rhetorical purpose that is the unfortunate legacy of too much schooling: to report *all* the knowledge there is on a topic.

The distinction between exigence and purpose is important. For example, a student's research might address a community's need to know more about the best method of teaching grammatical tense in English to speakers of other languages. Precisely how the student addresses that need—the specific goals she sets to influence her readers—remains hers to determine. A complete solution to the exigence is highly unlikely, but a rhetorical purpose that zeroes in on part of the problem or re-frames the problem is possible: for example, the student might test a variety of extant teaching approaches in order to narrow down the candidates for 'best method', or demonstrate that different approaches are required for different language groups, or set out to challenge the efficacy of the dominant approach, and so on.

To help students develop a sharper sense of their rhetorical purpose, I ask them to think (and write) about the effect they wish to have on readers: how they want readers to think or feel or act differently *after* they have read the dissertation. I point out that a complete reversal of position—'changing' someone's mind—is rare, and that more subtle effects are more realistic: encouraging readers to re-think their positions; seeding doubt about a widely-held view; proposing an alternative interpretation of a phenomenon; raising new questions about a theory or practice; advocating a new approach. Students sometimes think they need paradigm-shifting research, but a more modest and specific rhetorical purpose allows students to focus and direct their research questions, their methodologies, and their literature reviews.

Student writing often *reports* or *describes* or *tells*. To prompt a wider range of choices, I ask them to write detailed purpose statements drawing freely from a long list of the rhetorical actions that writing can perform, including: propose, argue, convince, summarize, amuse, direct, speculate, recommend, advise, illustrate, encourage, persuade, dissuade, influence, advocate, expose, counsel, endorse, question, demand, imagines, mediate, provoke, review, mediate, and so on. 'Argue' is one action that each thesis must perform.

It is well worth the student's and the supervisor's time to identify explicit, active goals—and to return to them often for revision.

Such explicit rhetorical goals can be set for chapters and other sub-sections of the dissertation, as well, and reviewed as the text grows and changes. A useful technique before students begin drafting, sometimes known as a *descriptive outline*, has students write a summary for the main sections of each dissertation chapter; for every section, the students describe (in writing) what the section will *say*—that is, what content it will have—and what the section will *do*—that is, how it will affect or influence the readers and advance the author's overall rhetorical purpose. And, as noted above, a review of journal articles or dissertations will often allow students to pinpoint an author's explicit statement of purpose and to identify the goals of the text's separate sections.

ETHOS: THE CHARACTER OF THE SPEAKER

When we write, we write as someone, and we write from some position. We are socially and self-identified in a wide variety of ways, of course, but in writing we are rhetorically identified as inquirers, advocates, sceptics, defenders, experts, and/or novices, and we write as members of theoretical camps, schools of thought, and methodological traditions. As others have noted (e.g., Thomson & Kamler, 2013), writing is identity work: we represent ourselves in and through our texts, and we signal our affiliations as well. The author is present in even the driest of scientific texts—making claims, agreeing with some researchers, refuting others, speculating, concluding, and otherwise positioning themselves in an ongoing disciplinary conversation. Bazerman (1988) nicely demonstrates this with a close rhetorical analysis of Crick and Watson's famous article on the structure of DNA. Thesis-writers citations and their approval or critique of others' research locates them in disciplinary debate, and the quality of their claims makes them sound confident, strident, cautious, boastful, or possibly even delusional. The rhetorical term for this is *ethos*—the character of the speaker—and developing it challenges students.

The transition from academic spectator to academic player is a fundamental identity transformation during the doctorate. After a lifetime as a student reporting other people's debates, doctoral students are expected to join the debate, to take a position, to signal affiliations, to question others' work, and to speak with the voice of authority. Anyone who has supervised a PhD student knows how daunting this can be. Feeling the need for certainty, but uneasy about the risk of exposure that textual presence brings, students sometimes resort to broad, unattributed claims ('Many people are dissatisfied with current . . .') or claims in the passive voice ('It is widely known that . . .'). Similarly, they either boost their own claims well past a point justified by their data ('This is irrefutable proof that . . .') or hedge them into insignificance to avoid sounding brash ('This might imply a possible trend . . .')—students thus troubled could consult Hyland (2004) for guidance on boosting and hedging.

Helping students find the right tone and tenor is a difficult and subtle task. Directing students to journal articles and exemplary dissertations, supervisors can ask: Does the author sound convincing? trustworthy? authoritative? boastful? combative? How has the author achieved that quality? What word choice and syntax show that they respect the authors they cite, or that they discount the work of others? Do they sound quarrelsome or belligerent, or is their voice collaborative and modest? And a key question: Do their claims seem warranted, or more forceful than their data justify? This sort of close textual analysis uncovers the presence and voice of the author throughout the text.

Dense sentence structure and multisyllabic words might be unavoidable at certain moments in scholarly writing, but the best academic prose is accessible and engaging. A simple trick here is to have students read their work out loud, preferably to a listener who can comment on their understanding of the text. But the very act of reading aloud should draw students' attention to overly-long sentences, dense sections, extended noun phrases, and multisyllabic words, or ponderous, pretentious prose.

BREAKING THE PROBLEM DOWN: THINKING RHETORICALLY FROM START TO FINISH

A student who sees the dissertation as a rhetorical task within a scholarly community, who can identify an exigence in need of solution in that community, and who can formulate a timely and focussed rhetorical purpose for the dissertation has a far better sense of direction or purpose. But that clarity of thought and action needs to be sustained over the long haul, from the early days of searching for a topic through the hard work of reading, research, writing, re-writing, and defending. Here, too, ideas from rhetoric can be helpful.

In the classical tradition, rhetoric was seen as having five canons or arts. They were *invention*, *arrangement*, *style*, *memorization*, and *delivery*. The logic in the sequence captures a movement from early thinking about a topic (invention) through to the provision of a finished product (delivery). In rhetoric's switch from oral to written texts, and the reduced concern with memorizing for oration, the first three of the canons were re-invented. One new version of the rhetorical canons was a three-stage model—pre-writing, writing, revision.

Although the model is rather simplistic and lock-step, writing clearly does evolve from the blank page to the finished text; overt awareness of progression will give more control over the work behind the emerging dissertation. Initially, to encourage invention, students should explore their topics by reading and talking about them, and by doing the sort of writing that promotes thinking and creativity. I ask students to keep a writer's notebook, in which they can jot ideas, try out arguments, define key terms, experiment with scholarly forms of expression, or just log their thinking process.

This is the stage at which students are finding their scholarly communities and their own interest niche. And they are also discovering the exigencies that motivate that community: the problems that spark rhetorical response in journals, books, conferences, and classrooms. To be helpful at this phase, supervisors can act as cultural brokers, helping students find their way in their new disciplinary world. This is a good time to be analyzing journals with students: identifying key thinkers and ideas in the community's debates, pointing out the exigencies that motivate research, and drawing students' attention to authors' statements of rhetorical purpose.

When students begin to write their dissertations, they need help with classical rhetoric's *arrangement*, which we might consider structure or organization. This is the point at which students need help formulating a realistic rhetorical purpose. The temptation for students after all the reading, thinking, and research they've done is to write about *everything* they know, and a sense of purpose allows then to determine what to select from all that knowledge, and how to use it to fulfill their goals. Constant attention at this stage to the student's imagined readers and rhetorical aspirations will help keep them on track. It will effectively teach them to be critically analytical.

And finally, revising before submission, concern with *style* becomes paramount. *Style* is not superficial, but related to the writer's character—the *ethos* of the text—and to the quality of the argument. Here, supervisors can help students find the appropriate tone and tenor. Do they sound trustworthy? Authoritative? Do they display the modesty that characterizes so much good scholarly prose, or are they cocky and aggressive? Are their claims in line with their data? Again, as representatives of the scholarly community, supervisors are in an ideal position to read as others will read, to imagine the community's response, and to help students understand that response.

The approach described in this chapter is fundamentally utilitarian. Although the word *rhetoric* might evoke high style oration, its deep roots and current applications are eminently practical. A rhetorical perspective on communication has existed for over 5,000 years for good reason: it works. It understands discourse as a way to act in and on the world, and it allows the writer to gain a strong sense of focus and direction. And, finally, it can assist supervisors in the important and difficult task of mentoring new colleagues.

ACKNOWLEDGEMENT

I would like to thank Dr. Dawn Allen for her invaluable help in the writing of this chapter.

* * *

Fostering identity development—things to do

- When proposed topics seem potentially disturbing in terms of a candidate's identity, discuss the risks, and how you will work together to mitigate them, early on.
- Be aware that non-traditional students may find identity transition traumatic—be open to alternative approaches (e.g. ways culturally different from your own).
- Take time to know the 'whole student', particularly, but not limited to, those from indigenous or other cultures: help them make a bridge between worlds by being open to culturally-based ways of knowing and expressing ideas alongside more traditional academic methodologies.
- Encourage experimentation with academic writing styles where appropriate (e.g. give permission to write messy drafts/use first person 'I' in early stages), followed by open conversation about disciplinary conventions vis-à-vis scope for personal voice.
- Establishing functioning peer writing groups is worth the effort in terms of assisting the candidate's growing pains through identity transition.
- Notice when your students are finding identity transition discombobulating, acknowledge their discomfort, and then talk about how such pain signals transitional growth and development.
- Encourage students to reflect on their own writing (what's working, what's not going so well), as a way to hone critical acumen and audience awareness.

Conclusion

Susan Carter and Deborah Laurs

This book intersects theory, practice, experience and literature in supporting research writing. Multiple perspectives and areas of expertise highlight different aspects of this multi-faceted practice. As Brookfield (2006: 1) notes, the 'multilayered complexity of teaching' activates '[p]assion, hope, doubt, fear, exhilaration, weariness, colleagueship, loneliness, glorious defeats, hollow victories, and, above all, the certainties of surprise and ambiguity'; supervision teaching upholds such a complex mixture of experience. We make the case that academics need heightened awareness of the complexity of research writing; they also need practical strategies to survive and thrive as pressure for increasing research supervision and timely completion squeezes more tightly.

Having launched with a litany of supervisor and student complaints, together with a review of literature highlighting the problematic nature of doctoral writing feedback and a dearth of guidance on how to do it well, we finish this compilation of voices from the field with our most important point: the potential for supervision of doctoral writing to be one of the richest academic experiences of all.

We admit that, because our original purpose was to inform the design of in-house workshops for academics (Susan) and for students (Deborah), we initially focused on identifying difficulties and tensions to address. Yet many survey respondents also highlighted positive elements: supervisors found the experience *'enjoyable'* (16 mentions), *'satisfying'* (11), *'pleasurable'* (7), and a *'joy'* (5) in and of itself. These sentiments were also shared by students, who characterized feedback as *'good'* (30 mentions), *'encouraging'* (19) and *'constructive'* (15), particularly when supervisors acknowledged the iterative nature of thesis writing and associated 'researcher-development' processes. In the words of one student, *'Knowing someone had my back, not just in terms of getting the thesis done, but also for my future career, was great.'* A supervisor aptly summed up the energizing possibilities of doctoral supervision: *'It's one-to-one teaching, which is the most satisfying form of pedagogy I know . . . I really like the intellectual spark.'* Our book, then, seeks to help supervisors fan students' intellectual sparks, offering practical strategies to enrich all aspects of the doctoral writing feedback relationship.

Bibliography

Adcroft, A. (2011) 'The mythology of feedback', *Higher Education Research and Development*, 30(4): 405–419.

Aitchison, C. (2009) 'Writing groups for doctoral education', *Studies in Higher Education*, 34(8): 905–916.

Aitchison, C. (2010) 'Learning together to publish: writing group pedagogies for doctoral publishing', in C. Aitchison, B. Kamler and A. Lee (eds) *Publishing Pedagogies for the Doctorate and Beyond*, London: Routledge, 83–100.

Aitchison, C. (2014) 'Learning from multiple voices: feedback and authority in doctoral writing groups', in C. Aitchison and C. Guerin (eds) *Writing Groups for Doctoral Education and Beyond: Innovations in Practice and Theory*, London: Routledge, 51–64.

Aitchison, C. (2015) 'Writing the practice/practise the writing: writing challenges and pedagogies for creative practice supervisors and researchers', *Educational Philosophy and Theory: Incorporating ACCESS*. Online: doi: 10.1080/00131857.2015.1035629

Aitchison, C. (2017) 'Research writing: purposes, practices and pedagogies in contemporary times', in M. Fourie-Malherbe, R. Albertyn, C. Aitchison and E. Bitzer (eds) *Postgraduate Supervision in the Knowledge Society: Possibilities and Futures*, Stellenbosch, South Africa: SUN MeDIA Publishers, 33–49.

Aitchison, C. and Guerin, C. (2014) *Writing Groups for Doctoral Education and Beyond: Innovations in Theory and Practice*. London: Routledge.

Aitchison, C. and Lee, A. (2006) 'Research writing: problems and pedagogies', *Teaching in Higher Education*, 11(3): 265–278.

Aitchison, C. and Lee, A. (2010) 'Writing in, writing out: doctoral writing as peer work', in M. Walker and P. Thomson (eds) *The Routledge Doctoral Supervisor's Companion: Supporting Effective Research in Education and the Social Sciences*, London: Routledge, 260–269.

Aitchison, C. and Mowbray, S. (2015) 'Doctoral writing markets: exploring the grey zone', in T. Bretag (ed.) *Handbook of Academic Integrity*, Singapore: Springer, 287–301.

Aitchison, C. and Paré, A. (2012) 'Writing as craft and practice in the doctoral curriculum', in A. Lee and R. Danby (eds) *Reshaping Doctoral Education: International Approaches and Pedagogies*, London: Routledge, 12–25.

Aitchison, C., Catterall, J., Ross, P.L. and Burgin, S. (2012) ' "Tough love and tears": learning doctoral writing in the sciences', *Higher Education Research Development*, 31(4): 435–447.

Aitchison, C., Kamler, B. and Lee, A. (eds) (2010) *Publishing Pedagogies for the Doctorate and Beyond*. London: Routledge.

Ali, A. and Kohun, F. (2007) 'Dealing with social isolation to minimize doctoral attrition: a four stage framework', *International Journal of Doctoral Studies*, 2(1): 33–49.

Allan, C. (2011) 'Exploring the experience of ten Australian honours students', *Higher Education Research Development*, 30(4): 421–433.

American Psychological Association (APA) (2012) *Ethical Principles of Psychologists and Code of Conduct, Standard 8.* Online: www.apa.org/ethics/code/index.aspx

Anderson, C., Day, K. and McLaughlin, P. (2006) 'Mastering the dissertation: lecturers' representations of the purposes and processes of Master's level dissertation supervision', *Studies in Higher Education*, 31(2): 149–168.

Anderson, J., Huggins, V. and Winfield, L. (2015) 'Exploring the experience and support needs of part-time Masters' students', in P. Kneale (ed.) *Masters Level Teaching, Learning and Assessment*, London: Palgrave, 43–53.

Andrews, R. (1995). *Teaching and Learning Argument*. London and New York: Cassell.

Archer, L. (2008) 'Younger academics' constructions of "authenticity", "success" and "professional identity"', *Studies in Higher Education*, 33(4): 385–403.

Aspland, T. and O'Donoghue, T. (1994) 'Quality in supervising overseas students?', in Y. Ryan (ed.) *Quality in Postgraduate Education*, London: Kogan, 59–76.

Association of American Universities (1998). *Committee on Graduate Education Report and Recommendations*. Washington, DC: AAU.

Austin, A.E. (2002) 'Creating a bridge to the future: preparing new faculty to face changing expectations in a shifting context', *The Review of Higher Education*, 26(2): 119–144.

Australasian Qualifications Framework Advisory Board (2007) *Australasian Qualifications Framework Implementation Handbook*. 4th edn, Carlton, Victoria: Impact Printing.

Babad, E.Y., Inbar, J. and Rosenthal, R. (1982) 'Pygmalion, Galatea, and the Golem: investigations of biased and unbiased teachers', *Journal of Educational Psychology*, 74(4): 459–474.

Badenhorst, C. and Guerin, C. (2016) *Research Literacies and Writing Pedagogies for Masters and Doctoral Writers*. Leiden: Brill Publishing.

Baker, M. (2014) 'He Ariaiatanga Whakangawari no te Maori: He Rangimarietanga i Tua o Te Arai: A theory of Maori palliation: A peaceful journey through the Veil' (Unpublished PhD thesis, University of Auckland, Auckland, New Zealand). Online: https://researchspace.auckland.ac.nz/handle/2292/21507

Bamberg, B. (1983) 'What makes a text coherent?' *College Composition and Communication*, 34(4): 417–429.

Bandura, A. (1997) *Self-Efficacy: The Exercise of Control*. New York: Freeman.

Baptista, A., Frick, B.L., Holley, K., Remmik, M., Tesch, J. and Åkerlind, G. (2015) 'The doctorate as an original contribution to knowledge: considering relationships between originality, creativity, and innovation', *Frontline Learning Research*, 3(3): n.p.

Barnacle, R. and Dall'Alba, G. (2013) 'Beyond skills: embodying writerly practices through the doctorate', *Studies in Higher Education*, 39(7): 1139–1149.

Barrett, E. (2007) 'Foucault's "what is an author": towards a critical discourse of practice as research', in E. Barrett and B. Bolt (eds) *Practice as Research: Approaches to Creative Arts Enquiry*, London: I.B. Tauris & Co., 135–146.

Barrett, E. and Bolt, B. (eds) (2007). *Practice as Research: Approaches to Creative Arts Enquiry*. London: I.B.Tauris & Co.

Barton, E. (1993) 'Evidentials, argumentation, and epistemological stance', *College English*, 55(7): 745–769.

Basturkmen, H. and von Randow, J. (2014) 'Guiding the reader (or not) to re-create coherence: observations on postgraduate student writing in an academic argumentative writing task', *Journal of English for Academic Purposes*, 16: 14–22.

Basturkmen, H., East, M. and Bitchener, J. (2014) 'Supervisors' on-script feedback comments on drafts of dissertations: socialising students into the academic discourse community', *Teaching in Higher Education*, 19(4): 432–445.

Bazerman, C. (1981) 'What written knowledge does: three examples of academic discourse', *Philosophy of the Social Sciences*, 11(3): 361–387.

Bazerman, C. (1988) *Shaping Written Knowledge: The Genre and Activity of the Experimental Article in Science*. Madison, WI: University of Wisconsin Press.

Benesch, S. (2000) *Critical English for Academic Purposes: Theory, Politics and Practice*. Mahwah, NJ: Lawrence Erlbaum.

Bennich-Björkman, L. (1997) *Organising Innovative Research: The Inner Life of University Departments*. Oxford: Pergamon IAU Press.

Berkenkotter, C. and Huckin, T.N. (1998) *Genre Knowledge in Disciplinary Communication: Cognition, Culture, Power*. Hillsdale, NJ: Lawrence Erlbaum.

Bhabha, H. (1994) *The Location of Culture*. London: Routledge, 85–92.

Biber, D. and Barbieri, F. (2007) 'Lexical bundles in university spoken and written registers', *English for Specific Purposes*, 26(3): 263–286.

Biggs, M. and Büchler, D. (2009) 'Supervision in an alternative paradigm', *TEXT: The Journal of Writers and Writing Courses*, 13(2). Online: www.textjournal.com.au/speciss/issue6/Biggs&Buchler.pdf

Bitchener, J. (2010) *Writing an Applied Linguistics Thesis or Dissertation: A Guide to Presenting Empirical Research*. Houndsmill, UK: Palgrave Macmillan.

Bitchener, J. (2012) 'The potential of written corrective feedback for SLA', *Journal of Second Language Writing*, 21(4): 348–363.

Bitchener, J. (2013) *A Guide to Supervising Non-Native English Writers of Theses and Dissertations: Focusing on the Writing Process*. New York: Routledge.

Bitchener, J. and Basturkmen, H. (2006) 'Perceptions of the difficulties of postgraduate L2 thesis students writing the discussion section', *Journal of English for Academic Purposes*, 5(1), 4–18.

Bitchener, J. and East, M. (2014) 'Feedback practices and motivations of applied linguistics thesis supervisors in New Zealand and Australian universities', paper presented at the 17th World Congress of Applied Linguistics: One World, Many Languages, Brisbane, 10–15 August.

Bitchener, J. and Ferris, D. (2012) *Written Corrective Feedback in Second Language Acquisition and Writing*. New York: Routledge.

Bitchener, J. and Storch, N. (2016) *Written Corrective Feedback for L2 Development* (Vol. 96). Bristol, UK: Multilingual Matters.

Bitchener, J., Basturkmen, H. and East, M. (2010) 'The focus of supervisor written feedback to thesis/dissertation students', *International Journal of English Studies*, 10(2): 79–97.

Bitchener, J., Basturkmen, H., East, M. and Meyer, H. (2011) *Best Practice in Supervisor Feedback to Thesis Students*. Online: https://akoaotearoa.ac.nz/best-practice-supervisor-feedback

Bitzer, L. (1968) 'The rhetorical situation', *Philosophy and Rhetoric*, 1, 1-14

Black, P., Harrison, C., Lee. C., Wiliam, D. and Marshall, B. (2002) *Working Inside the Black Box: Assessment for Learning in the Classroom*. London: King's College London.

Boice, R. (1990) *Professors as Writers*. Stillwater, OK: New Forums.

Bolker, J. (1998) *Writing Your Dissertation in Fifteen Minutes a Day: A Guide to Starting, Revising, and Finishing Your Doctoral Thesis*. 1st edn, New York: H. Holt.

Bolt, B. (2014) 'Beyond solipsism in artistic research: the artwork and the work of art', in E. Barrett and B. Bolt (eds) *Material Inventions: Applying Creative Arts Research*, London: I.B. Tauris, 22–37.

Boote, D.N. and Beile, P. (2005) 'Scholars before researchers: on the centrality of the dissertation literature review in research preparation', *Educational Researcher*, 34(6): 3–15.

Boud, D. and Lee, A. (2009) *Changing Practices of Doctoral Education*. London: Routledge.

Boud, D. and Molloy, E. (2013) *Feedback in Higher and Professional Education: Understanding It and Doing It Well*. London: Routledge.

Boulter, C. and Denicolo, P. (2002) 'Assessing the PhD: a constructive view of criteria', paper presented at the UK Council for Graduate Education Symposium on Research Degree Examining, London.

Bourke, S., Hattie, J. and Anderson, L. (2004) 'Predicting examiner recommendations on PhD theses', *International Journal of Educational Research*, 27(4): 178–194.

Braine, G. (2002) 'Academic literacy and the nonnative speaker graduate student', *Journal of English for Academic Purposes*, 1(1): 59–68.

Brett, J. (1991) 'The bureaucratization of writing: why so few academics are public intellectuals', *Meanjin*, 50(4): 513–522.

Brodin, E.M. and Avery, H. (2014) 'Conditions for scholarly creativity in interdisciplinary doctoral education through an Aristotelian lens', in E. Shiu (ed.) *Creativity Research: An Inter-Disciplinary and Multi-Disciplinary Research Handbook*, London: Routledge, 273–294.

Brookfield, S.D. (2006) *The Skillful Teacher: On Technique, Trust, and Responsiveness in the Classroom*. 2nd edn, San Francisco, CA: Jossey-Bass.

Brophy, J.E. (1983) 'Research on the self-fulfilling prophecy and teacher expectations', *Journal of Educational Psychology*, 75(5): 631–661.

Buissink-Smith, N., Hart, S. and van der Meer, J. (2013) ' "There are other people out there!": successful postgraduate peer groups and research communities at a New Zealand university', *Higher Education Research and Development*, 32(5): 695–705.

Burchfield, R.W. (ed.) (1996) *Fowler's Modern English Usage*. Oxford: Clarendon Press.

Burke, S.B. (2010) 'The construction of writer identity in the academic writing of Korean ESL students: A qualitative study of six Korean students in the U.S.' (Unpublished PhD thesis, Department of English, Indiana University of Pennsylvania, USA). Online: http://search.proquest.com/docview/839877923?pq-origsite=gscholar

Butt, M. (2013) 'One I made earlier: on the PhD by publication', *TEXT: The Journal of Writers and Writing Courses*, 17(2). Online: www.textjournal.com.au/speciss/issue22/Butt.pdf

Cadman, K. (1997) 'Thesis writing for international students: a question of identity', *English for Specific Purposes*, 16(1): 3–14.

Caffarella, R.S. and Barnett, B.G. (2000) 'Teaching doctoral students to become scholarly writers: the importance of giving and receiving critiques', *Studies in Higher Education*, 25(1): 39–52.

Can, G. and Walker, A. (2011) 'A model for doctoral students' perceptions and attitudes toward written feedback for academic writing', *Research in Higher Education*, 52(5): 508–536.

Canagarajah, A.S. (2015) ' "Blessed in my own way": pedagogical affordances for dialogical voice construction in multilingual student writing', *Journal of Second Language Writing*, 27: 122–139.

Carrigan, M. (2015, 7 April) 'Life in the accelerated academy: anxiety thrives, demands intensify and metrics hold the tangled web together', *Impact of Social*

Sciences Blog. Online: http://blogs.lse.ac.uk/impactofsocialsciences/2015/04/07/life-in-the-accelerated-academy-carrigan/

Carson, E. (2007) 'Helping candidates manage their candidacy', in C. Denholm and T. Evans (eds) *Supervising Doctorates Downunder: Keys to Effective Supervision in Australia and New Zealand*, Camberwell, Victoria: ACER Press, 54–61.

Carter, S. (2008) 'Examining the doctoral thesis: a discussion', *Innovations in Education and Teaching International*, 45(4): 365–374.

Carter, S. (2011) 'Doctorate as genre: supporting thesis writing across campus', *Higher Education Research Development*, 30(6): 725–736.

Carter, S. (2015, 27 November) 'The literature review for beginners: writing while still uncertain', *DoctoralWriting SIG* blog. Online: https://doctoralwriting.wordpress.com/2015/11/27/the-literature-review-for-beginners-writing-while-still-uncertain/

Carter, S. and Kumar, V.M. (2016) '"Ignoring me is part of learning": supervisory feedback on doctoral writing', *Innovations in Education and Teaching International*, 54(1): 68–75. Online: www.tandfonline.com/doi/full/10.1080/14703297.2015.1123104

Carter, S. and Laurs, D.E. (eds) (2014) *Developing Generic Support for Doctoral Students: Practice and Pedagogy*. London and New York: Routledge.

Carter, S. and Laurs, D., with Chant, L., Higgins, R., Martin, J., Teaiwa, T. and Wolfgramm-Foliaki, 'E. (2016) *Giving Feedback on Doctoral Writing: A Guide for Supervisors and Advisors*. Wellington, NZ: Ako Aotearoa. Online: https://akoaotearoa.ac.nz/doctoral-writing-feedback

Carter, S. and Pitcher, R. (2010) 'Extended metaphors for pedagogy: using sameness and difference', *Teaching in Higher Education*, 15(5): 579–589.

Carter, S., Blumenstein M. and Cook, C. (2013) 'Different for women?: the challenges of doctoral study', *Teaching in Higher Education*, 18(4): 339–351.

Carter, S., Kelly, F. and Brailsford, I. (2012) *Structuring Your Research Thesis*. Houndmills, Basingstoke, UK: Palgrave MacMillan.

Carter, S., Kensington-Miller, B. and Courtney, M. (2017) 'Supervision seminars and discipline difference: academic developer blind spots to supervisor learning', *Journal of Applied Academic Practice*.

Cayley, R. (2011, 9 February) 'Reverse outlines', *Explorations of Style: A Blog about Academic Writing*. Online: https://explorationsofstyle.com/2011/02/09/reverse-outlines/

Cayley, R. (2013, 22 August) 'Social media and expertise', *Explorations of Style: A Blog about Academic Writing*. Online: http://explorationsofstyle.com/2013/08/22/social-media-and-expertise/

Cayley, R. (2013, 18 December) 'Confronting the anxiety of academic writing', *Explorations of Style: A Blog about Academic Writing*. Online: https://explorationsofstyle.com/2013/12/18/confronting-the-anxiety-of-academic-writing/

Cayley, R. (2014, 18 December) 'The craft of revision', *Explorations of Style: A Blog about Academic Writing*. Online: https://explorationsofstyle.com/2014/12/18/the-craft-of-revision/

Cayley, R. (2017, 31 January) 'Metadiscourse', *Explorations of Style: A Blog about Academic Writing*. Online: https://explorationsofstyle.com/2017/01/31/metadiscourse/

Chang, P. and Tsai, C.C. (2014) 'EFL doctoral students' conceptions of authorial stance in academic knowledge claims and the tie to epistemic beliefs', *Teaching in Higher Education*, 19(5): 525–542.

Chanock, K. (2007) 'What academic language and learning advisers bring to the scholarship of teaching and learning: problems and possibilities for dialogue with the disciplines', *Higher Education Research and Development*, 26(3): 269–280.

Chant, L. (2013) 'Hauora Kotahitanga. Maori health experiences as models for co-operative co-existence between Indigenous and non-Indigenous peoples' (Unpublished PhD thesis, University of Auckland, Auckland, New Zealand). Online: http://hdl.handle.net/2292/20440

Cirillo, F. (n.d.) *The Pomodoro Technique*. Online: http://pomodorotechnique.com/get-started/

Computing Research and Education Association of Australasia (CORE) (1999) *Guidelines on Research Practice in Computer Science*. Online: www.core.edu.au/code-of-conduct

Connell, R.W. (1985) 'How to supervise a PhD', *Vestes*, 2: 428–431.

Conrad, L. (2007) 'Developing the intellectual and emotional climate for candidates', in C. Denholm and T. Evans (eds) *Supervising Doctorates Downunder: Keys to Effective Supervision in Australia and New Zealand*, Camberwell, Victoria: ACER Press, 36–44.

Cooley, L. and Lewkowicz, J. (1997) 'Developing awareness of the rhetorical and linguistic conventions of writing a thesis in English: addressing the needs of ESL/EFL postgraduate students', in A. Duszak (ed.) *Culture and Styles of Academic Discourse*, Berlin: Mouton de Gruyter, 113–140.

Cornelius, S. and Nicol, S. (2016) 'Understanding the needs of Masters dissertation supervisors: supporting students in professional contexts', *Journal of Perspectives on Applied Academic Practice*, 4(1): 2–12.

Cortes, V. (2004) 'Lexical bundles in published and student disciplinary writing: examples from history and biology', *English for Specific Purposes*, 23(4): 397–423.

Cotterall, S. (2011) 'Doctoral students writing: where's the pedagogy?', *Teaching in Higher Education*, 16(4): 413–425.

Cotterall, S. (2013) 'More than just a brain: emotions and the doctoral experience', *Higher Education Research and Development*, 32(2): 174–187.

Cotterall, S. (2014) 'The mythical community of practice', in S. Carter and D. Laurs (eds) *Developing Generic Support for Doctoral Students: Practice and Pedagogy*, London and New York, Routledge, 75–77.

Currie, P. (1998) 'Staying out of trouble: apparent plagiarism and academic survival', *Journal of Second Language Writing*, 7(1): 1–18.

Dawson, S., Tan, J.P.L. and McWilliam, E. (2011) 'Measuring creative potential: using social network analysis to monitor learners' creative capacity', *Australasian Journal of Educational Technology*, 27(6): 924–942.

D'Cruz, H. and Jones, M. (2014) *Social Work Research in Practice*. 2nd edn, London: Sage.

Delamont, S., Atkinson, P. and Parry, O. (2004) *Supervising the Doctorate*. Maidenhead, UK: Open University Press.

Deng, L. (2012) 'Academic identity construction in writing the discussion and conclusion section of L2 theses: case studies of Chinese social science doctoral students', *Chinese Journal of Applied Linguistics*, 35(3): 301–323.

Denholm, C. and Evans, T. (eds) (2007). *Supervising Doctorates Downunder: Keys to Effective Supervision in Australia and New Zealand*. Camberwell, Victoria: ACER Press.

Denicolo, P. (2003) 'Assessing the PhD: a constructive view of criteria', *Quality Assurance in Education*, 11(2): 84–91.

Denicolo, P. (2004) 'Criteria for assessing the written thesis in Social Science', in P. Tinkler and C. Jackson (eds) *The Doctoral Examination Process: A Handbook for*

Students, Examiners and Supervisors. Buckingham, UK: Open University Press, 114–116.

Denzin, N.K. and Lincoln, Y.S. (2008) *Strategies of Qualitative Inquiry*. Thousand Oaks, CA: Sage

Dong, Y. (1998) 'Non-native graduate students' thesis/dissertation writing in science: self reports by students and their advisors from two UD institutions', *English for Specific Purposes*, 17(4): 369–390.

Downes, S. (2012) 'Connectivism and connective knowledge: Essays on meaning and learning networks', *Stephen Downes Web* http://online.upaep.mx/campusTest/ebooks/CONNECTIVEKNOWLEDGE.pdf

Dunleavy, P. (2003) *Authoring a PhD: How to Plan, Draft, Write, and Finish a Doctoral Thesis or Dissertation*. Houndmills, Basingstoke, UK and New York: Palgrave Macmillan.

Dweck, C. (2012) *Mindset: How You Can Fulfil Your Potential*. London: Hachette.

East, M., Bitchener, J. and Basturkmen, H. (2012) 'What constitutes effective feedback to postgraduate research students?: the students' perspective', *Journal of University Teaching and Learning Practice*, 9(2): Article 7. Online: http://ro.uow.edu.au/jutlp/vol9/iss2/7

Elbow, P. (1973) *Writing without Teachers*. Oxford and New York: Oxford University Press.

Elbow, P. (1989) 'Toward a phenomenology of freewriting', *Journal of Basic Writing* 8(2): 42–71. Online. Available at: http://wac.colostate.edu/jbw/v8n2/elbow.pdf

Elbow, P. (1998a) *Writing with Power: Techniques for Mastering the Writing Process*. Oxford and New York: Oxford University Press.

Elbow, P. (1998b). *Writing without Teachers*. 25th anniversary edn, New York: Oxford University Press.

Engebretson, K., Smith, K., McLaughlin, D., Seibold, C., Teret, G. and Ryan, E. (2008) 'The changing reality of research education in Australia and implications for supervision: a review of the literature', *Teaching in Higher Education*, 13(1): 1–15.

Engles-Schwarzpaul, A.C. (2015) 'The ignorant supervisor: about common worlds, epistemological modesty and distributed knowledge', *Educational Philosophy and Theory*, 47(12): 1250–1264.

Entwistle, N. (2005) 'Learning outcomes and ways of thinking across contrasting disciplines and settings in higher education', *The Curriculum Journal*, 16(1): 67–82.

Evans, D., Gruba, P. and Zobel, J. (2011) *How to Write a Better Thesis*. 3rd edn, Melbourne, Victoria: University of Melbourne Press.

Falchikov, N. and Boud, D. (2007) 'Assessment and emotions: the impact of being assessed', in D. Boud and N. Falchikov (eds) *Rethinking Assessment in Higher Education: Learning for the Longer Term*, London: Routledge, 144–156.

Feldman, R.S. and Theiss, A.J. (1982) 'The teacher and student as Pygmalions: joint effects of teacher and student expectations', *Journal of Educational Psychology*, 74(2): 217–223.

Ferris, D. (2003) *Response to Student Writing: Implications for Second Language Students*. Mahwah, NJ: Lawrence Erlbaum.

Ferris, D.R. and Hedgcock, J. (2014) *Teaching L2 Composition: Purpose, Process, and Practice*. 3rd edn, New York: Routledge.

Finch, G. (2000). *Linguistic Terms and Concepts*. Houndsmill, Basingstoke, UK: Macmillan Press.

Fisher, K. (2012) 'Peer support groups', in C. Denholm and T. Evans (eds) *Supervising Doctorates Downunder: Keys to Successful Doctoral Study in Australia and New Zealand*, Camberwell, Victoria: ACER Press, 45–53.

Flaherty, A.W. (2004) *The Midnight Disease: The Drive to Write, Writer's Block and the Creative Brain*. Boston, MA and New York: Houghton Mifflin Harcourt.

Flower, L. (1989) *Problem-Solving Strategies for Writing*. Chicago, IL: Harcourt Brace Jovanovich.

Fox, M.F. and Mohapatra, S. (2007) 'Social-organizational characteristics of work and publication productivity among academic scientists in doctoral-granting departments', *Journal of Higher Education*, 78(5): 542–571.

Freestone, P. and Connell, L. (2014, 15 October) 'Drop and give me 20,000 (words)!', *The Thesis Whisperer* blog. Online: http://thesiswhisperer.com/2014/10/15/6589/

Frick, B.L. (2009) 'Improving students' learning outcomes: what about doctoral learning outcomes?', in C. Nygaard, N. Courtney and C.W. Holtham (eds) *Improving Students' Learning Outcomes*, Copenhagen: CBS Press, 33–48.

Frick, B.L. (2010) 'Creativity in doctoral education: conceptualising the original contribution', in C. Nygaard, N. Courtney and C.W. Holtham (eds) *Teaching Creativity: Creativity in Teaching*, Faringdon, UK: Libri Publishing, 15–32.

Frick, B.L., Brodin, E.M. and Albertyn, R.M. (2014) 'The doctoral student–supervisor relationship as a negotiated learning space', in L. Scott-Webber, J. Branch, P. Bartholomew and C. Nygaard (eds) *Learning Space Design in Higher Education*, Faringdon, UK: Libri Publishing, 241–262.

Garbus, J. (2005) 'Tutoring graduate students in the writing center', *Academic Exchange Quarterly*, 9(3): 172–174.

Gardezi, A. and Nesi, H. (2009) 'Variation in the writing of economics of students in Britain and Pakistan: the case of conjunctive ties', in M. Charles, D. Pecorari and S. Hunston (eds) *Academic Writing: At the Interface of Corpus and Discourse*, London: Continuum, 236–250.

Gardner, S.K. (2008) ' "What's too much and what's too little?": the process of becoming an independent researcher', *The Journal of Higher Education*, 79(3): 326–350.

Gelling, L. and Rodríguez-Borrego, M.A. (2014) 'Originality in doctoral research', *Nurse Researcher*, 21(6): 6–7.

Gere, A.R. (1987) *Writing Groups: History, Theory, and Implications*. Carbondale, IL: Southern Illinois University Press.

Ginn, F. (2014) ' "Being like a researcher": supervising Masters dissertations in a neoliberalizing university', *Journal of Geography in Higher Education*, 38(1): 106–118.

Glatthorn, A.A. (1998) *Writing the Winning Dissertation: A Step-by-Step Guide*. Thousand Oaks, CA: Corwin.

Godden, V. (2016) 'Embodying entanglement', unpublished manuscript.

Golde, C.M. (2005) 'The role of the department and discipline in doctoral student attrition: lessons from four departments', *The Journal of Higher Education*, 76(6): 669–799.

Golde, C., Bueschel, A., Jones, L. and Walker, G.E. (2006) 'Apprenticeship and intellectual community: lessons from the Carnegie Initiative on the Doctorate', in *Conference Proceedings of the National Conference on Doctoral Education and the Faculty of the Future*, Ithaca, NY: The Carnegie Foundation for the Advancement of Teaching.

Goode, J. (2007) 'Empowering or disempowering the international Ph.D. student?: constructions of the dependent and independent learner', *British Journal of Sociology of Education*, 28(5): 589–603.

Goodson, P. (2012) *Becoming an Academic Writer: 50 Exercises for Paced, Productive, and Powerful Writing*. Los Angeles, CA: Sage.

Gopen G. and Swan, J. (1990) 'The science of scientific writing', *American Scientist*, 78(6): 550–558.

Grammarly (2016) *Better Writing Made Easy*. Online: https://www.grammarly.com

Grant, B.M. (2003) 'Mapping the pleasures and risks of supervision', *Discourse: Studies in the Cultural Politics of Education*, 24(2): 173–188.

Grant, B.M. (2005) 'The pedagogy of graduate supervision: figuring the relations between supervisor and student' (Unpublished PhD thesis, University of Auckland, Auckland, NZ). Online: http://hdl.handle.net/2292/295

Grant, B.M. (2006) 'Writing in the company of other women: exceeding the boundaries', *Studies in Higher Education*, 31(4): 483–495.

Grant, B.M. (2008) 'Agonistic struggle: master–slave dialogues in humanities supervision', *Arts and Humanities in Higher Education*, 7(1): 9–217.

Grant, B.M. (2016) 'Living with ghosts: enabling identities for Pākehā supervisors of Māori doctoral students', *New Zealand Journal of Educational Studies*, 51(1): 113–124. doi:10.1007/s40841–016–0044–1

Grant, B.M. and Graham, A. (1994) ' "Guidelines for discussion": a tool for managing postgraduate supervision', in O. Zuber-Skerritt and Y. Ryan (eds) *Quality in Postgraduate Education*, London: Kogan Page, 165–177.

Gray, T. (2015) *Publish and Flourish: Become a Prolific Scholar*. 2nd edn, Las Cruces, NM: Teaching Academy, New Mexico State University.

Green, B. (2005) 'Unfinished business: subjectivity and supervision', *Higher Education Research and Development*, 24(2): 151–163.

Guerin, C. (2013) 'Rhizomatic research cultures, writing groups and academic researcher identities', *International Journal of Doctoral Studies*, 8: 137–150.

Guerin, C. (2013, 1 September) 'Literature reviews: trust yourself!', *DoctoralWriting SIG* blog. Online: https://doctoralwriting.wordpress.com/2013/09/01/literature-reviews-trust-yourself/

Guerin, C. (2014) 'The gift of writing groups: critique, community and confidence', in C. Aitchison and C. Guerin (eds) *Writing Groups for Doctoral Education and Beyond: Innovations in Practice and Theory*, London: Routledge, 128–141.

Guerin, C. (2016) 'Connecting the dots: writing a doctoral thesis by publication', in C. Badenhorst and C. Guerin (eds) *Research Literacies and Writing Pedagogies for Masters and Doctoral Writers*, Studies in Writing Series, Leiden: Brill, 31–50.

Guerin, C. and Green, I. (2015) ' "They're the bosses": feedback in team supervision', *Journal of Further and Higher Education*, 39(3): 320–335.

Guerin, C. and Picard, M. (2012) 'Try it on: voice, concordancing and text-matching in doctoral writing', *International Journal for Educational Integrity*, 8(2): 34–45.

Guerin, C., Aitchison, C. and Carter, S. (2016) 'Networks, nodes and knowledge: blogging to support doctoral candidates and supervisors', in M. Fourie-Malherbe, C. Aitchison, E. Bitzer and R. Albertyn (eds) *Postgraduate Supervision in the Knowledge Society: Possibilities and Futures*, Stellenbosch, South Africa: SUN MeDIA Publishers, 269–282.

Guerin, C., Xafis, V., Doda, D.V., Gillam, M., Larg, A., Luckner, H., Jahan, N., Widayati, A. and Xu, C. (2013) 'Diversity in collaborative research communities: a multicultural, multidisciplinary thesis writing group in Public Health', *Studies in Continuing Education*, 35(1): 65–81.

Haas, S. (2014) 'Pick-n-mix: a typology of writers' groups', in C. Aitchison and C. Guerin (eds) *Writing Groups for Doctoral Education and Beyond: Innovations in Practice and Theory*, London: Routledge, 30–47.

Hakkarainen, K. (2013) 'Mapping the research ground: expertise, collective creativity, and shared knowledge practices', in H. Gaunt and H. Westerlund (eds) *Collaborative Learning in Higher Music Education: Why, What, and How*, Farnham, UK: Ashgate, 13–26.

Hamilton, J. and Carson, S., with Ellison, E.R. (2013) *12 Principles for the Effective Supervision of Creative Practice Higher Research Degrees, Dispatches from the Field.* Sydney, NSW: Australian Government, Office for Learning and Teaching. Online: http://eprints.qut.edu.au/66223/

Hardy, C. and Clughen, L. (2012) 'Writing at university: student and staff expectations', in L. Clughen and C. Hardy (eds) *Writing in the Disciplines: Building Supportive Cultures for Student Writing in UK Higher Education*, Bingley, UK: Emerald, 25–54.

Harris, M.J. and Rosenthal, R. (1986) 'Four factors in the mediation of teacher expectancy effects', in R.S. Feldman (ed.) *The Social Psychology of Education: Current Research and Theory*, Cambridge: Cambridge University Press, 91–114.

Hart, C. (1998) *Doing a Literature Review: Releasing the Social Science Research Imagination.* London: Sage.

Hart, C. (2005) *Doing Your Masters Dissertation: Realizing Your Potential as a Social Scientist.* London, Thousand Oaks, CA, New Delhi and Singapore: Sage.

Hartzband, P. and Groopman, J. (2010) 'Untangling the web: patients, doctors, and the internet', *New England Journal of Medicine*, 362(12): 1063–1066.

Haswell, R.H. (1986) 'Minimal marking', *College English*, 45(6): 600–604.

Hattie, J. and Timperley, H. (2007) 'The power of feedback', *Review of Educational Research*, 77(1): 81–112.

Healey, M., Lannin, L., Stibbe, A. and Derounian, A. (2013) *Developing and Enhancing Undergraduate Final Year Projects and Dissertations.* York, UK: Higher Education Academy.

Helms-Park, R. and Stapleton, P. (2003) 'Questioning the importance of individualized voice in undergraduate L2 argumentative writing: an empirical study with pedagogical implications', *Journal of Second Language Writing*, 12(3): 245–265.

Hinkel, E. (2003) 'Adverbial markers and tone of L1 and L2 students' writing', *Journal of Pragmatics*, 35(7): 1049–1068.

Hirvela, A. and Belcher, D. (2001) 'Coming back to voice the multiple voices and identities of mature multilingual writers', *Journal of Second Language Writing*, 10: 83–106.

Hofstede, G., Hofstede, G.J. and Minkov, M. (2010) *Cultures and Organizations: Software of the Mind: Intercultural Cooperation and Its Importance for Survival.* New York: McGraw Hill.

Holbrook, A. and Bourke, S. (2004) 'An investigation of PhD examination outcomes in Australia using a mixed method approach', *Australian Journal of Educational and Development Psychology*, 4: 153–169.

Holbrook, A., Bourke, S. and Fairbairn, H. (2015) 'Examiner reference to theory in PhD theses', *Innovations in Education and Teaching International*, 52(1): 75–85.

Holbrook, A., Bourke, S., Fairbairn, H. and Lovat, T. (2008) 'Examiner comment on the literature review in Ph.D. theses', *Studies in Higher Education*, 32(3): 337–356.

Holbrook, A., Bourke, S., Fairbairn, H. and Lovat, T. (2014) 'The focus and substance of formative comment provided by PhD examiners', *Studies in Higher Education*, 39(6): 983–1000.

Holbrook, A., Bourke, S., Lovat, T. and Dally, K. (2004a) 'Investigating PhD thesis examination reports', *International Journal of Educational Research*, 41(2): 98–120.

Holbrook, A., Bourke, S., Lovat, T. and Dally, K. (2004b) 'Qualities and characteristics in the written reports of doctoral thesis examiners', *Australian Journal of Educational and Development Psychology*, 4: 126–145.

Holbrook, A., Bourke, S., Lovat, T. and Fairbairn, H. (2008) 'Consistency and inconsistency in PhD thesis examination', *Australian Journal of Education*, 52(1): 36–48.

Holdaway, E., Deblois, C. and Winchester, I. (1995) 'Supervision of graduate students', *Canadian Journal of Higher Education*, 25(3): 1–29.

Holmes, J. and Riddiford, N. (2009) 'Talk at work: interactional challenges for immigrants,' in V.K. Bhatia, W. Cheng, B. Du-Babcock and J. Lung (eds) *Language for Professional Communication: Research, Practice and Training*, Hong Kong: City University of Hong Kong, Asia-Pacific LSP and Professional Communication Association and The Hong Kong Polytechnic University, 217–234.

Humphrey, R. and Simpson, B. (2012) 'Writes of passage: writing up qualitative data as a threshold concept in doctoral research', *Teaching in Higher Education*, 17(6): 735–746.

Hunt, A. (2005) *Your Research Project: How to Manage It*. London and New York: Routledge.

Hyland, K. (2004) *Disciplinary Discourses: Social Interactions in Academic Writing*, Ann Arbor, MI: University of Michigan Press.

Hyland, K. (2007) *Genre and Second Language Writing*. Ann Arbor, MI: University of Michigan Press.

Hyland, K. (2008a) 'As can be seen: lexical bundles and disciplinary variation', *English for Specific Purposes*, 27(1): 4–21.

Hyland, K. (2008b). 'Disciplinary voices: interactions in research writing', *English Text Construction*, 1(1): 5–22.

Hyland, K. (2009) *Academic Discourse*. London: Continuum.

Hyland, K. (2013) 'Writing in the university: education, knowledge and reputation', *Language Teaching*, 46(1): 53–70.

Hyland, F. and Hyland, K. (2001) 'Sugaring the pill: praise and criticism in written feedback', *Journal of Second Language Writing*, 10(3): 185–212.

Hyland, K. and Tse, P. (2004) 'Metadiscourse in academic writing: a reappraisal', *Applied Linguistics*, 25(2): 156–177.

Ilgen, D.R., Fisher, C.D. and Taylor, M.S. (1979) 'Consequences of individual feedback on behavior in organizations', *Journal of Applied Psychology*, 64(4): 349–371.

International Committee of Medical Journal Editors (2009) *Uniform Requirements for Manuscripts Submitted to Biomedical Journals: Writing and Editing for Biomedical Publication*. Online: www.icmje.org/

Ivani , R. (1998) *Writing and Identity: The Discoursal Construction of Identity in Academic Writing*. Amsterdam: John Benjamins.

Ivani , R. and Camps, D. (2001) 'I am how I sound: voice as self-representation in L2 writing', *Journal of Second Language Writing*, 10(1–2): 3–33.

Jackson, D. (2013) 'Completing a PhD by publication: a review of Australian policy and implications for practice', *Higher Education Research & Development*, 32(3), 355–368.

Jaworski, K. (2015) 'Stuck between two languages: the ethics of writing a doctoral dissertation in the English language', in L. Bryant and K. Jaworski (eds) *Women Supervising and Writing Doctoral Theses: Walking on the Grass*, Lanham, MD: Lexington Books, 71–83.

Johnson, E.M. (2013) '"Previously I thought writing was writing": reflections on doctoral writing spaces', in S. Frielick, N. Buissink-Smith, P. Wyse, J. Billot, J. Hallas and E. Whitehead (eds) *Research and Development in Higher Education: The Place of Learning and Teaching* (Vol. 36), Auckland: HERDSA, 233–242.

Johnson, E.M. (2014) 'Doctorates in the dark: threshold concepts and the improvement of doctoral supervision', *Waikato Journal of Education*, 19(2): 69–82.

Johnson, L., Lee, A. and Green, B. (2000) 'The PhD and the autonomous self: gender, rationality, and postgraduate pedagogy', *Studies in Higher Education*, 25(2): 135–147.

Johnston, S. (1997) 'Examining the examiners: an analysis of examiners' reports on doctoral theses', *Studies in Higher Education*, 22(3): 333–347.

Jones, A. (1999) 'The limits of cross-cultural dialogue: pedagogy, desire, and absolution in the classroom', *Educational Theory*, 49(3): 229–316.

Kamler, B. (2008) 'Rethinking doctoral publication practices: writing from and beyond the thesis', *Studies in Higher Education*, 33(3): 283–294.

Kamler, B. (2010) 'Revise and resubmit: the role of publication brokers', in C. Aitchison, B. Kamler and A. Lee (eds) *Publishing Pedagogies for the Doctorate and Beyond*, London: Routledge, 64–82.

Kamler, B. and Thomson, P. (2006) *Helping Doctoral Students Write*. London and New York: Routledge.

Kamler, B. and Thomson, P. (2008) 'The failure of dissertation advice books: toward alternative pedagogies for doctoral writing', *Educational Researcher*, 37(8): 507–514.

Kamler, B. and Thomson, P. (2014) *Helping Doctoral Students Write: Pedagogies for Supervision*. 2nd edn, London: Routledge.

Kempenaar, L. and Murray, R. (2016) 'Writing by academics: a transactional systems model for academic writing behaviours', *Higher Education Research and Development*, 35(5): 940–950.

Kidman, F., Chu, C., Ferdandez, S. and Abella, I. (2015) *Māori Scholars and the University*. Wellington: Ngā Pae o te Māramatanga.

Kierein, N.M. and Gold, M.A. (2000) 'Pygmalion in work organizations: a meta-analysis', *Journal of Organizational Behaviour*, 21(8): 913–928.

Kiley, M. (2009) 'Identifying threshold concepts and proposing strategies to support doctoral candidates', *Innovations in Education and Teaching International*, 46(3): 293–304.

Kiley, M. (2010) 'Creativity in research education: is it a threshold concept or just a good thing?', paper presented at the 3rd Biennial Threshold Concepts Symposium, Sydney, July 2010.

Kiley, M. (2014) 'Now I know why I have been knocking my head against a brick wall: doctoral candidates and stuck places', in C. O'Mahony, A. Buchanan, M. O'Rourke and B. Higgs (eds) *Threshold Concepts: From Personal Practice to Communities of Practice: Proceedings of the National Academy's Sixth Biennial Conference and the Fourth Threshold Concepts Conference*, Dublin: NAIRTL, 73–77.

Kiley, M. and Mullins, G. (2004) 'Examining the examiners: how inexperienced examiners approach the assessment of research theses', *International Journal of Educational Research*, 41(2): 121–135.

Kiley, M. and Wisker, G. (2008) ' "Now you see it, now you don't": identifying and supporting the achievement of doctoral work which embraces threshold concepts and crosses conceptual thresholds', paper presented at the Threshold Concepts: From Theory to Practice conference, Queen's University, Kingston, Ontario, Canada, 18–20 June.

Kiley, M. and Wisker, G. (2009) 'Threshold concepts in research education and evidence of threshold crossing', *Higher Education Research and Development*, 28(4): 431–441.

Kiley, M., Boud, D., Manathunga, C. and Cantwell, R. (2011) 'Honouring the incomparable: honours in Australian universities', *Higher Education*, 62(5): 619–633.

King, S. (2001) *On Writing*. London: Hodder and Stoughton.

Knowles, M.S., Holton, E.F. and Swanson, R.A. (2011) *The Adult Learner*. 7th edn, London: Routledge.

Kovach, M.E. (2010) *Indigenous Methodologies: Characteristics, Conversations, and Contexts*. Toronto, ON: University of Toronto Press.

Kozar, O., Lum, J.F. and Benson, P. (2015) 'Self-efficacy and vicarious learning in doctoral studies at a distance', *Distance Education*, 36(3): 448–454.

Kumar, M. and Kumar, V. (2009) 'Recursion and noticing in written feedback', *European Journal of Social Sciences*, 12(1): 94–99.

Kumar, V. and Stracke, E. (2007) 'An analysis of written feedback on a PhD thesis', *Teaching in Higher Education*, 12(4): 461–470.

Lamott, A. (1995) *Bird by Bird: Some Instructions for Writing and Life*. New York: Anchor.

Lanham, R.A. (1992) *Revising Prose*. 3rd edn, New York: Macmillan.

Lantolf, J. (ed.) (2000) *Sociocultural Theory and Second Language Learning*. Oxford: Oxford University Press.

Lantolf, J. (2005) 'Sociocultural and second language learning research: an exegesis', in E. Hinkel (ed.) *Handbook of Research in Second Language Teaching and Learning*, Mahwah, NJ: Lawrence Erlbaum, 335–353.

Larsson, K. and Hansson, H. (2011) 'The challenge for supervision: mass individualization of the thesis writing process with less resources', paper presented at Online Educa Berlin, 17th International Conference on Technology Supported Learning & Training, 30 November–2 December.

Laurs, D.E. (2010) 'Collaborating with postgraduate supervisors', in V. van der Ham, L. Sevillano and L. George (eds) *Shifting Sands, Firm Foundations: Proceedings of the 2009 Annual International Conference of the Association of Tertiary Learning Advisers of Aotearoa New Zealand (ATLAANZ)*, Auckland: ATLAANZ, 18–30.

Lave, J. and Wenger, E. (1991) *Situated Learning: Legitimate Peripheral Participation*. Cambridge: Cambridge University Press.

Lavelle, E. and Bushrow, K. (2007) 'Writing approaches of graduate students', *Educational Psychology*, 27(6): 807–822.

Lee, A. (2008) 'How are doctoral students supervised?: concepts of research supervision', *Studies in Higher Education*, 33(4): 267–281.

Lee, A. (2012) *Successful Research Supervision: Advising Students Doing Research*. London and New York: Routledge.

Lee, A. and Murray, R. (2015) 'Supervising writing: helping postgraduate students develop as researchers', *Studies in Higher Education*, 52(5): 558–570.

Lee, A. and Williams, C. (1999) 'Forged in fire: narratives of trauma in postgraduate research education', *Southern Review*, 32(1): 6–26.

Leonard, D., Becker, R. and Coate, K. (2005) 'To prove myself at the highest level: the benefits of doctoral study', *Higher Education Research and Development*, 24(2): 135–149.

Li, S. and Seale, C. (2007) 'Managing criticism in Ph.D. supervision: a qualitative case study', *Studies in Higher Education*, 32(4): 511–526.

Li, Y. and Casanave, C.P. (2012) 'Two first-year students' strategies for writing from sources: patchwriting or plagiarism?', *Journal of Second Language Writing*, 21(2): 165–180.

Löfström, E. and Pyhältö, K. (2015) ' "I don't even have time to be their friend!": ethical dilemmas in Ph.D. supervision in the hard sciences', *International Journal of Science Education*, 37(16): 2721–2739.

Lovitts, B.E. (2005) 'Being a good course-taker is not enough: a theoretical perspective on the transition to independent research', *Studies in Higher Education*, 30(2): 137–154.

Lovitts B.E. (2006) 'Making the implicit explicit: faculty's performance expectations for the dissertation', in P.L. Maki and N.A. Borkowski (eds) *The Assessment of*

Doctoral Education: Emerging Criteria and New Models for Improving Outcomes, Sterling, VA: Stylus, 163–196.

Lovitts, B.E. (2007) *Making the Implicit Explicit: Creating Performance Expectations for the Dissertation*. Sterling, VA: Stylus.

Lovitts, B.E. (2008) 'The transition to independent research: who makes it, who doesn't, and why', *The Journal of Higher Education*, 79(3): 296–325.

Lowry, S. (2014) 'Strategies for artists becoming writers: tackling the written component of practice-based research in the creative and performing arts (a report from the regions)', in L. Ravelli, B. Paltridge and S. Starfield (eds) *Doctoral Writing in the Creative and Performing Arts*, Faringdon, UK: Libri Publishing, 337–352.

Maher, M.A., Feldon, D.F., Timmerman, B.E. and Chao, J. (2014) 'Faculty perceptions of common challenges encountered by novice doctoral writers', *Higher Education Research and Development*, 33(4): 699–711.

Manathunga, C. (2007) 'Supervision as mentoring: the role of power and boundary crossing', *Studies in Continuing Education*, 29(2): 207–221.

Manathunga, C. (2010) 'Critical transcultural exchanges: educational development for supervisors', in M. Walker and P. Thomson (eds) *The Routledge Doctoral Supervisor's Companion: Supporting Effective Research in Education and the Social Sciences*, London: Routledge, 76–87.

Manathunga, C. (2014) *Intercultural Postgraduate Supervision: Reimagining Time, Place and Knowledge*, London and New York: Routledge.

Mantai, L. (2015) 'Feeling like a researcher: experiences of early doctoral students in Australia', *Studies in Higher Education*, 42(4): 636–650. Online. Available at: http://srhe.tandfonline.com/doi/pdf/10.1080/03075079.2015.1067603?needAccess=true

Matsuda, P.K. (2001) 'Voice in Japanese written discourse: implications for second language writing', *Journal of Second Language Writing*, 10(1–2): 35–53.

Matsuda, P.K. (2015) 'Identity in written discourse', *Annual Review of Applied Linguistics*, 35: 140–159.

Maua-Hodges, T. (2001) 'Tivaevae', unpublished paper, Victoria University, Wellington, New Zealand.

Mauch, J.E. and Park, N. (2003) *Guide to the Successful Thesis and Dissertation: A Handbook for Students and Faculty*. 5th edn, New York and Basel, Switzerland: Marcel Dekker.

Maunder, R.E., Gordon-Ginlayson, A., Callaghan, J. and Roberts, A. (2012) 'Behind supervisory doors: taught master's dissertation students as qualitative apprentices', *Psychology Learning and Teaching*, 11(1): 30–38.

McAlpine, L. and Amundsen, C. (2011) 'Making meaning of diverse experiences: constructing an identity through time', in L. McAlpine and C. Amundsen (eds) *Doctoral Education: Research-Based Strategies for Doctoral Students, Supervisors and Administrators*, Dordrecht, the Netherlands: Springer, 173–183.

McAlpine, L., Jazvac-Martek, M. and Hopwood, N. (2009) 'Doctoral student experience in education: activities and difficulties influencing identity development', *International Journal for Researcher Development*, 1(1): 97–109.

Mccaskill, M.K. (1990, 1 January) *Punctuation, Grammar and Capitalization: A Handbook for Technical Writers and Editors*. Online: http://ntrs.nasa.gov/search.jsp?R=19900017394

McCulley, G.A. (1985) 'Writing quality, coherence and cohesion', *Research in the Teaching of English*, 19(3): 269–282.

McCulloch, A. and Loeser, C. (2016) 'Does research degree supervisor training work?: the impact of a professional development induction workshop on supervision practice', *Higher Education Research and Development*, 35(5): 968–982.

McGagh, J., Marsh, J., Western, M., Thomas, P., Hastings, A., Mihailova, M. and Wenham, M. (2016) *Review of Australia's Research Training System*, Melbourne, Victoria: Australian Council of Learned Academies.

McKenzie, D.F. (2005) 'Reducing attrition rates for Māori students', *Journal of Developmental Education*, 18(3): 12–14.

McKinley, E., Grant, B.M., Middleton, S., Irwin, K. and Williams, L.T. (2009) 'Supervision of Māori doctoral students: a report', *MAI Review*, 1: 1–12.

McKinley, E., Middleton, S., Grant, E., Irwin, K. and Williams, L.T. (2011) 'Working at the interface: indigenous students' experience of undertaking doctoral studies in Aotearoa New Zealand', *Equity and Excellence in Education*, 44(1): 115–132.

Mewburn, I. (2011) 'Troubling talk: assembling the PhD candidate', *Studies in Continuing Education*, 33(3): 321–332.

Mewburn, I. (2012, 8 May) 'The valley of shit', *The Thesis Whisperer* blog. Online: https://thesiswhisperer.com/2012/05/08/the-valley-of-shit/

Mewburn, I. (2012, 6 July) 'Personal learning net(WORKS)', *The Thesis Whisperer* blog. Online: https://thesiswhisperer.com/2012/07/06/personal-learning-networks/

Mewburn, I. and Thomson, P. (2013) 'Academic blogging is part of a complex online academic attention economy, leading to unprecedented readership', *LSE Impact Blog*. Online: http://blogs.lse.ac.uk/impactofsocialsciences/2013/12/12/academic-attention-economy/

Mewburn, I., Osborne, L. and Caldwell, G. (2014) 'Shut up and write! Some surprising uses of cafés and crowds in doctoral writing', in C. Aitchison and C. Guerin (eds) *Writing Groups for Doctoral Education and Beyond: Innovations in Practice and Theory*, London: Routledge, 399–425.

Meyer, E. (2014a) 'Navigating the cultural minefield', *Harvard Business Review*, May: 119–124.

Meyer, E. (2014b) *The Culture Map: Breaking Through the Invisible Boundaries of Global Business*. New York: Public Affairs.

Meyer, J.H.F. and Land, R. (2005) 'Threshold concepts and troublesome knowledge (2): epistemological considerations and a conceptual framework for teaching and learning', *Higher Education*, 49(3): 373–388.

Meyer, J.H.F. and Land, R. (2006a) 'Threshold concepts and troublesome knowledge: issues of liminality', in J. Meyer and R. Land (eds) *Overcoming Barriers to Student Understanding: Threshold Concepts and Troublesome Knowledge*, London: Routledge, 19–32.

Meyer, J.H.F. and Land, R. (eds) (2006b) *Overcoming Barriers to Student Understanding: Threshold Concepts and Troublesome Knowledge*. London: Routledge.

Micciche, L.R. (2011) 'Toward graduate-level writing instruction', *College Composition and Communication*, 62(3): 477–501.

Middleton, S. and McKinley, E. (2010) 'The gown and the korowai: Māori students and the spatial organisation of academic knowledge', *Higher Education*, 29(3): 229–243.

Morley, L. (2003) *Quality and Power in Higher Education*. Maidenhead, UK: Society for Research in Higher Education and Open University Press.

Morrison, T. (1992) *Playing in the Dark: Whiteness and the Literary Imagination*. Cambridge, MA: Harvard University Press.

Moses, I. (1992) 'Role perception rating scale', in I. Moses (ed.) *Research Training and Supervision: Proceedings from the ARC and AVCC sponsored conference*, Canberra: NBEET.

Mullins, G. and Kiley, M. (2002) '"It's a PhD, not a Nobel Prize": how experienced examiners assess research theses', *Studies in Higher Education*, 27(4): 369–386.

Murray, R. (2006) *How to Write a Thesis*. 2nd edn, Maidenhead, UK: Open University Press.

Murray, R. (2011) *How to Write a Thesis*. 3rd edn, Maidenhead, UK: Open University Press.

Murray, R. (2015a) *Writing in the Social Spaces: A Social Processes Approach to Academic Writing*. London: Routledge.

Murray, R. (2015b) *Writing for Academic Journals: How Can a Structured Writing Retreat Help?* Wiley Exchanges Open Access. Online: https://hub.wiley.com/community/exchanges/discover/blog/2015/09/17/writing-for-publication-how-can-a-structured-writing-retreat-help

Murray, R. (2016) *How to Write a Thesis*. 4th edn, Maidenhead, UK: Open University Press.

Murray, R. and Moore, S. (2006) *The Handbook of Academic Writing*. Maidenhead, UK: Open University Press/McGraw Hill.

Murray, R. and Newton, M. (2009) 'Writing retreat as structured intervention: margin or mainstream?', *Higher Education Research and Development*, 28(5): 527–539.

Netsinghe, R. and Southcott, J. (2015) 'A juggling act: supervisor/candidate partnership in a doctoral thesis by publication', *International Journal of Doctoral Studies*, 10: 167–185.

New Zealand Qualifications Authority (2001) *National Qualifications Framework*. Wellington: New Zealand Qualifications Authority.

O'Connell, F. and Jin, L. (2001) 'A structural model of literature review: an analysis of Chinese postgraduate students' writing,' paper presented at the BALEAP Conference, Sheffield Hallam University, Sheffield, UK.

Onwuegbuzie, A.J. and Collins, K.M.T. (2001) 'Writing apprehension and academic procrastination among graduate students', *Perceptual and Motor Skills*, 92(2): 560–562.

Paltridge, B. (2003) 'Teaching thesis and dissertation writing', *Hong Kong Journal of Applied Linguistics*, 8(2): 78–96.

Paltridge, B. and Starfield, S. (2007) *Thesis and Dissertation Writing in a Second Language: A Handbook for Supervisors*. London and New York: Routledge.

Paré, A. (2010) 'Making sense of supervision: deciphering feedback', in P. Thomson and M. Walker (eds) *The Routledge Doctoral Student's Companion: Supporting Effective Research in Education and the Social Sciences*, London: Routledge, 107–115.

Paré, A. (2011) 'Speaking of writing: supervisory feedback and the dissertation', in L. McAlpine and C. Amundsen (eds) *Doctoral Education: Research-Based Strategies for Doctoral Students, Supervisors and Administrators*, Dordrecht, the Netherlands: Springer, 59–74.

Paré, A. (2014) 'Writing together for many reasons: theoretical and historical perspectives', in C. Aitchison and C. Guerin (eds) *Writing Groups for Doctoral Education and Beyond: Innovations in Practice and Theory*, London: Routledge, 18–29.

Parry, S. (2007) *Disciplines and Doctorates*. Dordrecht, the Netherlands: Springer.

Pecorari, D. (2003) 'Good and original: plagiarism and patchwriting in academic second-language writing', *Journal of Second Language Writing*, 12(4): 317–345.

Pecorari, D. and Shaw, P. (2012) 'Types of student intertextuality and faculty attitudes', *Journal of Second Language Writing*, 21(2): 149–164.

Percy, A. (2011) 'Making sense of learning advising: an historical ontology' (PhD thesis, University of Wollongong, Wollongong, Australia). Online: http://ro.uow.edu.au/cgi/viewcontent.cgi?article=4363&context=theses

Perry, C. (2013) *Efficient and Effective Research: A Toolkit for Developing Research Students and Researchers*. Adelaide, South Australia: AIB Publications.

Perry, S.K. (1999) *Writing in Flow: Keys to Enhanced Creativity*. Cincinnati, OH: Writer's Digest Books.

Petersen, E.B. (2012) 'Monsters astray in the flesh: a layered exploration of the im/possibilities of resistance-work in the neoliberalised university', paper presented at the Academic Identities Conference, Auckland, July.

Petersen, E.B. (2014) 'Re-signifying subjectivity?: a narrative exploration of "non-traditional" doctoral students' lived experience of subject formation through two Australian cases', *Studies in Higher Education*, 39(5): 823–834.

Phillips, E.M. and Pugh, D.S. (2005) *How to Get a PhD*. 4th edn, Maidenhead, UK: Open University Press.

Picard, M. and Guerin, C. (2011) '"Be original, but not too original": developing academic voice through innovative use of text-matching and concordancing software', in C. Nygaard, N. Courtney and C. Holtham (eds) *Beyond Transmission: Innovations in University Teaching*, Faringdon, UK: Libri Publishing, 221–234.

Pilcher, N. (2011) 'The UK postgraduate Masters dissertation: an "elusive chameleon"?', *Teaching in Higher Education*, 16(1): 29–40.

Pinker, S. (2014) *The Sense of Style: The Thinking Person's Guide to Writing in the 21st Century*. New York: Viking.

Plucker, J.A., Beghetto, R.A. and Dow, G.T. (2004) 'Why isn't creativity more important to educational psychologists?: potentials, pitfalls, and future directions in creativity research', *Educational Psychologist*, 39(2): 83–96.

Presthus, W. and Bygstad, B. (2014) 'Strawberry analysis: writing a paper-based PhD', *Norsk Konferanse for Organisasjoners Bruk av IT*, 22(1): n.p. Online: http://ojs.bibsys.no/index.php/Nokobit/article/view/46

Prior, P. (2001) 'Voices in text, mind, and society: sociohistoric accounts of discourse acquisition and use', *Journal of Second Language Writing*, 10(1–2): 55–81.

Pyhältö, K., Stubb, J. and Lonka, K. (2009) 'Developing scholarly communities as learning environments for doctoral students', *International Journal of Academic Development*, 14(3): 221–232.

Reynolds, D. (2007) 'Restraining Golem and harnessing Pygmalion in the classroom: a laboratory study of managerial expectations and task design', *Academy of Management Learning and Education*, 6(4): 475–483.

Rheingold, H. (2013) *Crap Detection Mini-Course*. Online: http://rheingold.com/2013/crap-detection-mini-course/

Richardson, L. (2000) 'Writing: a method of inquiry', in N.K. Denzin and Y.S. Lincoln, (eds) *The Handbook of Qualitative Research*, 2nd edn, Thousand Oaks, CA: Sage, 923–948.

Rizvi, F. (2010) 'International students and doctoral students in transnational spaces', in M. Walker and P. Thomson (eds) *The Routledge Doctoral Supervisor's Companion: Supporting Effective Research in Education and the Social Sciences*, London: Routledge, 158–170.

Roberts, L.D. (2015) *Guide for New Supervisors of Honours and Coursework Dissertation Students*. Online. Available at: www.dissertationsupervision.org

Robins, L. and Kanowski, P. (2008) 'PhD by publication: a student's perspective', *Journal of Research Practice*, 4(2): Article M3. Online: http://jrp.icaap.org/index.php/jrp/article/view/136/154

Robinson-Pant, A. (2010) 'Internationalisation of higher education: challenges for the doctoral supervisor', in M. Walker and P. Thomson (eds) *The Routledge Doctoral Supervisor's Companion: Supporting Effective Research in Education and the Social Sciences*, London and New York: Routledge, 147–157.

Rose, M. and McClafferty, K. (2001) 'A call for the teaching of writing in graduate education', *Educational Researcher*, 30(2): 27–33.

Rosenthal, R. and Jacobson, L. (1968) *Pygmalion in the Classroom*. New York: Holt, Rinehart and Winston.

Shalley, C.E. (1991) 'Effects of productivity goals, creativity goals, and personal discretion on individual creativity', *Journal of Applied Psychology*, 76(2): 179–185.

Sharmini, S., Spronken-Smith, R., Golding, C. and Harland, T. (2015) 'Assessing the doctoral thesis when it includes published work', *Assessment and Evaluation in Higher Education*, 40(1): 89–102.

Shi, L. (2004) 'Textual borrowing in second-language writing', *Written Communication*, 21(2): 171–200.

Silvia, P.J. (2007) *How to Write a Lot: A Practical Guide to Productive Academic Writing*. Washington, DC: American Psychological Association.

Silvia, P.J. (2010) *How to Write a Lot: A Practical Guide to Productive Academic Writing*. 6th edn, Washington, DC: APA Life Tools.

Silvia, P.J. (2015) *Write It Up: Practical Strategies for Writing and Publishing Journal Articles*. Washington, DC: American Psychological Association.

Sinclair, J., Barnacle, R. and Cuthbert, D. (2014) 'How the doctorate contributes to the formation of active researchers: what the research tells us', *Studies in Higher Education*, 39(10): 1972–1986.

Smith, L.T. (1997) 'Decolonising intellectual identity: Māori/woman/academic', in M. Peters (ed.) *Cultural Politics and the University*, Palmerston North: The Dunmore Press, 192–210.

Smith, L.T. (1999) *Decolonizing Methodologies: Research and Indigenous Peoples*. London: Zed Books.

Smith, L.T. (2007) 'Getting the story right—telling the story well, indigenous activism—indigenous research', in A.T.P. Mead and S. Ratuva (eds) *Pacific Genes and Life Patents: Pacific Indigenous Experiences and Analysis of the Commodification and Ownership of Life*, Wellington: Call of the Earth (Llamado de la Tierra) and The United Nations University Institute of Advanced Studies, 74–81.

Smith, M. (1997) 'Using markings to respond to writing', *The English Journal*, 86(2): 79–80.

Sommers, N. (2006) 'Across the drafts', *College Composition and Communication*, 58(2): 248–257.

Sperling, M., Appleman, D., Gilyard, K. and Freedman, S. (2011) 'Voice in the context of literacy studies', *Reading Research Quarterly*, 46(1): 70–84.

Spratt, J. and Florian, L. (2014) 'Developing and using a framework for gauging the use of inclusive pedagogy by new and experienced teachers', in C. Forlin and T. Loreman (eds) *Measuring Inclusive Education*, Bingley, UK: Emerald, 263–278.

Starfield, S. (2010) 'Fortunate travellers: learning from the multiliterate lives of doctoral students', in M. Walker and P. Thomson (eds) *The Routledge Doctoral Supervisor's Companion: Supporting Effective Research in Education and the Social Sciences*, London: Routledge, 138–146.

Starfield, S., Paltridge, B., Ravelli, L.J. and Nicholson, S. (2012) 'Doctoral writing in the visual and performing arts: two ends of a continuum', *Studies in Higher Education*, 37(8): 989–1003.

Starr, S.L. (1999) 'Layers of silence, arenas of voice: the ecology of visible and invisible work', *Computer Supported Cooperative Work*, 8(1): 9–30.

Stracke, E. (2010) 'Undertaking the journey together: peer learning for a successful and enjoyable PhD experience', *Journal of University Teaching and Learning Practice*, 7(1): 1–10.

Stracke, E. and Kumar, V. (2010) 'Feedback and self-regulated learning: insights from supervisors' and PhD examiners' reports', *Reflective Practice*, 11(1): 19–32.

Stracke, E. and Kumar, V. (2014) 'Realising graduate attributes in the research degree: the role of peer support groups', *Teaching in Higher Education*, 19(6): 616–629.

Strauss, P. (2012) ' "The English is not the same": challenges in thesis writing for second language speakers of English', *Teaching in Higher Education*, 17(3): 283–293.

Strunk, W., Jr and White, E.B. (2011) *The Elements of Style*. Project Gutenberg. Online: www.gutenberg.org/files/37134/37134-h/37134-h.htm

Swales, J. (1986) 'Citation analysis and discourse analysis', *Applied Linguistics*, 7(1): 39–56.

Swales, J. (1996) 'Occluded genres in the academy: the case of the submission letter', in E. Ventola and A. Mauranen (eds) *Academic Writing: Intercultural and Textual Issues*, Amsterdam: John Benjamins Publishing, 45–58.

Swales, J.M. and Feak, C. (2004) *Academic Writing for Graduate Students: Essential Tasks and Skills*. 2nd edn, Ann Arbor, MI: University of Michigan Press.

Sword, H. (2007) *The Writer's Diet*. Auckland: Pearson Education.

Sword, H. (2009) 'Writing higher education differently: a manifesto on style', *Studies in Higher Education*, 34(3): 319–336.

Sword, H. (2012) *Stylish Academic Writing*. Cambridge, MA: Harvard University Press.

Sword, H. (2016) *The Writer's Diet: A Guide to Fit Prose*. Chicago, IL: University of Chicago Press.

Sword, H. (2017) *Air & Light & Time & Space: How Successful Academics Write*. Cambridge, MA: Harvard University Press.

Tardy, C.M. (2012) 'Current conceptions of voice', in K. Hyland and C.S. Guinda (eds) *Stance and Voice in Written Academic Genres*, New York: Palgrave Macmillan, 34–48.

Thaman, K.H. (1993) 'Culture and the curriculum in the South Pacific', *Comparative Education*, 29(3): 249–260.

Thaman, K.H. (2003) 'Culture, teaching and learning in Oceania', in K.H. Thaman (ed.) *Educational Ideas from Oceania*, Suva Fiji: Institute of Education, USP, 3–12.

Thaman, K.H. (2009) 'Towards cultural democracy in teaching and learning with specific references to Pacific Island nations (PINs)', *International Journal for the Scholarship of Teaching and Learning*, 3(2): 1–9.

Theodore, R., Tustin, K., Kiro, C., Gollop, M., Taumoepeau, M., Taylor, N., Chee, S.-T., Hunter, J. and Poulton, R. (2016) 'Māori university graduates: indigenous participation in higher education', *Higher Education Research and Development*, 38(3): 604–618.

Thesen, L. (2014) ' "If they're not laughing, watch out!": emotion and risk in postgraduate writing groups', in C. Aitcheson and C. Guerin (eds) *Writing Groups for the Doctorate and Beyond: Innovations in Practice and Theory*, London and New York: Routledge, 172–176.

Thompson, P. and Tribble, C. (2001) 'Looking at citations: using corpora in English for academic purposes', *Language Learning and Technology*, 5(3): 91–105.

Thomson, P. and Kamler, B. (2013) *Writing for Peer Reviewed Journals: Strategies for Getting Published*. New York: Routledge.

Thomson, P. and Kamler, B. (2016) *Detox Your Writing: Strategies for Doctoral Writers*. London: Routledge.

Thornley, J. (2014) 'Island home country—on the possibility of praxis between "artefact" and "exegesis" in the creative arts doctorate: a case study', in L. Ravelli, B. Paltridge and S. Starfield (eds) *Doctoral Writing in the Creative and Performing Arts*, Faringdon, UK: Libri Publishing, 135–155.

Thow, M. (2015) *How to Be Healthy at Work: For People Doing PhDs and Other Higher Degrees, Academics, Teachers and Office Workers Who Sit a Lot*. Raleigh, NC: Lulu.com.

Tinkler, P. and Jackson, C. (2004) *The Doctoral Examination Process: A Handbook for Students, Examiners and Supervisors*. Maidenhead, UK: Open University Press.

Toulmin, S., Reike, R. and Janik, A. (1984) *An Introduction to Reasoning*. New York: Macmillan.

Trafford, V.N. and Leshem, S. (2002) 'Starting at the end to undertake doctoral research: predictable questions as stepping stones', *Higher Education Review*, 34(4): 43–61.

Trafford, V.N. and Leshem, S. (2008) *Stepping Stones to Achieving Your Doctorate: By Focussing on Your Viva from the Start*. Maidenhead, UK: Open University Press.

Trafford, V.N. and Leshem, S. (2009) 'Doctorateness as a threshold concept', *Innovations in Education and Teaching International*, 46(3): 305–316.

Truss, L. (2003) *Eats, Shoots and Leaves: The Zero Tolerance Approach to Punctuation*. London: Profile Books.

Turman, P.D. (2001) '"I'm fooling them all": the examination of the imposter phenomenon in the undergraduate instructor assistant experience', *Journal of Graduate Teaching Assistant Development*, 8(3): 123–131.

Turner, G. (2015) 'Learning to supervise: four journeys', *Innovations in Education and Teaching International*, 52(1): 86–98.

UK Research Councils (n.d.) *Joint Statement of the Research Councils'/AHRC's Skills Training Requirements for Research Students*. Online: www.leeds.ac.uk/rsa/assets/pdfs/research,traininganddevelopment/students/JointSkillsStatementJSS.pdf (accessed 12 January 2016).

United Kingdom Quality Assurance Agency for Higher Education (2008) *The Framework for Higher Education Qualifications in England, Wales and Northern Ireland*. Mansfield, UK: Linney Direct.

University of Auckland (2012) *Statute for the Degree of Doctor of Philosophy*. Online: www.calendar.auckland.ac.nz/en/progreg/regulations-doctor-of-philosophy/phd.html

University of Auckland (n.d.) *Postgraduate Supervision Guidelines/Doctoral Supervision Policy and Procedures*. Online. Available at: www.auckland.ac.nz/en/students/academic-information/postgraduate-students/postgraduate-policies-guidelines-and-forms/doctoral-policies-and-guidelines/supervision.html

Vaioleti, T. (2006) 'Talanoa research methodology: a developing position on Pacific research', *Waikato Journal of Education*, 12: 21–34.

Vostal, F. (2016) *Accelerating Academia: The Changing Structure of Academic Time*. Basingstoke, UK: Palgrave Macmillan.

Walker, M. and Thomson, P. (eds) (2010) *The Routledge Doctoral Supervisor's Companion: Supporting Effective Research in Education and the Social Sciences*. London and New York: Routledge.

Wallace, M. and Wray, A. (2016) *Critical Reading and Writing for Postgraduates*. 3rd edn, London: Sage (companion website: study.sagepub.com/wallaceandwray3e).

Wang, T. and Li, L.Y. (2011) '"Tell me what to do" vs. "guide me through it": feedback experiences of international doctoral students', *Active Learning in Higher Education*, 12(2): 101–112.

Ware, M. and Monkman, M. (2008) *Peer Review in Scholarly Journals: Perspective of the Scholarly Community: An International Study*. London: Publishing Research Consortium.

Wegener, C., Meier, N. and Ingerslev, K. (2016) 'Borrowing brainpower—sharing insecurities: lessons learned from a doctoral peer writing group', *Studies in Higher Education*, 41(6): 1092–1105.

Wellington, J. (2010) 'More than a matter of cognition: an exploration of affective writing problems of post-graduate students and their possible solutions', *Teaching in Higher Education*, 15(2): 135–150.

Wellington, J. (2013) 'Searching for "doctorateness"', *Studies in Higher Education*, 38(10): 1490–1503.

Wenger, E. (1998) *Communities of Practice: Learning, Meaning, and Identity*. Cambridge: Cambridge University Press.

White, B. (2011) *Mapping Your Thesis: The Comprehensive Manual of Theory and Techniques for Masters and Doctoral Research.* Camberwell, Victoria: ACER Press.

Williams, C. and Lee, A. (1999) 'Forged in fire: narratives of trauma in PhD supervision pedagogy', *Southern Review: Communication, Politics and Culture*, 32(1): 6–26.

Williams, J.M. (1990) *Style: Toward Clarity and Grace*. Chicago, IL: University of Chicago Press.

Williams, J.M. (2007) *Style: Lessons in Clarity and Grace*. 9th edn, New York: Pearson Longman.

Winokur, J. (1987) *Writers on Writing*. Baltimore, MD: Port City Press.

Wisker, G. (2008) *The Postgraduate Research Handbook*. Basingstoke, UK and New York: Palgrave Macmillan.

Wisker, G. (2012) *The Good Supervisor: Supervising Postgraduate and Undergraduate Research for Doctoral Theses and Dissertations*. Basingstoke, UK and New York: Palgrave Macmillan.

Wisker, G. (2014) 'Voice, vision and articulation: conceptual threshold crossing in academic writing', in C. O'Mahony, A. Buchanan, M. O'Rourke and B. Higgs (eds) *Threshold Concepts: From Personal Practice to Communities of Practice: Proceedings of the National Academy's Sixth Biennial Conference and the Fourth Threshold Concepts Conference*, Dublin: NAIRTL, 169–174.

Wisker, G. and Savin-Baden, M. (2009) 'Priceless conceptual thresholds: beyond the "stuck place" in writing', *London Review of Education*, 7(3): 235–247.

Wisker, G., Cheng, M. and Morris, C. (2010) '"Nudging": conceptual threshold crossing in doctoral learning journeys', paper presented at the SRHE Conference, Newport, December 2010. Online: www.srhe.ac.uk/conference2010/abstracts/0256.pdf

Wisker, G., Kiley, M. and Aiston, S. (2006) 'Making the learning leap: research students crossing conceptual thresholds', in M. Kiley and G. Mullins (eds) *Quality in Postgraduate Research: Knowledge Creation in Testing Times*, Canberra, ACT: CEDAM, The Australian National University, 195–201.

Wisker, G., Robinson, G., Trafford, V., Warnes, M. and Creighton, E. (2003) 'From supervisory dialogues to successful PhDs: strategies supporting and enabling the learning conversations of staff and students at postgraduate level', *Teaching in Higher Education*, 8(3): 383–397.

Wolfgramm-Foliaki, 'E. (2016a) 'Under the mango tree: lessons for the insider-outsider researcher', *Journal of Perspectives in Applied Academic Practice*, 4(3). Online: http://jpaap.napier.ac.uk/index.php/JPAAP/article/view/165

Wolfgramm-Foliaki, 'E. (2016b) '"Do not assume we know": perspective of Pacific Island first in the family students', in L. J. Santamaría and A. P. Santamaría (eds) *Culturally Responsive Leadership in Higher Education: Promoting Equity, and Improvement*, London and New York: Routledge, 123–135,

Woodward-Kron, R. (2007) 'Negotiating meanings and scaffolding learning: writing support for non-English speaking background postgraduate students', *Higher Education Research & Development*, 26(3): 253–268.

Woolf, V. (2002) *A Room of One's Own*. London and New York: Penguin Modern Classics.

Yancey, K.B. (ed.) (1994) *Voices on Voice: Perspectives, Definitions, Inquiry*. Urbana, IL: National Council of Teachers of English.

Yeats, W.B. (1956) 'Adam's curse', in *The Collected Poems of W.B. Yeats*. New York: Macmillan.

Yeh, C.C. (2010) 'New graduate students' perspectives on research writing in English: a case study in Taiwan', *Journal of Academic Language and Learning*, 4(1): A1–A12.

Yeh, S.F. (2012) 'A qualitative study of mature Taiwanese writers' development of voice and positioning' (Unpublished PhD thesis, Indiana University of Pennsylvania, Indiana, USA). Online: http://knowledge.library.iup.edu/cgi/viewcontent.cgi?article=2028&context=etd

Yeh, S.F. (2015) 'Mature Taiwanese writers' development of writing and voices between different academic environments', *Advances in Language and Literary Studies*: 6(5): 197–208.

Zamel, V. (1995) 'Strangers in academia: the experiences of faculty and ESL students across the curriculum', *College Composition and Communication*, 46(4): 506–521.

Zeegers, M. and Barron, D. (2008) 'Discourses of deficit in higher degree research supervisory pedagogies for international students,' *Pedagogies: An International Journal*, 3(2): 69–84.

Zhao, C.G. and Llosa, L. (2008) 'Voice in high-stakes L1 academic writing assessment: implications for L2 writing instruction', *Assessing Writing*, 13(3): 153–170.

Zhou, J. (1998) 'Feedback valence, feedback style, task autonomy, and achievement orientation: interactive effects on creative performance', *Journal of Applied Psychology*, 83(2): 261–276.

Zinsser, W. (1980) *On Writing Well: An Informal Guide to Writing Non-Fiction*. New York: Harper and Row.

Zinsser, W. (1988) *Writing to Learn*. New York: Quill.

Index

Printed in Great Britain
by Amazon

65833409R00158